BIG AND BRIGHT

BIG AND BRIGHT

DEEP IN THE HEART OF TEXAS

HIGH SCHOOL FOOTBALL

GRAY
LEVY

Taylor Trade Publishing

Lanham • Boulder • New York • London

Published by Taylor Trade Publishing
An imprint of The Rowman & Littlefield Publishing Group, Inc.
4501 Forbes Boulevard, Suite 200, Lanham, Maryland 20706
www.rowman.com

Unit A, Whitacre Mews, 26-34 Stannary Street, London SE11 4AB, United Kingdom

Distributed by NATIONAL BOOK NETWORK

British Library Cataloguing in Publication Information Available

Library of Congress Cataloging-in-Publication Data
Levy, Gray, 1968-
  Big and bright : deep in the heart of Texas high school football / Gray Levy.
      pages cm
  "Distributed by NATIONAL BOOK NETWORK"—T.p. verso.
  ISBN 978-1-63076-089-2 (cloth : alk. paper) — ISBN 978-1-63076-090-8 (electronic)
  1. Football—Texas. 2. School sports—Texas. 3. Football players—Texas. I. Title.
  GV959.52.T4L48 2015
  796.332'6209764—dc23

                                                          2015014225

Printed in the United States of America

CONTENTS

ACKNOWLEDGMENTS

Writing a book with as many moving parts as *Big and Bright* takes the help and support of many people. As a teacher and coach who'd never written anything longer than a newsletter, many could have told me I was biting off more than I could chew, taking on such a project (a real possibility). Everyone mentioned here took me and my idea seriously, and for that I am very grateful.

The first professional I approached with my idea was Reno, Nevada, author Suzanne Morgan Williams. I want to thank her for being so generous with her time and her advice about getting this project off the ground.

Starting out I had tremendous interest but very little knowledge of Texas high school football. As finding the right teams would be the heart of this book, I need to recognize Travis Stewart, managing editor of "The Bible of Texas Football," *Dave Campbell's Texas Football* magazine; Carl Padilla, unofficial oddsmaker and founder of the Padilla Poll, an online service bought by coaches statewide; and Chris Koetting, head coach of Canadian High School in the Panhandle. All were instrumental in leading me to the eleven programs featured in this book.

My initial edits were done by Terri and Cory Farley, a Reno author and newspaper columnist, respectively, who turned a rambling mess into something resembling an actual book. I owe them tremendously for their patience and exhaustive suggestions. Without them, this book could never have been published.

I also owe a thank you to my agent, Richard Curtis, who saw something in my work and agreed to represent me. Another thank you goes to Rick Rinehart and Taylor Trade for agreeing to publish *Big and Bright*.

Nothing would have been possible without the backing of the head coaches. I owe them the ultimate debt for allowing unlimited access to their programs. The same gratitude goes out to the many assistant coaches at each school for letting me sit in on meetings, film sessions, and locker room talks, and stand on practice fields and game-day sidelines. These are great men, and I would be proud and privileged to have my kid play for any of them.

Finally, I need to thank my family. My parents deserve appreciation and love for supporting me in giving up teaching to follow my passion. Lastly, to my wife, Terri, a special thank you for granting me five months on the road and for her love, support, and patience in putting this thing together. Thanks for everything. I love you and appreciate all you've done for me.

INTRODUCTION

"When people move to town, they ask me three questions, 'What's the work like, where will I live, and what kind of high school football do you have here?' That's just Texas."

—Randy Boyd, contractor in Port Lavaca, Texas.

Texas is different. Texans never tire of reminding themselves where they live. There's the ever-present Texas Pride, with Lone Star flags and Texas silhouettes on everything from motel waffle irons and T-shirts to neon signs. Texas stars decorate the front of many homes, and all three American car companies have special Texas models of their pickup trucks. The Rangers baseball team is the only team with its location (TEXAS) on both away *and* home jerseys. Texas school children recite both the Pledge of Allegiance *and* the Texas Pledge every morning, and many football teams decorate their helmets with the state's iconic outline. There's the immense size, making it possible to drive 800 miles from north to south or east to west within its borders. There are the stereotypical caricatures of the state and its people; big cowboy hats and boots, steer horns on hoods of Cadillacs and oil wells. In reality, Texas has a diverse culture, giving each part of the state its own distinct feel. There is the unique history, the Alamo, war with the Comanches, and the fact that Texas was a separate nation for ten years. There's the food: BBQ, Mexican food, fried chicken, Whataburger, and Dr Pepper. But maybe the one thing that makes Texas Texas, from the Panhandle to the Rio Grande Valley, from El Paso to Beaumont, is high school football.

In 2012, I took a trip though Texas to explore the best high school football in the country. Other states have outstanding programs, but no one does high school football like Texas. I came because I'd become disillusioned with the changing priorities of public education and hoped to restore my faith. I came because here, high schools are still the seat of community pride, while schools elsewhere have become faceless testing factories offering mediocre extracurricular activities as an afterthought. I came to see how the sport I love looks when it's given all it needs to thrive. Finally, I came to find the truth about whether schools exploit kids for the entertainment and community pride of adults.

Texas football has been compared to a religion, but it's much more than that. Texas may be the most religious state in the Union, but like most everything here, its religion is diverse. Football overcomes cultural differences and binds Texans together. The Dallas Cowboys are a statewide institution; the Houston Texans have a local following. The college programs have passionate supporters, but nothing is as absolute as the hold the high school game has on the communities, suburban neighborhoods, and big and small towns.

Starting early in the twentieth century, the cultural importance of high school football here has far surpassed that found throughout most of the country. Football culture is an artifact of Texas' unique and violent history. Most of the 1800s consisted of a succession of wars fought on Texas soil, first with Mexico, then with the Comanche and Kiowa, then with the Union, and finally, again, with the Indians. No other state was a combat zone for so long. In Texas, American civilization first butted up against both the Spanish empire and the warlike, nomadic Plains Indians. The threat of violence was part of daily life on a frontier stretching the width of the state, from the Rio Grande to the Red River. It wasn't until the 1880s that the western two-thirds of the state became safe enough for settlement. Toughness was necessary for making a life here and became part of the Texans' character. Settlements along the frontier survived by pulling together, creating strong community ties. Just one generation removed from a century of hardship, it isn't surprising that a sport celebrating toughness and teamwork would be embraced by the people of Texas.

The game first took root in isolated towns in West Texas, places like Breckinridge, Cisco, and Brownwood, where high schools represented communities the way college squads represent states. This mindset is still strong in the Lone Star State. In rural areas, the town and the team are synonymous. Often the relationship between fans and the high school team is more personal than that of the pro or college fan. These are *their* boys, representing their town. The community has watched these kids grow up and takes personal pride in their performance. Pro and college games are spectacles and diversions, but the high school games are about family and community. In Texas, it's still accepted wisdom that football builds boys into men and can lift a school and community in ways no other activity can. Texans simply see the sport differently. In Texas, high school football still matters.

The difference can be seen immediately, from a landing airplane or by driving down the highway. Huge, poured concrete stadiums designed to hold ten to twenty thousand people, bleachers with seatbacks, and video replay scoreboards are commonplace. The norm for a Texas high school football program is far above what is exceptional in any other state. The best high school stadiums in most states would be run-of-the-mill 3A facilities in Texas, while the top Texas facilities are superior to those at many colleges in other parts of the country.

Most schools in Texas have a fieldhouse for athletic teams. Locker rooms for each team and a large group coaches' office, with separate desks for assistant coaches, are always part of the layout. A large laundry room, training room, and weight room are also always on-site.

The facilities demonstrate how Texans view the game and its importance. What would seem ostentatious elsewhere looks natural here. Games are important and attending them is a cherished civic function. It's only right that proper facilities are built. As impressive as the architecture is, however, the real differences are much more significant.

After twenty-two years as a high school football coach in Reno, Nevada, my career hit a dead end after a disagreement with my school's administration. I spent a year teaching without coaching, but found it unrewarding and dull. It was time to try something new, so I retired. My love of high school football was still strong, and deep down, I'd long been drawn to seeing the game at its highest level, in Texas.

Ever since I'd read *Friday Night Lights* as a young coach, I'd been intrigued by the idea of a place where high school football was still a priority. I'd worked with several Texas transplants and could hardly believe their stories of year-round athletic periods with fifteen coaches and hundreds of kids working on football skills, where schools drew tens of thousands to games. For many, including the author of *Friday Night Lights*, this prioritization of football has been seen as misguided and destructive. But *FNL* was written twenty-five years ago and only covered one program. I wondered whether Permian of 1988 was representative of Texas today. I was curious about the different permutations of what is the "national game" of this huge and diverse state. Is there any commonality to how this model shapes young Texans from different backgrounds?

In organization, scope, or reach, no other nation has anything like high school football. If the quote by Wellington after the Battle of Waterloo is to be believed, the British owed their defeat of Napoleon to "the playing fields of Eton" as much as any formal military training. With its greater cultural relevance, how much more have Americans been shaped by their experience on the gridiron? No place could better answer that question than Texas.

Despite negative stereotypes about Texas high school football, I wondered if it could be a model of how to balance academics and athletics in public education. My gut told me that Texas might be onto something. Learning the details of the Texas model seemed like a fascinating way to spend a year.

What would a football program look like when a coach has every resource at his disposal? There were a million things I wanted to do when I was coaching, but couldn't because they weren't affordable, I had too little help, or the players were too raw. In Texas, coaches usually have the tools to prepare teams without making compromises. This was a dream situation for me and something I wanted to see firsthand. I'd never done anything like this before, and the thought of devoting a year to roaming around Texas watching high school football was both scary and exciting. Excitement won out.

I loaded my Ford Focus with two suitcases, a cooler, a laptop, notebooks, a camera, a video recorder, and an audio recorder and headed to San Antonio, site of the Texas High School Coaches Association Convention, Coaching School, and All-Star Game. I crossed into Texas on August 25 and, but for a few days, would not leave until three days before Christmas.

The excitement is just starting as I arrive. *Dave Campbell's Texas Football* magazine, "The Bible of Texas Football," came out a few weeks ago, the seven-on-seven tournaments are done, and the first day of practice is only days away. Summer vacations are wrapping up; coaches are spending time with family before the five-month marathon is about to begin. After an off-season of lifting weights, playing lesser sports, and coaches being hired, fired, and changing schools, seventeen weeks of the best high school football in the country is gearing up. In big cities and tiny ranch towns on the West Texas plains, in the piney woods of East Texas, on the oil field, in upper-middle-class suburbs of the Metroplex, in the Hill Country, and down south in the Rio Grande Valley, social calendars will soon revolve around local teams. Rich, poor, black, Hispanic, and Anglo (in Texas, "Anglo" is the common term, rather than white or Caucasian), Texans are united by a passion for high school football.

For a lifelong educator who'd lost faith in the system, my hope was that, in Texas, I'd find a place where schools still teach rather than test. I hoped to find a place where complete education is still valued and respected, a place where pride can still be seen and where communities still come together to display their best on autumn Friday nights.

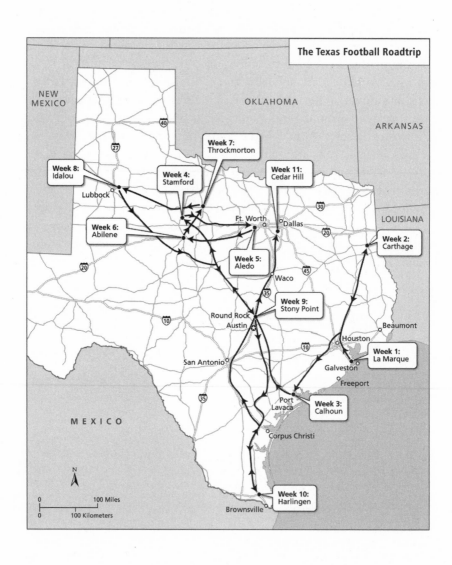

The Texas Football Roadtrip

NEW MEXICO

OKLAHOMA

ARKANSAS

Week 7:
Throckmorton

Week 8:
Idalou

Week 4:
Stamford

Week 11:
Cedar Hill

Lubbock

Ft. Worth   Dallas

LOUISIANA

Week 6:
Abilene

Week 2:
Carthage

Week 5:
Aledo

Waco

Week 9:
Stony Point

Beaumont

Round Rock
Austin

Houston

Week 1:
La Marque

San Antonio

Galveston

Freeport

MEXICO

Port
Lavaca

Week 3:
Calhoun

Corpus Christi

N

0   100 Miles
0   100 Kilometers

Week 10:
Harlingen

Brownsville

1

THE CHAMPIONSHIP DRUG
Week One: La Marque Cougars

"CTS"

"La Marque is a dying town." It's something heard from residents, teachers, coaches, and administrators when describing this community just across the causeway from Galveston Island. It's easy to see when driving the main drag between I-45 and the oil refineries marking its border with Texas City. La Marque isn't an urban ghetto but a suburban one, with the feel of a neglected country town. Coming into town, I pass weedy vacant lots where nothing will ever be built and half-empty neighborhoods of abandoned homes and boarded up businesses. The well-tended and tidy blocks that make the backbone of the town are only a few blocks from the main drag. These are neighborhoods of stubborn people refusing to join the white flight that's taken so many of their neighbors to the more affluent communities of Texas City, Friendswood, and League City up the interstate toward Houston.

Typical of a small Texas town, the cultural center of La Marque is the high school. Old-timers talk about the La Marque High School they grew up with. The school had been a melting pot, the best of what desegregation was supposed to be. La Marque was a well-rounded school then, excelling both athletically and academically. Locals were proud to have La Marque High School represent them and happy to send their kids there. This was before the economy and Hurricane Ike ran most of the whites and many affluent black families out of town. Team pictures lining the hallway outside the coaches' office tell the story: predominately Anglo teams during the 1970s, becoming blacker as the years go by. Now, the economy, the storms, pressure from the state government, and bureaucratic infighting between the townspeople and the La Marque Independent

1

School District (LMISD) have led to talk about the school being shut down. The successful football program and its traditions are all that's left of a once thriving school.

Back when a man could make a good living with blue-collar skills, La Marque was a solid working-class community of people who'd come to service the oil industry. The refineries are still here, but the economic downturn has hit hard. The plants no longer run at full capacity and cutbacks have meant layoffs. Layoffs lowered property values and resulted in a poorer tax base for the LMISD, accelerating white flight as residents moved to send their kids to more prosperous schools. The vicious cycle is complete when perceived failure of the schools further erodes property values.

While much of what La Marque was has disappeared, one important thing remains: an outstanding football program with amazing young athletes, raised to understand and respect the traditions of Cougar football.

People in La Marque take pride in those traditions. La Marque boys are taught at a young age about the flags flying behind the north end zone at Etheredge Stadium, five on tall flagpoles for state championship wins and five on shorter ones for state final appearances. Boys begin their education in La Marque football at five years old, when they pad up for the peewee Cougars. This isn't a place that pretends winning *isn't* important, that football is just about going out and playing. From the time they start competing, La Marque boys know winning *is* important and expected. And they do win. In peewee, junior high, freshman, JV, and varsity, Cougar athletes usually play up to expectations. By the time they reach high school, they know how to win, expect to win, and know how winning feels. Beyond simple desire, La Marque is blessed with dazzling athletes. This is a regular stop for college coaches recruiting in the Houston area, and every year La Marque grads go to college with football scholarships.

Since it began playing during the 1930s, La Marque had fielded mostly middling teams. La Marque's rise to elite status began when the black school, Lincoln High School, closed and La Marque integrated in 1970. Throughout the 1970s and early '80s, La Marque often made the playoffs but rarely advanced. La Marque had always been a good football town, but it was during the post-segregation period that the program became central to the community.

"People saw what could be done when they combined Lincoln and La Marque together into one outstanding high school," Mike Lockwood, a proud 1971 graduate of the first integrated senior class, told me. The community took pride in those teams and in the school during those years. There was much to be proud of, too: La Marque was recognized not only for football but also for having one of the best academic programs in the state.

During the 1970s and early '80s, La Marque became a quality, respected program, but there's a huge gulf between being "respected" and being one of the handful of teams on the statewide radar by competing for a state championship. Under coach Hugh Massey, La Marque crossed that gulf in 1986. In what spare time he had, he was a volunteer assistant for the United States Football League's Houston Gamblers, where he was one of the innovators of the run-and-shoot offense. In 1986, the Cougars took off, winning district and advancing three rounds into the playoffs. Tragically, however, Massey wouldn't see the payoff. That weekend, before the regional championship game, he was killed in an auto accident while returning to La Marque from a meeting in Galveston. An assistant coach took over and led the Cougars through the remainder of the playoffs, taking them to their first championship game, where they lost to Plano in the finals. After that first taste of the big game, there was no going back. Expectations changed. Winning district wasn't enough. The Cougars had been to the "Promised Land" and needed to get back.

The next head coach, Larry Nowotny, a Massey assistant, left in 1998, and La Marque hired Alan Weddell in 1990. He immediately predicted to the press, "We are not just going to win some football games, we're going to win some championships." During the Weddell era, winning championships became the expectation at La Marque. In his eight years, La Marque won three state championships and made it to the title game five straight times, bringing the flag total at Etheredge Stadium to six.

Larry Walker succeeded Weddell. Walker led the Cougars to their sixth straight championship appearance in 1998, but a 31-8 record over the next three seasons didn't satisfy the supporters and he was let go after the 2001 season. During the 1990s, La Marque recorded 127 victories, more than any other program in the state. Bryan Erwin replaced Walker. In his five years at La Marque, Coach Erwin posted a record of 65-8, winning two state titles. Erwin led the Cougars to their fourth title in 2003, completing an undefeated season by beating Denton Ryan in a triple-overtime championship game, 43-35. In 2005, a victory over Waco brought a fifth championship flag to Etheredge.

Winning a championship in the 4A inevitably brings lucrative offers from richer Independent School Districts (ISDs), and in 2007 Erwin left La Marque to take a 5A job in the Metroplex. This dynamic brought in Chris Jones, who was hired away from Class 2A Refugio. Jones lasted one year at La Marque. His 2007 team went 9-3, but by now Cougar fans expected more. Many weren't convinced Jones had what it took to coach at what had become a very tough school. The Coogs were winning, but some saw an inability to discipline his squad correctly and worried that the lack of discipline would cost them when facing tough opponents deep in the playoffs.

Cougar fans let their displeasure be known late in the season. Despite a 7-0 record, La Marque supporters were chanting, "We want a new coach," during the week eight game after the Cougars started slowly. Things got worse when the Cougars were bounced by Lumberton in the second round. By now, this early an exit from the playoffs wasn't tolerable, and Coach Jones resigned. It's accepted around La Marque that he was pressured to go. Anonymous threats and "For Sale" signs were punched into the Jones' yard. "The kids thought he was overwhelmed by the fanaticism of the place," a local booster told me.

Darrell Jordan replaced Jones as coach in 2008. After two poor seasons, his 2010 squad limped into the playoffs, fourth in district, but advanced to the state finals, falling to Aledo at Cowboys Stadium. Despite making it to state, locals say Jordan had lost control of the team and the confidence of the community. They believe the 2010 team went to state *despite* coaching, not because of it.

A local businessman told me, "He didn't understand how to handle these kids and he didn't want to be a part of the community. In 2010 we barely made the playoffs, then went all the way to the state finals, but only because the parents stepped in." Once again, La Marque was looking for a coach.

La Marque is a tough place to coach. The people can be unforgiving and quick to second-guess. Expectations are always high and failure to meet those expectations is often fatal. "We've been to the big dance ten times with five different coaches over the last twenty years. We know we have the talent to get there, it's just a matter of finding the right coach," said Lockwood, a member of the hiring committee in 2010. He's right, but it also takes the right person to do the job with the bar set so high. Even the peewee success can be a double-edged sword for the high school coach. On the plus side, kids develop an expectation of winning long before arriving at the high school, and they're taught football skills at a young age. But youth coaches make a core group of somewhat knowledgeable football men, people who know enough to quickly second-guess what's going on with the high school team. To coaches, these are the worst back-seat drivers, seeing the mistakes without being privy to all the factors that caused them.

That said, the job has a strong allure. At La Marque, a coach knows he'll have outstanding athletes and a passionate, football-savvy following. There are only so many programs in Texas that have legitimate shots of winning it all. Coaches don't advertise this, but the ceiling at a particular school is generally known. At La Marque, the sky's the limit. An ambitious coach, if he can weather the storms and gain the people's confidence, can count on competing at the highest level of Texas football, and the possibility of coaching a state championship team is worth the risk for many.

Outsiders see La Marque as a suburb of Houston or Galveston, but it sees itself as a small town, self-contained and proud of its identity. In small-town Texas, local boosters often have influence within the football program. These people are important in getting the community behind the program.

Coaches come and go, but the boosters remain. Lockwood is a lifelong resident and a graduate of La Marque's class of 1971. "Papa Coog," as he fittingly describes himself, owns a local lumberyard, but his real passion is Cougar football. According to Lockwood, "Best way I can explain it is that La Marque football is up there with God and family. When we win a championship, this town changes, the people change. It's like a drug: once you've been to the big show, you just gotta get back."

Lockwood started the Coogsports.net website. He also produces a local telecast of La Marque games, shown on a local community access station and YouTube. Lockwood has become the most important middleman between the program and the community, not an unimportant role considering the friction between coaches and the people of La Marque. When it came time to find a new coach in 2010, Lockwood was one of ten on the hiring committee.

Lockwood explained what the committee was hoping to find. "We were looking for four basic things. One: restore the program. Two: restore discipline, which had gotten out of control between 2007 and 2010. Three: be a father figure to many of the student-athletes. And four: plan to stay in La Marque for a number of years."

This is a poor school, full of kids with dysfunctional family lives. Well over 60 percent of the students come from economically disadvantaged homes. Basic needs like food, shelter, and safety are not a given. Crime and drug abuse are common. Coaching here requires more than just coaching ability; coaches must be mentors and social workers at La Marque. The committee wanted a coach who would go into the homes and work with church leadership.

Supporters of La Marque football had been embarrassed by the behavior of some of their teams. Behavior was the main reason Jordan was gone despite leading his team to state. The committee selected ten candidates to interview from the thirty-four who applied. Lockwood described how it went down.

"Dr. Mike Jackson drew the short straw for Saturday's interviews, the last one of the day. Now think about that. . . . ten committee members already having listened to nine other candidates, only taking a one-hour lunch break, and it was almost ten o'clock on a Saturday night. I had maybe three viable candidates, but no one really hit the right note yet. In walks Jackson with two six-packs of Red Bull. . . . plops [one] down in front of five committee members on the right side of the half-moon table and the other six-pack on the other side. He comes out firing: 'OK everyone wake up. . . . I'm going to show and tell you how I am the best candidate for the job.' I turned around and looked at my buddy and whispered, 'Where in the hell has this guy been all day?'

"Jackson passed out a small brochure [most other candidates handed out a book] of who he was, who he is, and what he would do starting day one in La Marque. Before the first question was asked he told us a short introductory story. It went something like this: 'You probably want to know if I can handle the pressure of coaching in La Marque. Well, I passed the test of handling pressure many years ago when I was a young head coach at the age of twenty-five. My team was in the state title game, we were behind, it was fourth-and-goal at the eight-yard line. I didn't have any timeouts left, with twenty-five seconds to call the final play of a game that would define me as a coach for many years to come.'

"Silence . . . then more silence . . . we [the committee] are all hinged on his next statement. He holds up his state title ring. My buddy to the right bruised my ribs with his elbow after hearing this opening statement. Either the man was a mind reader, stole the questionnaire sheet, or did extensive research on what La Marque was looking for in a head coach/athletic director . . . but he nailed every question. I was ready to put the pads back on after forty years, go out, and knock the shit out of someone and say 'I am from La Marque and damn proud of it!' That's how a majority of us felt after his hour flew by."

In Jackson, the committee believed they found someone who knows how to win and do it the right way, putting a championship-caliber team on the field that La Marque supporters can be proud to call their own.

Jackson has the rare distinction of never having been an assistant coach. He started his career at the age of 22 at St. Paul Catholic in Shiner in 1991. In 1992, his Cardinals won the private school state championship. Later, Jackson took the job at Houston Saint Pius X and won another state title.

While there are many good private school teams in Texas, the real prestige and much better pay is in the University Interscholastic League (UIL). Jackson began moving up the ranks in the public schools. In 1999, he took Charlotte to the fourth round of the UIL playoffs. His father was diagnosed with cancer and he gave up coaching, for a time, taking a principal job in Houston to be near home during his dad's treatment. The cancer went into remission, and Jackson returned to coaching at Milby in 2004. From there, he moved to a 5A school in Houston, Chavez, in 2006.

Though he was successful at Chavez, taking the Lobos to the playoffs five years in a row, Jackson longed for another shot at a state championship, this time in the more competitive UIL. At Chavez, the ceiling was low. Making the playoffs is an achievement, but a state championship is unlikely for a Houston ISD, 5A school. At La Marque, the playoffs are a minimum expectation. Schools like La Marque, with its tradition and talent, are both tempting and dangerous for coaches. There's an opportunity for a ring, but coaches who fall short will soon be looking for new jobs.

Hopes are high this year; La Marque's declining enrollment has one positive side effect. Every two years, the governing body for Texas high school athletics, the UIL, realigns the nine classifications for athletics based on enrollment. The 245 largest schools play in the 5A, the next 245 go 4A, 245 are sent to the 3A. With the small schools, 2A is split into Division I and II, 1A is split into eleven-man D-I and II. Schools under 100 students have the option of playing six-man and are put into Division I and II based on enrollment. Biannual UIL realignment has moved the Cougars from the 4A to the 3A.

Because the movement into and around Texas is very volatile, with new schools opening in the suburbs and older schools getting smaller, teams commonly bounce between different classifications. New schools may be in 3A when they open and quickly find themselves in 5A as surrounding subdivisions grow. Other schools move to smaller classifications. Schools with stable populations may move up or down as the cutoff numbers are adjusted.

In Texas, there isn't much stigma attached to being in a lower division or added prestige to being in a higher one. Great 3A programs can beat many 5A schools, and poor 5A schools don't match up well with the best in the 3A. In 2011, Lake Travis was widely considered the best team in the state despite playing in the 4A. In 2012, the Cavaliers moved up to 5A while perennial 4A powers La Marque, Stephenville, El Campo, and Abilene Wylie dropped to 3A. The real difference between the classifications is the number of quality teams in each. The entire 3A may have twenty to thirty outstanding programs, the 4A has forty to fifty, and the 5A is a meat grinder where even mediocre non-playoff teams can be dangerous.

Jackson's first task was getting control of the program. "The inmates were running the asylum," Jackson tells me of the behavior of some Cougars during his first season in 2011. Jackson risked some tough games early, benching several starters for disrespecting teachers and others who were late for practice. Supporters grumbled, but a precedent was set; certain things simply wouldn't be tolerated. Behavior improved.

There have been hiccups. Relapses occurred during the Manvel semifinal game. The Cougars fell behind and kids began pulling in different directions, yelling at each other and losing composure. During the second half La Marque made it a game, scoring three touchdowns, but the comeback fell short and 2011 ended with a 38-35 loss.

That game is one reason for this year's optimism. Even in the loss, there were positive signs that a return to state may come as soon as this year.

Manvel has three times the enrollment of La Marque. They've moved to the 5A, while the Cougars will play in 3A. La Marque returns eight starters on defense. Only two offensive starters are back, but the Cougars have so much talent, the defense should carry them. If the team stays strong and healthy through a tough non-district schedule, the Cougars have a great shot at hanging a sixth championship flag in the end zone.

I drive in from Austin after making a circuit of the state. I'd spent the past weeks on the road, and I'm glad to spend an entire week in the same place. I arrive in La Marque for their zero week matchup against the Galveston Ball Tornados. Preparation begins on Friday afternoon when the Cougars return to La Marque after their final scrimmage against Friendswood. The offensive players meet in the large assistant coaches' office, while the defense gathers in an adjoining conference room to watch film of their just-completed scrimmage.

Many 3A teams have players working on both sides of the ball, but top-end programs in this classification field separate offensive and defensive units. As is typical in the top three classifications, freshmen at La Marque learn both offensive and defensive positions, but from sophomore to senior year, most players work exclusively on one side of the ball with a position coach, who also works only one position. Platooning teams have many advantages over teams playing "iron man" football. One-way players are fresher, exploding off the ball for each play, while two-way players pace themselves. Even more important is preparation: one-way players spend twice as much time as two-way players working on assignments and techniques of their position.

Football is the most complex sport in the world, full of unnatural skills and techniques only gained through meticulous coaching and endless repetition. Coaches who focus on teaching a handful of kids a few specific skills are more effective than those doing a little of everything. A running backs coach who's also the defensive coordinator may not have time to implement ball security drills, but a full-time running backs coach knows his career is tied to hanging onto the ball and teaches those techniques with a passion. In a district where many opponents have players going both ways, one-way players give La Marque a huge advantage.

As is usually true with early scrimmages, play against Friendswood is sloppy, but the coaches are generally happy.

"There is a reason every adult has 'coach' in front of his name," Jackson informs the inexperienced offense. "Don't hang your heads about the mistakes you made, we're going to coach you up. Remember, we're all pulling on the same rope." The defense played very well today. They are experienced, and their pursuit speed gave Friendswood problems. After about an hour of watching film, the critique ends and the kids leave. The coaches either hurry off to prepare for the first day of school Monday or begin watching the little Ball film they have. Kickoff isn't until Thursday, but the season has begun.

Saturday morning at 8:00, thirteen coaches meet to work out the game plan for Galveston Ball. The offensive coaches are in the main office, while the defensive staff is in the conference room. Usually this day involves watching lots of film. The offensive staff looks for tendencies of the upcoming opponent.

During week zero, finding much is always difficult. The only films are from Ball's scrimmages and last year's game. Teams don't run much of their offense during scrimmages, giving coaches little to work with. There's much guessing about personnel, but the coaches are confident about the scheme they'll see. G-Ball has a run-oriented attack, a triple I, with three running backs in the backfield. They're big but don't move well. On defense, the Tornadoes run a 3-4, and the offensive coaches aren't impressed by how Ball outside linebackers get to the flat. This could be huge. Getting the ball to the perimeter is a major part of La Marque's offense.

Coach Jackson's offense is all about speed and tempo. It uses elements of the spread, but the blocking is strongly rooted in wing-T philosophy. Instead of the zone blocking used by most spread teams, La Marque down blocks and pulls, blocking defenders at an angle and driving them laterally. Like the spread, however, the quarterback often acts as a running back and reads the pursuit, pulling the ball from the running back and taking off when he sees an opening. Like Chip Kelly's offense at the University of Oregon, the real key of the offense is the tempo. Coach Jackson says, "The one constant is the clock. Control the clock and you have a big advantage." The goal is to use tempo to dictate to the defense, getting to the ball quickly and snapping it as soon as it's set, not allowing the defense to regroup or switch personnel. Playing defense requires more energy than offense. Keep leaning on a team and their weaknesses become glaring. With great athletes, mismatches lead to big plays. La Marque never huddles, calling its plays from a wristband. Much practice time is spent running plays versus air (no defense), working at getting plays off faster. There is some second-guessing from the Cougar faithful about this offense; some fans would rather see a more wide-open attack, throwing the ball downfield instead of relying so much on the run and quick screen passes. The deep ball is in the scheme but may not fit this team very well. Quarterback Demun Mercer is an outstanding athlete and also dangerous running the ball, but the receiving corps has been unsteady, dropping many balls.

The defensive staff discusses adjustments and the offensive coaches talk about plays they'll run. It's a veteran staff; five of the thirteen assistants have been head coaches but were drawn to La Marque by the opportunity to work in a program with so much tradition and the chance to compete for a state championship. This is just a stop on the coaching carousel for many assistants, a chance to add a championship to their resumes before going on to other jobs. They make sacrifices to be here; assistant pay isn't very good and the facilities are poor. Low, swampy spots and mosquitoes cover the practice fields, and there's no true fieldhouse like those found at most 3A or above schools. The stadium, while considered "hallowed ground" by La Marque supporters, is old and has none of the modern trappings that have become common throughout Texas. There's no replay scoreboard or seatbacks at Etheredge, just fanatical support and tradition.

The offensive meeting is conducted by offensive coordinator John Launius and assistant offensive line coach Pete Gareri. The defensive meeting is run by defensive coordinator Mike Lawrence. Jackson briefly comes from his private office and talks to the coaches about personnel issues. Several players are on the fence between JV and varsity. Jackson keeps a light hand on the offensive side of the plan. He knows he's hired quality coaches and he doesn't step on their toes by interfering with the game plan. He spends most of Sunday in the fieldhouse, taking care of administrative details and meeting with Launius and Gareri privately, giving his input before they finalize the game plan.

It's a relatively quick day. As the season progresses, Saturdays can last until well after sunset. Without much film to base a plan on, today's meeting breaks up early in the afternoon. The coaches know their assignments and are expected to be ready for athletic period on Monday, the first day of school.

The Ball-La Marque rivalry goes back many years. Galveston is only separated from La Marque by a mile-long bridge. The annual non-district opener is known as the Clash of the Causeway. At one time the two teams were more evenly matched, but in recent years La Marque has taken control of the series. Hurricane Ike hammered both schools and communities in 2008. La Marque lost 600 residents, but neighboring Galveston took the bigger hit. Ball lost almost a quarter of its enrollment, and the city still hasn't fully recovered. While it may not be a great matchup on the field, the La Marque-G-Ball game is still important locally. Kids in La Marque grow up with kids from Ball, and many have relatives at the other school. Jackson says, "They may go 0-10, but you can count on Ball playing their best football of the year in this game."

The most significant difference between a Texas school day and a school day elsewhere is the schedule for student-athletes. Along with math and English, a Texan has athletic period, with the entire team and coaching staff. Athletics at La Marque is held fourth period; Monday, the players file into the coaches' offices for their initial scout of the Tornadoes. They look good in their school clothes; La Marque requires collared shirts and long pants. No sagging pants or electronics are allowed, and at least on the first day of school, the students conform. This is a short week for the Cougars. The UIL doesn't allow televised Friday night games. The Causeway Battle will be on TV and held on Thursday night, making it one of the first games of the 2012 season.

The offensive staff hands out packets and goes over the game plan in the office while the kids sit around the room. The plan is very simple; the goal for the week is to do a few things well. This unit is still inexperienced, taking baby steps. Launius tells the offensive unit, "In any game there will be peaks and valleys, highs and lows. When we get a low we can't hit the panic button. We just have to execute and play our tempo and we'll be fine."

Meanwhile, Lawrence and his staff meet with the defensive players in the mat room. Each player has been given a packet; a cartoon of a muscle-bound Panther tearing apart the bridge leading to Galveston is on the front page. The packet includes diagrams of every Ball formation and the plays run from each. As the kids leaf through the packet, Lawrence goes through personnel and alignment adjustments.

It's hot and muggy in Galveston County this week; thunderstorms have left the practice fields damp, with standing water in low spots. On my first visit, I learned a valuable lesson about foot protection in the humid parts of the state. After three hours of standing on the hot, soggy turf, my shoes were soaked through and my feet swollen to the point that it was painful to walk. Subsequently, I always made sure I had a fresh pair of shoes and socks handy.

The freshmen are outside for athletics the last period of the day. Several freshman coaches review special teams assignments as the varsity files out at 3:00. Jackson is already on the practice field. As always, he wears a baggy, dark blue pullover warm-up despite the stifling heat. He usually spends individual position time or "indy time" by himself. He doesn't coach a position, preferring to keep some distance, observing what his coaches teach and how players respond. Occasionally, he'll pull a kid from a drill to correct or discipline if he sees something to fix without stepping on toes.

La Marque has four practice fields, and after a short warm-up the defense and offense separate for individual drills. During the week the two units rarely work together. Today, as usual at La Marque, there's no contact during practice. After an indy period, the offense works on their tempo by running plays versus air, going through formations and plays they'll use against Ball. Over on the defensive field, Lawrence and his staff align to formations shown by a JV offense.

La Marque practices are broken into five-minute segments; a segment timer is propped up underneath the main filming tower behind the end zone of the offensive practice field. On a portable bleacher underneath the tower, Pastor Jerry Lee and several other local boosters enjoy the shade, talk about the days' events, and watch practice.

Alongside the tower is a large blue-and-white sign, listing the years the Cougars have won their district and how far each year's team advanced in the playoffs. Above those boxes are '95, '96, '97, '03, and '06, the years the Cougars won state championships.

The coaches are happy with today's practice. The first day of school can be tough. With the new routine of going to classes and practice, kids can become distracted and sluggish. Today, the Cougars look crisp and businesslike. After an hour and forty-five minutes, the varsity goes into the air-conditioned weight room for a quick workout. The JV stays outside to work on their own, now that their other role of preparing the varsity is over for the day.

After practice, coaches compare their new teaching schedules. Most are already apprehensive about the school year. In Texas, the norm is for coaches to teach one less academic class, because athletic period with their team is part of the teaching schedule. In many ISDs, a teacher/coach will actually have two fewer classes and be assigned to both freshman and varsity athletic periods.

But the La Marque ISD needs to cut corners. The state cut 10 percent of funds across the board on what it allocates to La Marque. With the local tax base being what it is, LMISD has to be creative in covering its needs. This week, the coaching staff learned one of the ways, one that will affect them. Instead of having athletic period on their teaching schedules, the coaches have their free, or conference period, aligned with athletic period. This means coaches won't get a break the entire school day. Running backs coach Justin Calvin dubbed this new period as "confreletic" period. The coaches joke about it, but it will make for some long days: showing up before school for position meetings, followed by a full class load, "confreletics" during their "free" period, and practice after school. The coaches will put in twelve hours before getting to catch up on other school responsibilities.

Tuesday morning at 6:45, Cougar players and coaches arrive an hour before school for position meetings. Coaches Gareri and Mike Janes meet the offensive line, going over blocking adjustments against Ball's 3-4 front. With only one starter returning, this is a raw group, but one with good size and natural ability. Gareri reminds them of the progression they should follow on each play. 1) Are they play-side or back-side? 2) What is their first step? 3) What is the snap count? If they know these three things, Gareri assures them they'll be fine against Ball. Baby steps for now. Things will get more complex later in the season, but right now, against this opponent, it's just about the basics.

During fourth-period athletics, the varsity changes into yellow T-shirts and blue shorts and goes to the weight room. The athletes are expected to sit down in straight lines before being led in a brief stretch. From there they come together for a chant and break into lifting stations by positions.

Today, some players are showing rough edges. Many are late and have forgotten nine coaches are in the room. There's a lot of joking and street talk. Launius sits patiently, watching and listening, looking at his watch as each late arriver enters, clearly unhappy with what he's seeing and taking mental notes. After the last player arrives, Launius calmly but firmly addresses the team. He tells them that it's unacceptable to take eighteen minutes to get changed and into the weight room. Five minutes should be plenty if they aren't wasting time in the hallways.

He addresses the language. He's aware of how kids talk when coaches aren't around. Nothing he can do about that, but he reminds them, "Nobody's going to hire someone yelling nigger, bitch, motherfucker, ho . . ." These kids represent the school, the coaches, and the town, and they need to present a better example. The reminder of how they *should* behave hits home. The young men respond well, the workout is short but intense, and they're soon lifting with nine coaches overseeing from various spots.

"Kids here don't need to be yelled at. They are good football kids, they know what to do, and they just need to be reminded every now and then," Lawrence tells me later.

Jackson isn't a screamer. His criticisms are commonly delivered in an, "I love you but you need to do better at . . ." way. He's firm and has absolute rules. Exceptions aren't made for star players. Jackson reminds the kids several times during Ball week that any trash talking will result in an immediate benching. The rest of the staff follows the head coach's lead. There is very little yelling at La Marque; discipline is meted calmly.

La Marque has traditionally had a lot of swagger, and their pregame warm-ups are partially designed to get under the skin of the opponent. One tradition is a distinctive kickoff team. It's as much a dance as anything: the players chant, swaying together, shoulder to shoulder, displaying a joy and intensity they're expected to play with. The whole demeanor of the Cougars can come across as arrogant to opponents, but it is also intimidating. The goal for the Cougar staff is to uncage the exuberance and give their players freedom to play with emotion without allowing that energy to cross the line into taunting and lack of control. It's a fine line.

One advantage of the Texas model is that it allows coaches to be themselves. It surprised my coaching friends in Reno that, in general, Texas coaches are less authoritarian than coaches elsewhere. In Texas, I rarely saw coaches openly ripping kids the way we sometimes did. From the first day of middle school through high school graduation, the young athlete has many coaches' eyes on him. When he's in the weight room, a coach is assigned to watch his group. When he's in math class, there's likely a coach down the hall, ready to tutor or apply consequences as needed. The student-athlete in a good program knows he'll be held accountable and learns early to act accordingly.

This isn't true in most other places. Most coaches meet the kids later in the process, have more of them, fewer assistants, and much less time. Often only one or two coaches see the kids during the offseason, and the weights teacher (usually the head coach) may be the only person at the school with a coaching role during the entire school year. With less time, teaching has to be done quickly and forcefully. Control isn't a given, and coaches might need to be the stereotypical "hardass" simply to keep the upper hand. In Texas, coaches work with their players every day for at least three years. They know them, not just as football players but as young men, and learn how best to reach them.

Seeing so many coaches and kids work closely together was a situation I could only envy. In Reno, under the best circumstances, five or six coaches work with a team. In Texas, the number was usually in double digits.

This is a short week and the practice schedule is condensed. On Tuesday, the Cougars wear full pads, but there isn't much hitting. Contact is controlled and run by position coaches during individual time. Janes drills the offensive line in second-level cut blocks using a stand-up dummy; this is not a high school drill found across the rest of the country because the technique is illegal in forty-eight states. (Texas and Maine are the only states that use the National Collegiate Athletic Association rule book instead of National High School Association rules. In addition to low blocking, this means a kickoff can be returned from the end zone, something not allowed by the NHSA book. Other differences include overtime, play clock, and some penalties.)

After indy, it's time for more tempo drill for the offense, lining up and running as many plays as possible during a two-segment (ten minutes) session. Liking what he sees, Jackson sends the offense inside. The defense continues to run through Ball's offensive plays. Coach David Montano directs the scout team, holding up the binder full of Ball plays in laminated sleeves, while Lawrence and defensive backs coach Toby Foreman make corrections. The defense stays out about ten minutes longer than the offense.

Wednesday's practice is very quick, just walk-throughs and special teams. Afterward, the players bring their helmets into the coaches' office to get their stickers: two Cougar paws with a star on each pad denoting the program's five titles. An American flag and a "CTS" to place on the bottom edge are also handed out. "CTS" stands for Coogs Take State, and is found on most of the practice gear, constantly reminding every player of the tradition and expectations of playing here.

A handful of youth coaches sit in pickups along the edge of the field and on the bleachers in the little shade provided by the filming tower during practice. Along with coaching the peewee teams, these coaches also run the varsity seven-on-seven team during the summer. (In Texas, high school coaches aren't allowed to coach during the summer when the seven-on-seven tournaments are held.) While La Marque lacks a lot, it always has an abundance of athletes. Success in youth football is all about the athlete. The team with the best kid on the field usually wins. La Marque boys and youth coaches are used to winning long before high school. High school coaching is limited to teachers, so many boosters hang around the fringes of the program, helping out wherever they can.

While the football program at La Marque is fighting to win another championship, the school and the entire LMISD are fighting for survival. Whether La Marque High School will still exist ten years from now is an open question. Rumors of the state taking over or the school shutting down are common in Galveston County. The perception is that La Marque is failing. Some wonder if the kids might be better served by closing the high school and sending them to Texas City High School a few miles up the road.

The poor economy helped lead the school to this perilous place. Political infighting among the school board, the superintendent, and community leaders has also caused friction. The *Galveston Daily News* regularly reports on squabbles within the community. The source of the fighting is hard to follow, but it reads like a soap opera and makes good copy. From the outside, the stories show a town tearing itself apart.

Recently, a school bond has been proposed to raise operating funds for the cash-strapped district. Instead of "pulling on the same rope," La Marque is fighting aboard a sinking ship. The bond faces an uphill battle. Accusations of incompetence, of a district that refuses to cut fat from its budgets, have been made. Locals claim that poor test scores by the district's students indicate poor management. All of this conveniently ignores the societal and economic factors that make success for the LMISD so difficult.

The third and perhaps most dangerous threat to the existence of LMISD might be the state of Texas itself.

Ecomet Burley has a tough job. As superintendent of the La Marque ISD, he's responsible for keeping this district afloat. The community has a falling tax base and a population that is getting smaller and older. In this climate Burley needs to convince skeptical voters to support a tax increase to cover the funding the state slashed. The situation in the community would be bad enough without additional pressure coming from Austin. LMISD has been labeled as unsatisfactory by the state's standardized testing protocol. Two years ago Texas cut 10 percent of educational spending across the board. More prosperous ISDs with higher-end homes aren't hurting as much because they get more money from property taxes. Schools like La Marque feel the squeeze most. La Marque lost $1.5 million in state funding in 2011, and this year it will lose $1.6 million.

At least as troubling as funding is the fact that the LMISD has been rated a failing school district by the state. This rating isn't based on reading, math, or science test scores. Under the Texas Assessment of Knowledge and Skills (TAKS), LMISD has shown steady improvement in all academic areas since 2006. La Marque is a transient community; students come and go. One criterion requires schools to maintain records on all students who've ever been enrolled. Here LMISD has been deemed inadequate.

Put simply, the LMISD is being dragged through the mud because it's lost track of too many former students. These students could be dropouts or living in Houston, Dallas, or anywhere. The LMISD is required to divert resources from the students who *are* attending to search for students who aren't. If the missing students aren't found, the district may be taken over by the state.

On the federal side, the academic scores have been acceptable, but the district is reaching a danger point with No Child Left Behind. According to federal law, LMISD schools must improve to 93 percent on reading proficiency to reach adequate yearly progress during 2012, a goal that may be unreachable.

"The purpose of testing should be to improve instruction, but it's become about sorting success from failure," said Burley.

Paraphrasing the Bible, Burley says, "When the Israelites were held captive by Pharaoh they were forced to make bricks for the Egyptians. The Israelites were given quotas to reach or they would face punishment. They told Pharaoh they needed more straw and mortar to reach the quota. Instead of listening to reason, Pharaoh got angry with the Israelites for their impertinence and stopped giving them any mortar or straw at all, expecting the same production. That is what the state is doing to us now."

True, except that the state isn't asking for the same production, but more. In 2012, Texas stopped using the TAKS system and began using a new protocol, the State of Texas Assessments of Academic Readiness, or STAAR. With STAAR, all students are required to pass a standardized test each semester to pass every course. The state spends $450 million on this testing protocol, ten times what the state of New York pays.

Professor Cynthia Osborne of the University of Texas' Lyndon B. Johnson School of Public Affairs believes the state will eventually allow some leeway on graduation requirements; otherwise, failure rates will be too high to endure. According to Osborne, the money component of state policy hurts poorer districts like LMISD disproportionately. "The Legislature cut 10 percent across the board, but at the same time the schools are being asked to do more with less." Testing has also become a drain on time: 34 of 180 school days are now devoted to testing in La Marque and the rest of Texas' public schools.

This "one size fits all" testing policy doesn't make sense for schools that vary in enrollment from eleven students to more than

6,000, and schools with as many different demographic, ethnic, and socioeconomic populations as imaginable. For smaller schools this has caused many problems. The superintendent at Throckmorton told me the school basically shuts down on testing days since it takes five of his seven high school teachers to administer the tests. The richer districts can continue to offer superior extracurricular programs through self-funding, but poorer districts find it harder to spend money on anything that doesn't directly aid testing requirements. In states where athletics aren't valued, budget crunches devastate programs. Even in Texas, some administrators don't seem to understand the positive impact quality coaches and extracurricular programs have on educational achievement. Moving from the traditional Texas model of athletics as part of education has caused problems in some big, multi-school ISDs.

When I started teaching, the commonly accepted mission of a high school was to provide a well-rounded education offering opportunities in the arts, music, industrial arts, and athletics as well as core academics. However, schools have become increasingly handcuffed by standardized tests. The false premise that school quality can be judged as you'd judge the profitability of a business, by placing a number on it, has taken hold. Government oversight puts schools under constant pressure to improve scores. With limited budgets, school must continually find additional resources to improve test-taking skills, because administration is judged on test scores.

I saw this mindset slowly take hold when I was teaching. Fine arts, music, industrial arts, foreign language, physical education (PE), and all extracurricular activities including athletics were sacrificed amid the desperation to meet sometimes impossible goals.

Seen from a distance, holding schools accountable looks like a positive thing, but only if success on standardized tests truly reflects actual learning. Studies dispute this premise. Teachers are pressured to teach narrow curriculums designed to prepare kids for testing. Are students best served when their English class focuses on memorizing definitions rather than reading literature? This is often what testing means at the classroom level. Teachers of "non-essentials" such as PE, athletics, the arts, or the trades have become steadily more marginalized to the point where many have been eliminated.

Increased government control of schools has created a system that sends one-dimensional graduates into an increasingly multidimensional world. A school can neglect everything but testing skills and be seen as exemplary by government agencies. Students are fatter, lazier, and know fewer survival skills than they did twenty years ago, but are better at defining obscure words.

Football is the one thing that binds La Marque High School and the entire community together. Remarkably, when asked what would happen to the school without its football program, people from the superintendent down question whether the school could survive at all. Knowing the struggles of this place, from funding to testing to the infighting within this town, it's hard to doubt that La Marque High School might not exist except for football.

One-third of the male students at La Marque play football. With extra attention from their coaches, grade point averages (GPAs), graduation rates, and test results among this group create the solid backbone of the school. Fourteen La Marque boys received football scholarships in 2011, including several who went to military academies and one who went to Dartmouth College. Defensive lineman Lawrence Montegut has been offered seven scholarships, including from Texas Tech University and Rice University. The graduation rate for football players at La Marque hovers just below 100 percent. Without football, how many of these kids would drop out as so many of their classmates have? Would these kids be likely to be motivated by academic success for its own sake? Where else can they see examples of hard work leading to success? As Superintendent Burley put it, "We're not ashamed that we produce championships. We use it to let our students know that if we can do it on the playing field, we can do it in the classroom."

Despite the depressed state of the school, outstanding coaches, who often are outstanding teachers, line up for the opportunity to teach and coach here. Would this happen without football? Principal Morris Gurnell, a former La Marque coach himself, gives Jackson and his staff high marks, not just for their work on the field but also for their teaching and academic mentoring.

Montegut, a senior, agrees: "You see your coaches in the halls every day. If you mess up, they're right there to guide you." Montegut credits the coaches and the values he learned playing football as a big reason he's an A student on his way to college. Take away what football brings to this school, and La Marque High School would have a tough time surviving.

Most of the community believes in the importance of the program, but issues crop up. Last year, there was a push to end coaching stipends, a move that would have effectively killed the football program. The athletic budget was cut 10 percent, in line with the other cuts, but the school board heeded the advice from Jackson and other supporters. It's difficult to argue that the entire athletic department isn't worth the 1.5 percent of the budget allocated to it. Still, this district will continue to make tough choices as the tax base dwindles and the state squeezes.

On game day, the players wear gold ties with the Cougars' logo embroidered in blue. During athletic period, they meet with position coaches for last-minute reminders. Again, they're warned not to say anything to opposing players if they want to stay in the game. Launius lets his players know how to deal with the well-meaning but sometimes distracting supporters in the stands, "Remember, you're at La Marque. Best fans in the world, but they also know everything." Coach Lawrence is very confident about tonight, telling his charges, "This defense, right now, is about where we were in the fifth or sixth week last year." Coach Jackson expects the Tornadoes to come out flying, but thinks they'll fade once the emotion settles down and as long as the Cougars don't give them an excuse to think they're in the game.

Several coaches recommend I go to the pep rally after school, saying a La Marque pep rally is unlike anything I've ever seen. It turns out I *have* seen its like before. The suggestive, rhythmic dancing by girls in skimpy sequined costumes may not be the norm in Texas, but I'd seen many similar high school groups in New Orleans during Mardi Gras. The crescent of coastal Texas including Galveston, Houston, and Beaumont has more in common with Tidewater, Louisiana, than other parts of its state. Texas is only one state, but it has more cultural regions than most countries.

After the rally, Cougar players come in for their game uniforms, navy blue jerseys with gold numbers, COOGS stitched below the neck, matching pants with "CTS" on the right hip, and blue socks. The players head to the cafeteria for a team meal and a short devotional by Pastor Lee before getting on the air-conditioned school buses that carry them two miles to the stadium.

Etheredge Stadium is impressive, but not because there's anything noteworthy about its architecture or size. The place is simple and functional: just two slopes of steel bleachers, an adequate press box, spartan locker rooms, a basic scoreboard, and a natural turf field. What's striking is the care taken preserving it. It must have been built fifty years ago, but the 11,000-seat stadium looks brand new. It's like a perfectly restored 1970 Dodge Dart—nothing showy, but there's clear reverence for the traditions this place holds. The field is perfectly manicured and stenciled, the Cougar paw painted at midfield for the game, as the buses arrive from La Marque at 5:00.

It's a hot and muggy evening in Galveston County. The players, coaches, and fans are already dripping sweat at kickoff. The stands are about half full. This is a rivalry game, but nobody expects much from G-Ball, and their fans don't travel well. Not one to overlook any opponent, Jackson has looked nervous all day. He's a deeply superstitious man; on the sideline he dresses all in black and has several game-day rituals he follows each week. A stick of gum is given to the same chosen assistant during warm-ups, and he always finds his young daughter in the stands holding up a personalized sign of support. A few years ago he wore something that wasn't black and his team lost. Since then, he's been careful to stick to his routines.

During his pregame talk, Jackson reminds the squad of a lineman challenge tug-of-war they lost to new 3A rival Coldspring this summer. Coldspring taunted them after the loss, "Welcome to 3A." To remind his team of this humiliation and hammer home the point that all must pull together to accomplish anything, Jackson brought a thick length of rope for a player to carry onto the field each week. "Don't let go of the rope" is the team's theme for the season.

Ball is big, but sluggish and slow. Their huge linemen don't get off the ball well, clogging the running lanes needed in their stack I offense. On the second offensive play, Mercer hits receiver Daniel Lee on a screen pass for 57 yards, giving the Cougars a 7-0 lead. After a Ball fumble, La Marque quickly capitalizes with another score to go up, 14-0. La Marque switches between their shotgun stretch formation to spread the field and an offset I to pound the ball.

While clearly the better team, La Marque is sloppy. In the 35-12 victory the Cougars are their own worst enemy. The inexperienced offense puts the ball on the ground eight times, leading to both

G-Ball scores. The defense is stifling, allowing nothing from the Tornadoes' ground attack. But Jackson looks nervous and sounds disappointed and angry after the game. The Cougars need to find running backs that can hang onto the ball.

"This is my two hundred thirteenth game as a head coach, and that was the most we have ever fumbled the ball . . . I know we're young on offense, but it's not an excuse. Hang on to the football. If you're not going to hang on to the football, you're not going to play." He knows they won't get away with mistakes like this in December.

I talk with Jackson later. I'm headed to Carthage in the morning and don't know when I'll next be in Houston-Galveston. Jackson is calmer now; he's put this game in perspective, and while they have a lot of work to do, he believes he has the pieces to make a run. He invites me back for the playoffs, promising the team will look much different in November and December.

After some shuffling, they solve the turnover problem. La Marque finishes 9-1. The only regular-season blemish is an overtime loss to Coldspring-Oakhurst in week three. The Cougars avenge this loss, beating Coldspring in a second-round playoff game at Reliant Stadium in Houston. La Marque's dream of a sixth state championship would be decided by a third-round matchup with the top-ranked Navasota Rattlers.

This game effectively decides the 3A championship, and the Cougars do not play well. They squander an early scoring chance, going four-and-out inside the Navasota 10. Two bad snaps on punts, including one in the end zone, lead to two Rattler scores. La Marque makes another huge mistake, fumbling on the 5-yard line. It's hard to believe Navasota is a 3A school; they are incredibly quick and sharp. Even so, without the mental mistakes, the Cougars might have won. After beating the Cougars, the Rattlers breeze through the rest of the playoffs. Their 31-20 victory over La Marque is their only challenge during their championship run.

It's a loss of composure shown by a few Cougar players and fans that is most disappointing. On the first play of the game a player is ejected for punching a Navasota player and it goes downhill from there. As soon as the Cougars get into trouble, some supporters abandon them and begin verbally attacking coaches and players. Players slam helmets into the ground in frustration. It's a sad and ugly scene as La Marque heads inside at halftime trailing by 11.

The coaches, Principal Gurnell, and Pastor Lee spend half the intermission just trying to convince the distraught Cougars the game can be won, as long as they clean up their mistakes. The coaches settle things down and might have turned things, had the Cougars gotten a big momentum-turning play in the second half. Unfortunately, early in the third, a second bad snap in the end zone leads to another Rattler score and composure is lost for good.

It's hard to watch; all the pride and hard work disappears. Ugly football is depressing for me, especially when a program I respect embarrasses itself. Principal Gurnell is livid. As another Cougar throws his helmet he comments about his disappointment with the young player. "He doesn't understand how to be a man."

A good football team looks indestructible, but in reality it's a delicate machine. If the right stress is applied, an unseen flaw can throw one gear and the whole thing flies apart. It takes only a few players to wreck everything. Tonight it's only four "broken gears" creating the collapse. Over thirty other kids play hard and keep their dignity to the end, but that isn't what's seen or what's remembered. Months later, I spoke with Foreman, the defensive backs coach, about the game.

"There's never an excuse for that. I was as embarrassed as I've ever been in my coaching career, but it was a complete shock to us. When we lost to Coldspring, nothing like that happened." Coaches can (and do) often talk about how to handle adversity, but until adversity is faced it's hard to know if those talks are getting through.

La Marque *had* faced adversity during the 2012 campaign, but not the loss of what they saw as their birthright. La Marque kids are raised to understand that winning championships is expected. The Cougar mystique isn't about winning district or bi-district; it's about getting to the "big show" and putting more flags up at Etheredge Stadium. Other teams look at a third-round playoff loss to an eventual state champion as a good year, but at La Marque, this team failed to live up to the "CTS" ideal expected by the entire community. They were coming up short of the goal set for them many years before. When the reality set in that there would be no flag this year, some weren't strong enough to handle it. One player lost his scholarship due to his behavior during the Navasota game; another was told he won't be welcomed back to the team until he and his father had a sit-down with Coach Jackson.

What is encouraging is how the community responded to their embarrassing night. On Coogsports.net few excused the behavior from the kids or the fans. "This is the second year in a row where we have gone a few rounds in the playoffs and have been involved in altercations that have no place on any football field and have put two black eyes on our program for all to see! It's getting to be quite embarrassing . . ." commented one poster.

"Papa Coog" commented on the fans, "I am very ashamed . . . of how our fans were . . . When the fans get so fanatical and start telling the players not to listen to those *#%@ & Coaches . . . then we have a lot of soul searching to do if we expect to regain any respect . . ."

Coach Jackson has taken steps, as well. Shortly before the 2013 season he told me, "All off-season we preached accountability and dealing with disappointment like a man. Monday at the first practice the kids were told that if we lose a game this year and they take off their shoulder pads, sulk, display poor sportsmanship, etc., their careers are over right then. If it occurs in the last game of the season like last year they will not receive their varsity letter, they will not be pushed for scholarships, will not be nominated for any postseason all-district, state, county awards, etc. . . . I have to do my best to make sure something like that never occurs again."

While the end was ugly, the season had positives, too. Regardless of what some in the community think, football is *not* only about winning championships. If it were, the thousands of teams that don't hoist trophies would be wasting time. The effort to win is important (anything worth doing should be done with that goal in mind), but sometimes the most important lessons are taught in defeat. The scholarships a *very* few receive are one tangible benefit football brings to student-athletes. Others are harder to point out. Teamwork, work ethic, discipline, commitment, and respect were taught and learned during the Cougars' eleven wins in 2012. The harsh lesson of what happens when those foundations are forgotten was taught during the season-ending loss to Navasota. These lessons aren't things taught in a classroom, but are at least as important.

Nine Cougar players from the 2012 squad signed letters of intent to play college football. Mercer would sign with Texas State

University and Montegut would choose University of Texas at El Paso (UTEP) over Rice. Several assistant coaches would leave for head jobs at other schools, but Jackson has had no problems finding quality replacements. In November 2012, the bond issue to raise operating dollars for the LMISD failed by a wide margin. Both Superintendent Burley and Principal Gurnell would leave the La Marque ISD at the end of 2012. The future is as up in the air as ever.

2

THE FINAL LESSON
Week Two: Carthage Bulldogs

"WE BELIEVE In God, In Family, In Our Community, In Our Ability To Win"

—Sign hanging in the hallway of the Carthage fieldhouse.

"The ultimate measure of a man is not where he stands in moments of comfort and convenience, but where he stands at times of challenge and controversy."

—Martin Luther King Jr. quote on a sign in the varsity locker room.

Before spending whole weeks anywhere, I visited each program in August during two-a-days. I wanted to introduce myself, check out the motel where I'd be staying, and most importantly, get a feel for the countryside. The circuit of all eleven schools took two weeks and added 5,000 miles to my odometer, but gave me a greater appreciation of the size and scope of terrain in Texas. During the regular season, most of the driving between cities would be done at night, after Friday night's game and the Saturday morning meetings. I love driving to new places, seeing different things, and trying to get an idea of how the people live in the places I pass. So I was excited to be getting my first look at East Texas when I left Houston and drove north to Carthage.

In this part of Texas, there's much more you can't see than what you can. East Texas is very different from where I'd just left. Houston-Galveston was coastal plains—flat, but big horizons. Leaving Houston, I was quickly swallowed by trees, with strips cut for power lines, natural gas installations, and the occasional town. Heading up to Carthage through Cleveland and Nacogdoches, I passed swampy ponds and endless expanses of trees, but never got a view of the surroundings. The flat topography and the trees keep the horizons close. This forest is different than those I know out west. In the

West, forests and mountains share the countryside; even in Central Texas, hills allow one a sense of the surroundings. Here, the feeling is claustrophobic, like looking up from the bottom of a shallow canyon, except the canyon is made of trees. I never see more than a few hundred yards into the distance. A trainer from these parts told me, "The difference between West Texas and East Texas is that in West Texas people like to see what's coming at them." During the evening and early afternoon, the sound of the bugs is so steady that I quickly stopped hearing it.

East Texas is part of the South in a way the rest of Texas isn't. The culture of the place is closer to neighboring Louisiana and Arkansas than the rest of the state. Unlike the big Texas cities, the speech patterns are southern. People here go to Shreveport for their shopping, not Dallas or Houston. The local sports section covers the New Orleans Saints and Louisiana State University (LSU) along with Texas teams.

I arrive in Carthage the Saturday of Labor Day weekend. The players have a three-day weekend, so the Bulldog coaches have decided to stretch out their work, giving the players Saturday and Sunday off. For the coaches, however, this is anything but an easy weekend. The extra day simply gives the coaches twenty-four extra hours to fix problems from last night.

Carthage lost a heartbreaker to Jacksonville last night. After the game, as usual, the coaches went to work breaking down the film, finishing up around 4:30 in the morning. Now, at 9:00 Saturday morning, defensive coordinator Darrin Preston and a few linebackers are in the fieldhouse watching the film. Preston is unhappy and looks disgusted as he repeatedly runs key plays on the screen. The linebackers and safeties are especially bad. The starting safety has a hairline fracture and will be out three weeks, and the backup isn't working out. The young replacement looks completely lost, dropping deep when he should come up and coming up when he needs to stay behind streaking receivers. The linebackers look tentative, going around blockers instead of taking them on and getting fooled by play-action. The defensive coordinator looks pained watching such poor execution, knowing the blown assignments were a factor in turning a very winnable game into a loss. Preston has been around long enough to know that the first game is usually full of glaring mistakes. Coaches often don't really know their team until they see them in a game, so it's often trial and error in finding the right eleven to put on the field. Knowing this doesn't make watching the Bulldogs blow the game any easier.

The staff worked so hard to put the Bulldogs in position to win, but somehow they couldn't find a way to finish, giving the game away again and again. The backbreaker came during the final minute. With a 3-point lead, a sophomore Carthage defensive back intercepted a pass along the sideline that should have ended the game. Instead of going down or out of bounds, the young Bulldog ran the ball back, cut across the field, and was stripped. Jacksonville recovered and, a few plays later, scored the winning touchdown. The coaches can't help but question themselves. With all the hours they put in and all the situations they prepared the team for, they'd never coached the defense about what to do when picking off a pass during the final minute with a lead.

Yes, the cornerback should have understood the situation, but the coaches know better than to expect a sophomore playing his first varsity game to be football savvy. Carthage just gave this game away, and it shows on Preston's face and in his body language. He sits hunched over and speaks slowly and sadly as though more than a zero week non-district game was lost. After about an hour of watching film, the defensive coordinator slowly tells the kids, with long pauses between phrases, "We gotta play aggressive . . . play assignments . . . and make plays . . . we're looking for the best eleven . . . we were up here half the night . . . juggling names . . . if you can't get it done in practice . . ." He leaves the last phrase hanging. Everyone knows changes will be made Monday.

The mood with the offensive coaches is slightly better. Returning starting quarterback Blake Bogenschutz had a poor game, overthrowing some open receivers, but Bogie threw twenty-nine touchdown passes and for almost 2,700 yards as a sophomore, so head coach Scott Surratt and the offensive staff aren't worried about a subpar opener. The young offensive line and running backs looked good. They were a few inches and stupid mistakes away from putting this game away, but at least, unlike the defense, they know they have the pieces they need. As Coach Surratt tells the offensive coaches during the personnel meeting on Sunday, "We have a hell of a lot more talent than last year, and a hell of a lot more up front."

Carthage is a clean little town of around 6,000, a traditional town square and a strip with restaurants, convenience stores, and other shops, surrounded by residential neighborhoods full of mostly well-kept homes peeking through the trees—nice, but not ostentatious. If there's anything remarkable about the city, it's the school itself. Only 741 students are enrolled, but it has the feel of a much bigger place. The gym is large; really it's three separate gyms, divided by folded up bleachers. The cafeteria, library, and classrooms are all spacious, airy, and modern. Natural gas money has made this one of the richest ISDs in the state, and bond issues have built this school into a showcase.

Bulldog Stadium isn't especially big by Texas standards, with 6,500 seats, but it's comfortable with seatbacks in the middle section for season ticket holders. Unlike many newer stadiums, it has a one-level press box.

"It was too crowded as soon as it opened," the radio play-by-play man tells me. A new replay scoreboard has just gone up in the north end zone. The scoreboard is a point of pride for the people of Carthage but seen in a different light by those who don't understand Texas football culture.

At 1,200 square feet, it is the largest high school video screen in the country. During a national recession, the scoreboard is an easy target for out-of-staters. The *Wall Street Journal*, *Sports Illustrated*, and Associated Press (AP) all ran stories on it. The *Wall Street Journal* didn't say it directly but implied this was another example of misplaced priorities in Texas. The story cited the $60 million, 18,000-seat stadium built in Allen as another example of high school football run amok in Texas.

It's easy and lazy to condemn Carthage for spending $750,000 on a luxury, pointing out things the money could be better spent on: math books, more teachers, or whatever. It's the same argument often made to deride any government spending one doesn't like. In fact, it's the same strategy used by the anti-bond people in La Marque: find what you consider waste and use this waste to argue against entire institutions.

It's hard to argue against this debating tactic without knowing the details. Here are a few of this case:

Carthage is a very rich school district, the third richest in Texas. While much of the country is in a recession, energy money has been very good to Panola County. In addition to the scoreboard, Carthage voters approved another bond raising $17 million for a new elementary school. The students in the Carthage ISD don't lack math books, quality teaching, or facilities. The money for the scoreboard came from a voter-approved bond issue specifically for a scoreboard. It is a luxury, but it's also *their* money; the schools are otherwise well supported and the scoreboard doesn't take away from anything else. That the people of Carthage are willing to support extracurricular programs extravagantly is nothing to apologize for, but something more places should be willing to do. It's a shame we don't see *Wall Street Journal* articles bringing attention to all the bond issues that *fail* in communities that refuse to support their schools as well as the people in Carthage.

This insinuation of amazing facilities taking a huge chunk of educational budgets in Texas is false. On average, less than 2 percent of Texas' education money goes to athletics. Not 20 percent, or 10, but 2 percent. It would be hard to argue that a system that does so much good for kids and communities isn't worth 2 percent of educational spending.

The fieldhouse is the most impressive part of the Carthage athletic complex. The building holds separate coaches' offices for the offensive and defensive staffs, meeting rooms, three locker rooms, a huge training room, and a spacious weight room. The entire complex is prewired for video, with ceiling-mounted projectors and motorized screens in all meeting rooms, offices, and locker rooms, allowing coaches to pull up practice and game film with the push of a few buttons. Playing at Carthage was "almost like a professional team or a really big D-I college team," I'm told by former Carthage quarterback Anthony Morgan. "I went off and played D-III and the experience was nothing like here. We had the best facilities hands down . . . brand new shoes every year . . . a great coaching staff."

The football program at Carthage has been respected, if not great, since its founding in 1923. During his twenty-eight years as head coach, Everett "Sleepy" Reynolds guided his Carthage squad to the playoffs thirteen times.

Since Surratt arrived in 2007, the Bulldogs have become a perennial contender in this tough part of the state. When college recruiters come to Texas, they generally focus on three areas: the Dallas-Fort Worth (DFW) Metroplex, Houston, and East Texas. In football circles East Texas is renowned for its incredible athletes. The brand of football played in East Texas has the reputation of being fast and physical. At Carthage these characteristics are definitely true. The Bulldogs also have great participation. Out of only 741 students, 180 play football, with fully one-third of the male student body suiting up for the Bulldogs. With speed, size, and outstanding fundamentals, at first glance, this is the most impressive of the eleven teams I cover in 2012. Defensive tackle Isaiah Golden has already committed to Texas A&M University, and next to him at the other defensive tackle spot, K'Aelin Ware is an outstanding lineman and student, with a 4.0 GPA.

Look a little closer, however, and you see the flaws that cost Carthage the Jacksonville game. The Bulldogs are talented but not deep. Much of the weekend is spent shuffling offensive and defensive players around, trying to fill the holes exposed during the zero week loss.

The coaching staff meets at 1:00 Sunday to begin preparing for their second game against the Lindale Eagles. The mood is pretty tight. The staff doesn't talk about it much, but losing as they did Friday makes for a long week. They haven't slept much, and are eager to get to work and solve problems exposed during the loss. Nobody will feel right again until they get back on the field.

Seven coaches meet in the defensive office, eight in the offensive room. The two staffs won't see each other until dinner. In the offensive office, the glass-fronted mini-fridge is filled with water and Diet Coke; the defensive coaches prefer Diet Dr Pepper. To get them through the long day, little cellophane packets of cheese crackers are on the conference tables of both offices.

Former head coach, now defensive assistant, Benny Mitchell passes a bag of roasted almonds around. It's common for coaches to bounce around Texas, but in small towns you often see a few who've stayed put, sometimes surviving through multiple head coaches. Mitchell has been at Carthage for forty years. On the offensive side, Dennis McLaughlin has been here almost as long. Preston has only been at Carthage for two years but has a long relationship with Coach Surratt; they grew up and coached together at Texas High. They also married identical twin sisters.

During weekend meetings coaches always look like they just rolled out of bed. Most wear gym shorts, T-shirts, and flip-flops as long as the weather allows, switching to jeans as it gets cold. The offensive coaches spend the early afternoon evaluating Lindale personnel, trying to find weak links. They make notes of the first step taken by each Lindale defender and determine the backups for each starter, little things the offensive coaches in the box upstairs might be able to relay down to the field to give them an edge.

In the defensive room, the coaches look at the fifteen formations Lindale ran during their zero week game against Tyler-Chapel Hill. Each formation is drawn on a whiteboard at the front of the office, along with a defensive alignment to use against it. Several coaches gather around this board whenever someone draws up a new proposed front, like chess players pondering strengths and weaknesses of a possible move. Other coaches enter the down and distance of all Lindale plays from the previous night into the computer scouting program.

After the data is entered, reports are printed showing what Lindale does on particular down-and-distance and formation situations. Next, the defensive staff looks at whether Lindale personnel changes give away their formation. Keying personnel groups (groups substituted together for particular formations; "heavy," for example, might be a package including two tight ends and two running backs) has become a big defensive priority in the higher classifications of Texas football. If a defense can determine the offensive formation from substitutions, they may be able to guess the play before the offense even breaks the huddle. Often a coach upstairs is assigned to watch the opponents' sideline and relay personnel groups down via headphone.

Back on the offensive side, the coaches work on their personnel packages. Of the teams I cover this season, Carthage runs the most complex offense. Offensive philosophies fall on a continuum between getting really good at a few things and having formations and plays to attack any weakness, front, or coverage a defense can devise.

Carthage is very far on the complex side of the spectrum. They run a pro-style offense with anything from zero to three backs, and operate out of shotgun or from under center. The quarterback can check out of any play and into another depending on the defense he sees when he comes to the line. They use multiple blocking schemes and regularly work on gadget plays for every possible scenario. By the end of the season, they'll have fifteen different personnel groups.

They can handle this complexity because of a veteran staff, incredible organization, and hard work. Football knowledge among the players is impressive. I have trouble following what's going on during the offensive meetings because the terminology and adjustments are so numerous. One of the first-year coaches tells me that after a month, he is just now starting to get a handle on the lingo.

The quality of coaching is also apparent during Bulldog practices. On top of being excellent athletes, Carthage players have superb football technique. The receivers are outstanding route runners, and the offensive linemen are big, strong, and use their feet well. Bogenschutz, the returning starting quarterback, is only a junior and rarely throws a poor pass.

Surratt is regarded by many in Carthage as an offensive genius. He isn't the offensive coordinator, but he coaches quarterbacks and is very involved with game planning. On this Sunday, he doesn't leave the offensive office until 4:30. He spends a few minutes with the defensive coaches finding out which offensive players the defensive staff wants to borrow, hoping to solve secondary problems. Surratt nixes one player, telling the defensive staff that he's just too valuable at receiver to split time, but approves the others Preston asks for.

Surratt started coaching in 1990 as a head baseball/football assistant coach at Redwater High School. After stops in Little Cypress-Mauriceville, Linden Kildare, and Waxahachie, he became the offensive coordinator at Texas High School in Texarkana in 1999. During his eight years at Texas High, he helped lead the Tigers to a state championship in 2002. While there he worked with current NFL quarterback Ryan Mallett, earning a reputation as an outstanding quarterbacks coach. After landing his first head job, at Carthage, in 2007, Surratt quickly took the Bulldogs from being respectable to being champions.

After an 8-2 regular season during his first year, the Bulldog program reached new heights in 2008, winning the first of three straight state championships.

"Coach Surratt is the best coach in the state of Texas. There may be some as good, but none better," said Pat Browning, a longtime Carthage High School administrator and coach.

Larry Allen, the "voice of the Bulldogs" on KGAS radio, agreed and explained how Surratt and his staff influenced what had been known as a baseball school.

"He changed the culture of the school from being happy going one or two rounds into the playoffs to expecting to win championships." Morgan, quarterback of two of those championship teams, told me of the atmosphere during the state runs: "Looking back . . . we were just so prepared for anything and had it in our mind that nobody could beat us."

It's late afternoon on Sunday and the offense is installing a new play package and personnel group, a three-back diamond formation that will let the offense zone block one way and attack the opposite edge with a lead block.

Sandwiches and chicken wings are delivered at 7:00. During and after dinner, the defensive coaches continue adjusting for the fifteen Lindale formations they've drawn up on the whiteboard. After dinner, the offense finishes the Lindale plan and begins grading every player for the Jacksonville game. The offensive staff watches each play from three angles while the coaches assess their position players. They're eight hours into their meeting.

Fans often fail to recognize just how important assistant coaches are. Football skills are so specialized and individualized that a head coach, no matter how knowledgeable, must trust his assistants to run their pieces of the big picture.

No sport compares to football when it comes to diverse skills and techniques. Every basketball player, regardless of position, uses the same basic skills. Baseball is slightly more specialized but doesn't come close to football with its twenty-two starting positions, each with specific and varied responsibilities. Football is uniquely challenging to coach because there is so little overlap in the skills. Quarterbacks and offensive linemen may wear the same uniform, but what they're taught and how they're coached is completely different. Trusted assistants usually have a lot of freedom. They choose the training methods, run the drills, and often decide who starts Friday night. While the head coach always retains veto power, on a quality staff such as Carthage's, it's rarely used.

Offensive and defensive coordinators effectively take the role of head coach on their side of the ball. Many head coaches are more involved on one side than the other, and Surratt, as an outstanding quarterbacks coach, is very involved with offensive planning. Other head coaches have a hand on the defensive side. However it's arranged, coordinators are responsible for deciding the game plan, designing practices, and making personnel and strategic decisions during the game. Just as a head coach can't be successful without good coordinators, the coordinators can't be successful without good position coaches. In effect, the staff forms a team within a team.

A strong head coach like Surratt attracts the quality assistants needed to be successful and engenders the loyalty to keep them. A head coach puts the complex pieces of the puzzle together and gets everything moving with purpose. The head coach also takes care of the details so the assistants can coach without any other concerns. Discipline, grades, parents, and interaction with the administration and public are all the responsibility of the head coach, and when done well, these are things the staff may not even notice.

Of course, as with a CEO or president, the buck stops with the head coach. If his assistants don't do their jobs well, the head coach takes the blame.

In the Bulldog fieldhouse, things start wrapping up at around 10:00. This is an early ending to their Sunday session. Later in the season as they have more film to watch, they often don't leave until after midnight. It's been fascinating to watch what's done during the meetings. Staffs made up entirely of professional coaches makes routine in Texas what's unusual elsewhere. As interesting as it is, by the time I leave the fieldhouse and head back to my motel, I'm exhausted.

Labor Day weekend means extra time to prepare because there's no school on Monday. Football teams, during the season, don't have holidays. Veterans Day, Columbus Day, and, for those fortunate enough still to be playing, Thanksgiving are all part of the commitment kids and coaches make. When I get to school at 8:00, the coaches are already watching film on their laptops and iPads. Others are at the conference table drawing up Lindale fronts, stunts, and coverages, putting diagrams in laminated sleeves and ordering them in binders for the JV defense to run this morning. On the offensive side there's a script of each inside run period play, another for seven-on-seven, and a third for full-team. With each script are corresponding binders of scout defenses to be run against each play. The same process is happening in the defensive office as they organize their scripts and scout binders.

At 9:00, the players arrive. Before hitting the field, they break into groups to watch the Jacksonville film. The defense watches together, crammed into the coaches' office. The offense splits by positions, the line, running backs, and receivers all going into separate rooms. Surratt takes the quarterbacks to his office to watch the film separately.

Carthage has fully separate offensive and defensive coaching staffs, but some players work two positions. For this reason, practice is split into focus periods. On Monday, the offense takes the early part of practice while defensive coaches work with the "white hats," or JV players, and varsity players in red helmets who play only defense. After the offense finishes, they switch and defense becomes the focus. The system allows every coach to work directly with sub-varsity kids instead of only using them to run opponents' plays for the varsity. Practice here is more physical than at other schools I visit. In August, I'd been amazed to see a full-speed inside run session where the players wore only T-shirts and shorts. It looked intense, but the coaches found it slow and sluggish. The Bulldogs work some "good on good" each week, matching the starting offensive players and defensive players, something many comparable programs never do.

Surratt is very involved during the offensive practice, coaching quarterbacks and overseeing the play script along with offensive coordinator Chris Smith. During defensive time, he takes a more distant view and is more approachable. By nature, he's an easygoing, good-natured country boy, but nothing about his approach to football is relaxed. Surratt's practices are well organized and he's an extremely hard worker with the reputation of working his Carthage squad into wins.

"If we have the same talent level as the other team, we'll win nine out of ten times," said Allen, Carthage's play-by-play man.

After about two and a half hours, at 12:30, the Bulldogs head into the cafeteria for a pizza lunch, then go back to the fieldhouse for their second film session of the day. This morning's practice was filmed from two angles, end zone and sideline. The two angles were intercut during lunch, ready for players to watch with position coaches so they can go over the mistakes made just hours earlier.

Among the biggest changes in football over the past twenty years is the use of technology. Football has been at the cutting edge of sports technology since coaches started using game film in the 1940s. The game is video friendly. Each play is a discrete event that can be classified a number of ways (right/left, strong/weak, pass/run, wideside/boundary, formation and play, down and distance). Using video to determine tendencies is a huge part of any opponent scout.

What will the opponent run on second-and-5? What coverage will they see when in a three-wide set? How often do they run to the wide side of the field from the right hash mark? Who's the weakest defensive end? These are some questions coaches work to answer. Unlike more fluid sports, coaches can use this information to implement specific strategies.

Scouting from film goes back to the days when the film was actually film that had to be developed and run through a projector. During the 1980s, VHS tapes became common. In the new millennium DVDs replaced tapes, and just recently digital video in conjunction with scouting software has become predominant.

Coaches usually trade recent films, eliminating the need for sending live scouts to every opponent. Each Texas district has its own rules, but most trade films from the past two games. Live scouting is still is used by many teams, with junior high coaches sent out to take notes on upcoming opponents.

Film, VHS, or DVD, the process is always basically the same. Coaches put on a game film and watch each play over and over, looking for little things to give their team an edge; offensive coaches look for weak players to attack and defensive coaches look for opponents' tendencies. Most would make tally sheets to keep track of formation or down-and-distance tendencies, but the information was incomplete and the process was time consuming.

The problem was with the huge amount of information on each film. This made it difficult to be systematic in a breakdown. A game has around 200 plays, each with a specific down and distance, either a run or pass, run from one of many formations, to the strong or weak side, to the right or left, with any of six players touching the ball, and involving the actions of twenty-two individuals. On defense, teams use multiple fronts and secondary coverages, and run different combinations of stunts and blitzes. There are literally thousands of recordable actions on each game film, and coaches have about a day and a half to find the clues that will make a difference.

Computers made a comprehensive approach possible and affordable. Scouting programs allow each play to be broken down various ways and filtered to show exact scenarios. Want to know what a team does on second-and-5? A few clicks and it's broken down, by percentage, right or left, strong or weak, run or pass, to what player. Push another button for all the second-and-5 plays they've run this year. Want to know tendencies from a specific formation? Another click separates out all plays run out of any particular formation. High school coaches can now put together detailed scouting reports and make weekly adjustments.

For many years several companies competed for the scouting software business. Recently this changed when Hudl, an Internet-based company, bought out most of its competition. Hudl's advantage was its use of the Internet instead of purchased software. Coaches don't buy the software now, but pay for use and storage. With Hudl, film trade with other schools is done over the Internet. Everything can be done from any Internet-connected device, meaning coaches can work from home or at the office, on laptops, iPads, or smartphones. This has changed the way many staffs meet. Instead of sitting around a screen watching film, as was once necessary, more work is done at home and coaches' office meetings are getting shorter.

While the Internet may have made meetings at Carthage a little shorter, the hours are still very long. Much still must be done by hand. After the kids leave at 2:30 on Monday, the coaches quickly start putting together Tuesday's practice plans, scripts, and binders.

On Tuesday, everyone is back in school after the three-day weekend. The football day starts at 11:30 with athletic period. The JV is in the weight room. The offense is outside working on their goalline package, and the defense is inside watching more Lindale film with Coach Preston. Coach Mitchell comes over from the school building and lets everyone know he's "stomped out a lot of ignorance today" during his social studies classes. Everyone congratulates defensive tackles coach Mark Brown on being named teacher of the week.

At Carthage, all fifteen coaches have both varsity/JV and freshman athletic periods in their teaching schedules. The freshman period is the last of the day. Varsity offensive or defensive coaches take turns working with the ninth-graders. Today, the defensive staff puts the freshmen through their drills. With freshmen at the end of the day, and the JV and the varsity afterward, the defensive coaches have three groups today. It's known in the defensive office as "Terrible Tuesday." The offensive coaches have their "Blue Monday," when it's their long day. To make it more terrible, this is the hottest week of the year, well above one hundred degrees, and the field turf feels even hotter. I walk outside to watch the freshmen work out, but I can take only fifteen minutes before heading back into the air-conditioned fieldhouse.

Wednesday is a lifting day for the varsity. Most programs in Texas lift either two or three days a week in-season. During game weeks, lifting at most schools is generally quick and intense, with multiple coaches overseeing each station. At athletic period on Wednesday, the varsity Bulldogs lift for twenty minutes, working through a circuit of bench press, parallel squats, power cleans, and military presses. Afterward they're back in meeting rooms watching more practice or game film with their coaches. The JV is outside today with other coaches, getting ready for their game tomorrow.

After-school practice is shorter than practice on Monday and Tuesday. The goal is to get everyone out of the fieldhouse by 6:30. The shorter Wednesday session was a conscious decision by Surratt to allow coaches and players time with their families. Coaches will have a long night Thursday with freshman and JV games in Lindale, and Friday with the varsity, so Surratt lets the coaches get home at a decent hour once a week.

Though football keeps both players and coaches away from home during the season, family is important to this staff. Many of the coaches' young sons hang out at practice and in meeting rooms, playing football in the back of the end zone as their fathers work. During games, many kids are on the sideline as ballboys. Secondary coach Mike Morgan has been here just a few years. He came from another East Texas town, bringing his son, who starred at quarterback on the 2009 and 2010 state championship teams. His younger son attends grade school and is often around the fieldhouse. Surratt and Preston's young boys are also regulars at the complex after their school day ends.

Family is a big reason Coach Surratt is still in Carthage. Winning three consecutive state titles in the 3A will inevitably lead to offers from higher classifications. Head coaching positions aren't subject to the typical teachers' pay scale. More money (up to the low six figures), and perks are often offered by schools trying to lure a successful coach. Coaching in Texas is anything but a stable profession and situations change quickly. A coach can never say never when it comes to a future move, no matter how much he likes his current job.

Surratt is comfortable in Carthage, and it would take a lot to convince him to leave. A few years ago he was offered a 5A job in the Metroplex, but as a father with two young kids, he couldn't see moving them for the sake of his career.

"This is a pretty good place to be. I'm a country boy. I might have thought different when I was single, but with kids, I don't know. Kids can get in trouble here, but you have to work a little more to find it," Surratt said.

A young Carthage graduate comes into the office before practice on Wednesday. He has a mental disability and has been around the Carthage program for years. As a student, the young man served as a manager. Since his graduation, he's helped coach Jim Milstead film and does odd jobs for the coaches. He's now in his twenties, and his mother has told him it's time to find a job. He's worried about losing his time with the team. Smith and Preston are consoling and reassure him that though he may not be there every day, "You will always be part of the family."

Several coaches discuss how they should handle this. They don't want to undermine his mother. They clearly want to do right by this young man. He *is* useful for the program, but the main reason he's around is that he loves it so much and letting him be a part of the program further carries out the coaches' mission of building better men. They decide to talk with his mother to determine the best way to support her.

Wednesday's practice always start with a quick sermon by the team's chaplain. Today, Pastor James McWright talks about the danger of pride. The players kneel and listen respectfully before breaking into their groups.

If anything, today is hotter than yesterday. Rather than fry on the hot artificial turf, I decide to sit with Coach Milstead, the school's tennis coach, who films practice from the air-conditioned press box, a good excuse to get out of the heat. Practice is quick and sharp and a little looser than Monday or Tuesday. The hard part of the week is done and everybody's eager to suit up for Lindale. The practice ends on a very light note as the two biggest linemen on the team have a 50-yard race while everyone cheers them on.

In Texas, varsity practice on Thursday is usually very short, and often players are entirely free after school. There are two reasons for this. First, athletic period gives the coaches enough time to work on the special teams adjustments, two-minute offense, and goal-line sessions that often make up pregame practices elsewhere. The second reason is the relationship between the JV and varsity in Texas. In many other places, schools have three separate staffs: freshman, JV, and varsity. They may use a common playbook, but each is a self-contained program. JV games are often played before varsity games on Friday night, further separating the JV from varsity, as this arrangement makes it hard for the varsity coaches to help the JV. Experience as a JV head coach is often a stepping stone for prospective head coaches in the West.

In Texas, the relationship between varsity and sub-varsity is much fuzzier. There's no such thing as a "JV head coach" here. Most coaches have varsity and JV responsibilities. At Carthage and the other ten programs I visited, there are no true JV coaches or JV practices. During the week, the JV serves as a scout team for the varsity, allowing varsity teams to work both offense and defense as the JV squads service varsity starting units.

Freshman ball is usually more separated. Most schools have between two and four freshman football coaches, but even here, things are closely aligned. The varsity staff is very involved with freshman athletes, coaching them during athletic periods and helping on the sideline during games.

A Texas sophomore is generally a better football player than a tenth-grader in other parts of the country. By the time they arrive at two-a-days their sophomore year, most Texans have had three full seasons learning the system during seventh, eighth, and ninth grade. They've also been through three years of athletic periods, including a year with the varsity staff during ninth grade. In 4A and 5A schools, they've had eighteen days in pads during spring ball as freshmen. It's common in Texas for a large handful of sophomores to play and start on quality varsity teams.

The system allows coaches to specialize and teams to run separate offenses and defenses. The fifteen coaches on the Carthage staff are good examples of this efficiency. In Nevada, fifteen coaches would be split between the three levels—maybe four freshman coaches, five JV, and six varsity. At Carthage, all fifteen have responsibilities on all three levels. It makes for long Thursdays, as many coaches help with sub-varsity games. The advantage to this system shows during varsity practices and on Friday nights, when every position has a full-time position coach.

Interestingly, the quality of training both helps and hurts a Texas prospect in getting scholarship offers. A Metroplex coach told me, "With kids from other states, the college coaches know they can coach them up and make them better football players. With the kids from here, coaches figure the kid is already playing at his potential, having come up through our systems."

The excellence of the Texas system is driven home during the JV game at Lindale Thursday evening. Carthage defeats the JV Eagles, but it's the level of play that stands out. This is the first JV game I see in Texas, and I'm blown away by the quality. Good stances, no sloppy penalties, tight spirals, good footwork by the linemen, a deep playbook, and no blown coverages. In short, it's solid, well-played football. These teams would beat big-school varsity squads in many states. It's more relaxed and informal than games I'd seen and coached back home. There's no band and the crowd is small, mostly consisting of parents. The use of varsity coaches also means the focus is on techniques and learning instead of winning, as is sometimes the case when there's a separate JV staff. Coaches are, by nature, competitive people, but varsity coaches working with JV kids have a different perspective of the purpose of sub-varsity than coaches trying to move up the ladder.

Thursday turns into a long night. Instead of riding the bus, I take the van with Smith and running backs coach Andre Granger. We should beat the buses back to Carthage. However, a young Bulldog running back breaks his hand during the game, and we take him to the emergency room in Longview. We finally get back after midnight. Not a problem for me, as my Friday routine during the regular season is to sleep late before checking out of the motel, since I always have a long drive. This week it's 300 miles to Port Lavaca. For the coaches, however, it means a very short night before a long game day.

Game day for coaches always feels endless. The work is done, and there's nothing to do but wait and watch the clock. Surratt spends most of the afternoon in his office. He looks tense. While always polite, he answers questions with short sentences and is in no mood for small talk. Though still a non-district game, tonight is important. The Bulldogs had high hopes going into the season; the coaches are confident but really don't know their team yet. The coaches assure me that the Bulldogs often play poorly in their first game, a fact backed by Surratt's career record. Despite a lifetime record of 62-11, he's only .500 for season openers.

"Just wait until you see us during the playoffs, you'll be amazed by the improvement we've made," several coaches say. Still, it's something that has to show on the field. As much as history keeps things in perspective, the only way to feel good again is to play well. Lindale is good; this game is no sure thing. An 0-2 start would be hard to swallow.

Some coaches stay busy with last-minute jobs. Coach Charlie Tucker, who's also the head basketball coach, sets up the headphone system. Coach Smith laminates the large play sheets each offensive coach carries. Tonight's game plan is broken into down-and-distance and situation groupings. During the game, offensive coaches upstairs in the coaches' box make notes on the sheets with felt-tip pens as they see what is and isn't working. Most of the other coaches find ways to keep themselves occupied during these long hours of nothing.

After a quick after-school pep rally, the team loads onto buses for a pregame meal at Brac's Steakhouse at 3:45. Then it's back to the fieldhouse to dress before position meetings at 5:25. Nothing new is discussed during these meetings; they're just a final chance for the coaches to remind players of tonight's adjustments.

The first personnel group hits the field at 6:15. It's still nearly one hundred degrees at kickoff. A good crowd of over 4,000 is in the stands. Lindale travels well, filling their side, despite being over one hundred miles from home. The Carthage side is three-quarters full.

It turns out the Bulldogs have nothing to worry about; they score on the opening drive and don't look back, routing the Eagles, 38-21. The defense plays very well, holding Lindale to just 169 yards on the ground. While still a work in progress, the Bulldogs show improvement over the previous week. It's something the staff needs to see this week.

Surratt quickly addresses the team, telling them he's happy about the improvement, but reminding them they still have a long way to go. The coaching staff spends a few minutes celebrating with their wives and families on the field before heading inside to start the laundry and begin breaking down tonight's film. The staff may not leave until 4:00 in the morning, but they won't mind after a win.

I'm introduced to coaches' wives, family members, and friends. The mother of the current quarterback proudly tells me her grandfather quarterbacked the Bulldogs in 1927. She regrets that he didn't live to watch his great-grandson play.

It's fun to be on a winning sideline. The happy atmosphere is hard to leave, but I have a long drive south toward Port Lavaca in coastal South Texas. I hit the road and listen to the postgame highlights on KGAS as I'm quickly swallowed by the dark forest on the two-lane highway heading toward Houston. I don't return to East Texas until December.

The Carthage Bulldogs finish the 2012 regular season with an 8-2 record, winning the District 20-3A title. During the early playoff rounds, I try to see as many of my teams as possible but the math works to keep me in the Metroplex more often than not.

I keep a close eye on the scores of all my teams, usually from the sideline of whatever game I'm at. I'm glad to see that while the Bulldogs have a few close calls during their first three rounds, they survive to the state semifinal game against top-ranked El Campo.

Early during the week of the semifinal, I return to Carthage and catch up with the Bulldogs as they prepare for El Campo. It's been a long time since Lindale week, and I find a very different scene than the one I left four months before. The early-season tension of a staff unsure of whether they're coaching a good team has disappeared. What the coaches told me was right: the Bulldogs did find their stride, improving week to week. They've positioned themselves to compete for a fourth state title. The staff seems confident about their game plan versus El Campo, but whatever happens, they know they've done their jobs.

Coach Mitchell had told me about his first visit to Cowboys Stadium for the state championship in 2010.

"I stood out in the middle of that field and called my wife and told her that I could stop coaching now, I've been to the Promised Land." He didn't stop coaching, but with a win on Friday night, he'll get to go again.

Those who've never been around teams deep in the playoffs might be surprised by the atmosphere. You'd expect the tension to ramp up higher with each step but the opposite is true. The competition gets tougher each week, but practice tension drops with each win. Most of the teaching is done; coaches don't get bent out of shape by little things anymore. They're more concerned with staying fresh than banging each other around. Nobody's going to learn how to hit at this point. If they haven't gotten it by now they never will.

There's also a sense of contentment. Survival to this point, being one of the final four teams still playing, means that whatever happens this Friday night, it's been a successful season. Practices are shorter and looser. Coaches are in a good mood, savoring time with players that they know will soon end. The team has seen almost everything they're going to see during the previous thirteen games and it doesn't take nearly as much time or energy to get them ready.

The El Campo Ricebirds have had a great first season in Class 3A after moving down from 4A. They're undefeated in thirteen games. The Carthage staff is confident, however; they feel their team matches up well. El Campo doesn't have a passing game worth mentioning but is outstanding on the ground. The Bulldogs are excellent against the run. Carthage also rose through a much tougher East Texas Region 3 than South Texas' Region 4. There's no lack of respect, though. As the saying goes, "There are no turkeys after Turkey Day," and the Bulldogs know they have to play well to win. But there's a sense of confidence that the Bulldogs will be playing in Cowboys Stadium on December 14 with a shot at their fourth state championship.

The semifinal game is played at Lamar University in Beaumont, over 150 miles from each school. El Campo travels well. About 4,000 supporters have made the trip, excited by the prospect of the Ricebirds making their first championship game. The El Campo fans are incredibly loud. Many have brought Clorox bottles half-filled with pennies or pebbles and painted in Ricebird blue. A rock-filled barrel on a spit is cranked by the El Campo cheerleaders on the sideline whenever the Bulldogs have the ball. The tumbling boulders against the steel drum are deafening.

On the Carthage side is a smaller but still respectable crowd of maybe 3,000 people. I heard several times during my week in Carthage that their supporters had gotten a little spoiled by the three championships, and many are waiting to travel to Arlington the following week.

The coaching staff was right. While the Ricebirds are an outstanding team, four well-executed quarters by the Bulldogs should win the game. But this season the Bulldogs have had a frustrating habit of not putting away teams when they have them down. In the bi-district round, Carthage narrowly avoided disaster, letting Palestine climb back from a big deficit before hanging on, 30-27. Against a team as good as El Campo, the failure to finish can be fatal.

Carthage is in complete control halfway through the fourth quarter, and I'm checking the score of Stephenville-Kilgore to see whom the championship will be against and making plans for Cowboys Stadium. But the Bulldogs can't come up with the one play they need to finish off the Ricebirds. Something the Texas high school playoffs have taught me is that, with teams this good, the ability to finish is often the difference between advancing and going home. Those still playing four weeks in are so disciplined and dangerous, situations that would make ordinary teams fold and start thinking about the offseason are often overcome if the team on top can't put a boot on the neck and finish the job.

After taking a 25-14 lead early in the fourth, the Bulldogs have many chances to put that boot on the neck but keep letting the Ricebirds up. The next two El Campo possessions end in turnovers. One good drive will finish the job, but the Bulldogs fail to capitalize either time they have the ball. Still, when El Campo takes possession with 7:10 left, deep in their own territory and down by 11, the game feels under control.

El Campo has thrown just eighty passes the entire season; down by two scores with time running out, it seems unlikely the Ricebirds have enough time or firepower.

The passes the Ricebirds throw during their comeback rarely connect but don't hurt them, either. One goes through the fingers of a Carthage defender when an interception will end the game. Several others hit the ground, helping the Ricebirds by stopping the clock. Meanwhile, El Campo continues to do what got them here, moving the ball on the ground and scoring a touchdown with 3:27 left. A successful two-point conversion makes the score 25-22 Carthage.

It's still Carthage's game to lose. A few first downs and the clock will run out. On second-and-long, the Bulldogs attempt a swinging gate play and the pitch is fumbled. The Ricebirds recover at Carthage's 9-yard line, and four plays later, on fourth-and-goal from the 2, retake the lead, 29-25, with 1:57 remaining.

With an offense as explosive as Carthage's, there's still hope. The Bulldogs quickly move to the El Campo 29-yard line, but two incomplete passes set up a fourth-and-3. A quarterback draw takes the ball to the marker; the chains are brought out. Short by an inch, and suddenly, the game and season are over.

At its best, football, for a brief moment, feels like the most important thing in the world to the men who coach it and the kids who play it. For the past five months, thousands of hours have been dedicated, and the people involved have spent more time with each other than their families. During the playoffs, everything is elevated; the highs of winning and moving on are amazing, but the lows are devastating. Suddenly, everything is taken away and all the work feels like it's been for nothing. Players realize they've just played their last game, many their last ever. The aftermath of a playoff loss is one of the few times you'll see teenage boys openly cry.

This is how it usually ends. Natural optimism and popular culture make winning championships seem almost normal, but in reality, for each Texas team celebrating the end of their playoff run, sixty-three others finish with shattered dreams. A huge majority of *successful* coaches go entire careers without ever finishing a campaign with a win.

Football is really about the life lessons it teaches the students who play it. How to deal with the crushing season-ending loss is the final lesson. Surratt and the staff show how to lose with dignity. Surratt gathers his team for the final time and tells them he's responsible: "I called it terrible. I'll take the blame."

He admonishes the few who lost composure, "You gotta have a little self control. What do you think I want to do right now? . . . I want to hide my face . . . I wanted to run off the field . . . I didn't want to shake nobody's hand. You think I wanna go tell that guy, 'y'all go win it'? . . . but we're going to act right." Holding his hat in his hand, he looks across the field to see the celebrating Ricebirds, looks down, shakes his head, and continues, "I'm going to blame myself, I promise you. Losers look for someone to blame, winners blame themselves . . . I'm not a winner tonight, we fell short. My fault." After a long pause to gather himself, he tells his team he's proud of them, thanking them for the effort, before leading them in the Lord's Prayer.

Surratt is still standing at midfield and looks sick when I say goodbye. He puts his hands on his knees as if trying to awaken from a nightmare. He can't believe what happened. But for all the pain, he's still a gentleman and apologizes for not getting me to Cowboys Stadium. I say goodbye to the assistant coaches, thank them for allowing me to hang around, and tell them I'm sorry about the loss, but what do you say to someone when all their work and dreams just came crashing down? Everyone's incredibly gracious, wishing me safe travels and thanking me for coming, but they're taking the loss just as hard as their boss.

My wife has told me how she hated coming up to me after a tough loss, and now I know how she felt. There is just nothing to say. "Sorry" doesn't feel like enough, and I feel helpless. My last image of the Carthage Bulldogs is watching the coaches stoically trying to be gracious and hold themselves together, continuing to mentor their kids, many of whom just saw their dreams and football careers come to an end. It will be a long offseason for the Bulldog coaches and returning players. This type of loss haunts you.

The shock will be overcome; this staff will be hard at work on Monday, assessing mistakes, finding improvements, and looking ahead to the 2013 team. The underclassmen will quickly transition from in-season workouts during athletic period to off-season and take new roles on the 2013 squad. The graduates of the program will also shake off the disappointing end of their season. While never forgetting or completely putting away what happened on that field in Beaumont, they'll use the lessons they learned during this season and eventually look back with pride on their accomplishments. The people of Carthage will be disappointed but will quickly turn to other things. However, none of this takes the sting out of the opportunity that slipped through their fingers on this Friday night.

I come to like and respect the people in each of these programs and towns I visit. Football kids and coaches are generally outstanding, hardworking people. Keeping objectivity is impossible. I was pulling just as hard for Carthage as many lifelong residents in the stands, and it hurts that I won't see them next week in Cowboys Stadium. Most of all, I feel awful for the coaches and kids. I know how hard they worked to get to this point and how it feels when it ends so suddenly. These are outstanding people and it's hard to watch them hurting. I'm sure El Campo has quality coaches and kids, as well, and deserve the success they've earned tonight, but I don't know them.

Another of my teams will be playing tomorrow afternoon in DFW, so I leave soon after the game ends. I drive about halfway to the Metroplex before stopping in Palestine for a few hours at a Super 8. Sleep is a long time coming, thinking about all the chances the Bulldogs had and how they let this one slip away.

3

WINNING THE OLD-FASHIONED WAY

Week Three: Port Lavaca
Calhoun High School Sandcrabs

"Having a place to go is a home. Having someone to depend on is a team. Having both is a Family."

—Sign on the wall in the Calhoun locker room.

Port Lavaca is proud of their team's unique nickname, but that wasn't always the case. Just a few years ago, there was talk in Calhoun County about ditching Sandcrabs for something more common and dignified, something that wouldn't make people laugh when they saw, "Home of the Fighting Sandcrabs" on the stadium's press box while driving up Highway 35. Pride in the school's athletic programs was low. There hadn't been many wins in recent years.

Steve Phillips, class of 1981, tells me, "When I was going to school here in the early '80s, it was parents, students, and friends of the family that would go to the games."

Lina Moore, another grad, said, "Literally, there was a time when you were embarrassed to say you were from Calhoun, you'd tell people and they'd laugh and say, 'We've heard about y'all.' They don't laugh anymore."

They don't laugh, and locals are now proud of their nickname instead of embarrassed by it. The H-E-B supermarket has a huge section of black-and-gold Sandcrab gear. Everywhere in Port Lavaca people proudly wear Calhoun T-shirts and hats. The change started not with great athletes, or even a great coach, but with the realization by leaders in this community that athletics could and should have a more important place in Port Lavaca.

Here in the Coastal Bend, at the northern edge of South Texas, Corpus Christi's Calallen and Gregory-Portland always had the support programs in Texas are known for, but Calhoun didn't. If Calhoun High School was known for anything besides its funny nickname, it was academics. The high school always got positive marks for its academic programs, but as the years and losses piled up, a feeling that something was missing began to grow. It wasn't just that the football program wasn't good; nobody wearing a Sandcrab uniform was. Basketball, baseball, girls' sports, it didn't matter; Calhoun was poor in everything. In Texas, academics *are* important, but schools represent communities as well as provide education. Moreover, for the education to be complete, the school must at least be competitive at other endeavors, and football is at the top of the pyramid. When football does well, other things fall into line.

The problem was priorities. The Calhoun County Independent School District had never cared about football or athletic success. This disinterest was reflected in the money allocated to bringing coaches to Port Lavaca when the coaching job opened. The pay was fine for coaches wanting a stepping stone to a better job, but not enough to attract quality candidates to a program that hadn't been to the state playoffs since 1961. Over the decades, many coaches came but left for better jobs or were let go for lack of success. When Larry Nichols was hired as the superintendent in 2000, the Sandcrabs had had just three winning seasons since 1960.

Nichols had a different vision for the high school, and along with several new school board members, decided athletic success needed to become a priority. The formula to turn things around was simple: allocate more money to attract better candidates for the head coach/athletic director (HC/AD) position. The Calhoun ISD raised the salary to make the Sandcrab job one of the better-paying positions in the 4A, and a different caliber of applicant began to apply.

The first coach Nichols hired didn't work out. Gary Davenport made improvements, but this program had long been down, and encouraging kids to play needed to be an emphasis. Coach Davenport told Superintendent Nichols, "We'll start winning when they start coming out, but I'm not going to go around begging anyone to play."

"He was the first coach we'd had in quite a while who understood it was about building a program, not just coaching a team," local contractor and booster Randy Boyd told me. Still, the program needed a promoter who would inspire kids to play, and Nichols decided a change needed to be made.

Richard Whitaker grew up in the East Texas town of Cushing, married his high school sweetheart, and went to college at Northwest State University in Louisiana on a track scholarship. He got his first coaching job at Kerens High School, before making the move that would define his career.

In 1990, Whitaker took a job at Aldine High School in Houston and became the offensive coordinator in 1995 under legendary coach Bill Smith.

While at Aldine, Whitaker learned the intricacies of the option offense. During his first season, the Mustangs won the 5A state championship, beating Arlington Lamar to finish with a perfect record. In 1999, Whitaker took his offensive system to his first head job at 4A Kingsville King High School, where he led the Brahmas to a 32-29 record over six years. When the job in Port Lavaca opened, Whitaker applied. He was a perfect fit, an outgoing, personable guy who'd make phone calls and go to players' homes to recruit, with an offensive philosophy that would work in Port Lavaca.

The option scheme goes back to the middle of the twentieth century and has deep Texas roots. Emory Bellard is attributed as one of its inventors, coaching the scheme out of the wishbone at San Angelo High. University of Houston coach Bill Yeoman is credited with modifying this offense to be used from different formations.

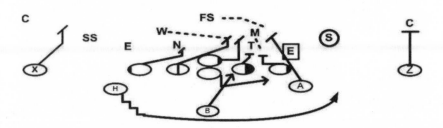

The option play has many variations, but the most common is a triple option. This play gives the quarterback three choices and two reads (defensive players the quarterback watches to decide what to do with the ball). After taking the snap from under center, the quarterback holds the ball out to the fullback heading up the middle and reads the first down lineman to see how he reacts. If he's out of position and there's a hole, the quarterback lets the fullback (B in the diagram) have the ball. If the defender (E) is in position to make a play on the fullback, the quarterback pulls the ball back and continues down the line. One defender is always purposely unblocked, usually the last man on the line of scrimmage (S). The unblocked player is the quarterback's second read. If the unblocked player attacks the quarterback, the quarterback pitches the ball to the third option, either a trailing halfback or wingback (H) who runs parallel and slightly ahead of the QB. If the unblocked defender goes to the pitch man, the QB keeps the ball and turns upfield.

Everything described above takes place in less than one second. It's beautiful to watch when run correctly, but the investment is enormous. The teamwork required to execute it well is arguably greater than any other scheme in football, and the skills are so specific to this offense that if it isn't successful, there's no reasonable fallback. Running the option means committing to an entire philosophy.

Superintendent Nichols was unsure this system would be successful at a school not known for great athletes. Calhoun is largely Hispanic, and doesn't have much size or speed. However, research showed the option might be a perfect solution. One of its main advantages is allowing smaller and slower teams to be successful through teamwork and execution instead of individual athleticism. Instead of relying on better athletes, this offense is built on precise and increasingly arcane rules and a disciplined approach.

An added bonus is that defenses hardly ever see it and rarely know how to defend it. Modern defenses aren't set up to defend against run-heavy offenses, replacing big gap-plugging defensive linemen with quicker, smaller players who can play from sideline to sideline. Like the more modern zone read, this offense allows a well-coached quarterback to recognize and take whatever's given by the defense. When run correctly, it's a very tough scheme to stop. This is the offense that allows the military academies to stay competitive playing D-I football despite being out-athleted almost every week. But running the option is a commitment. Everything—training, personnel decisions, terminology, blocking schemes, and even how the defense is run—is affected by this offense.

Whitaker had reservations about the Port Lavaca job; the facilities at Calhoun High School are nothing special by 4A standards. The weight room was an afterthought attached to the old competition gym. The coaches' offices are cramped and Sandcrab Stadium is showing its age. Nichols convinced Whitaker to make the leap, telling him, "It's not about the facilities, it's about the people." In Calhoun, Whitaker decided he had found people committed to giving him the tools to be successful and he took the job during the spring of 2005.

Shortly afterward, Boyd took the new coach up in one of his airplanes to show him the area his new school would draw from. Calhoun High doesn't only service the city of Port Lavaca, but all of Calhoun County. Kids come from up to thirty miles away. Building up the numbers of students playing in the program would be one of the first goals for Whitaker, and knowing the lay of the land would be important in selling a program that had been down so long.

Whitaker quickly went to work on changing the culture. His approach has three basic tenets: create a brotherhood, build a better work ethic, and implement his offensive philosophy. It takes time to turn around a traditional loser. During Whitaker's first season in 2005, the Sandcrabs finished 2-8 and had just eighty-three players in the program, very low numbers for the 4A.

Losing becomes a habit, just like winning, except losing is easier. Losing only requires the kids to continue what they've been doing. It's incredibly difficult to convince kids who've never been successful to buy in and do things differently. Heads are down and there's a deep belief that nothing will work. Convincing players that they'll become successful by running a 1950s offense in the twenty-first century takes a great motivator and salesman.

Whitaker was up to the task. The program turned the corner in 2006. The clinching win over Beeville at Sandcrab Stadium that delivered the first district title since 1961 was truly a watershed moment for this community.

"I compare it to 1980," Boyd told me, referring to the gold medal US Olympic hockey team. "You had a country that didn't feel good about themselves and you had a bunch of kids at Lake Placid that lifted a nation. I compare these kids and what they did for this county to what that hockey team did for this nation. Right [after we won] a norther blew in and people always say that it was the wind of change."

Something fundamental changed in Port Lavaca. Since 2005, the Sandcrabs have been to the playoffs seven straight years, winning five district titles, and the number of kids playing football has doubled. Before 2006, the seats at the Stadium were often empty, and fans didn't follow the Sandcrabs on the road. Since 2006, locals have begun arriving hours before games just to get a seat. Now people get off work early to make the trip to away games. On the road, Port Lavaca fans often outnumber those of the home team.

The change hasn't been limited to football. That first taste of success affected the town in many ways. As the rising tide lifts all boats, Calhoun's other programs have become successful, as well. In the five years before Whitaker arrived, volleyball was the only sport to make the playoffs. Since 2005, boys' basketball has been in the playoffs seven straight years, and the girls made their first playoff trip in twelve years. Softball has five playoffs appearances, and baseball has three. The boys' track team has won three district titles, and the girls finished second in district twice. Golf, cross-county, and powerlifting have also shown big gains.

The morale of Port Lavaca benefited as well. Moore, who's the principal at Travis Middle School, told me, "Everything about our community has totally changed across the board, girls, boys, everything. The football program was absolutely the beginning of the change. Kids used to skip practices and the parents made excuses; now the parents drag their kids there. Everybody is supportive of whatever needs to be done. It's been very exciting to watch the change. It has to do with doing the best at whatever. That atmosphere and that feeling is just everywhere. I can only see that it benefits the community in every shape, form, and fashion."

Sandcrab games have become important rallying points for the community, and playoff games take this to a whole other level. Calhoun has played at the Alamodome in San Antonio a number of times over the last five years.

"It's become like a second home," one booster proudly told me.

Moore says the atmosphere for these big games brings the town together like nothing else, "It's amazing what this has done for our community. It's like a class reunion from every year, people from all over the state of Texas come." Boyd tells me about the Uvalde game several years ago, "It was tremendous to look up and see between eight to ten thousand from a county that has less than twenty thousand."

Finally, improved athletics have positively impacted education, as well. "We've always had good academics. Has it gotten better? I have to say yes." Moore tells me what football has done for her middle school. "My kids [Travis Middle School kids] when they're in football, they behave better, their grades are better . . . it's a huge help. I wish the season was longer, to be honest."

The elementary school kids are included. They decorate the buses for the team for road games. Moore describes how the young kids respond when the Crabs visit: "It's like a superstar just walked in. Those little ones love being a part of it."

That kids can be successful without having tremendous talent is what drew me to high school football. As an undersized lineman during my high school years, I earned respect with work ethic and tenacity, something I couldn't have done sheerly with athletic ability. To me, what makes high school football the greatest game in the world is how it rewards effort. The turnaround at Port Lavaca exemplifies this.

Hard work, guts, teamwork, and smart organization can overcome better athletes in the high school game. In football, more than any other sport, the program that pays the higher price for success is likely to win. It's basic mathematics; factor in man-hours of practice, team-building activities, scouting, off-season lifting, lower-level preparation, net coaching experience, and booster club support and the program that puts in more hours usually wins.

To some extent, the same could be said for any activity, but the number of people involved makes the correlation between work and winning stronger in football than any other sport.

One great basketball player can take over a game in a way one football player can't. In baseball the law of averages means the superior team will win a higher percentage of the time over a long season, but anyone can win on a given day. Of course, luck is always involved, especially between evenly matched teams. Any sport has the element of chance built in. The ball bounces funny, quarterbacks can be "off," weather can impact results, and kickers have a huge impact. But among team sports, football has the highest parallel between preparation and success.

Football may be the fairest of sports, but it's a brutal, merciless fairness for the team on the wrong end of the equation. There are no second chances and usually no quick fixes. Adjustments to the program must be implemented during the off-season, and it may take years to determine whether they're effective. The absolute nature of the game causes sleepless nights for coaches. The success or failure of a coach is determined on ten Friday nights a year; success on those nights is decided by decisions made the other 355 days.

For me, and I'm sure for most coaches, what makes the wins so rewarding and the losses so crushing is the preparation invested. More than most sports, a single game is a test that exposes the overall quality of a program. When a coach wins, he knows he's accomplished something. The win proves he's taking things in the right direction. A loss means he must reevaluate what he does. For players, it's an amazing feeling when the sweat and blood they've invested over years pays off and they walk off the field knowing they've earned their triumph.

Boyd spoke to me about what a playoff win meant to his son.

"I'll never forget walking out into that field and looking into my son's eyes, just an exuberation of how happy you are yet how exhausted . . . he had just given his all, he looked at me and said, 'Dad, I love this feeling.' What was brought to this town more than anything was the knowledge and understanding of what that drug of achievement is . . . all these kids who have played understand what it takes to achieve."

I'm exhausted when I arrive in Port Lavaca on Saturday morning. Last night was the first of my long postgame drives. I'd left Carthage late the night before, getting about an hour past Houston before stopping for a few hours of sleep. Another few hours on the road this morning and I arrived on the coast during the Crab morning meeting. I realize now that the long late-night drives will be an ordeal for me. I'm not as young as I once was and my eyes don't handle dark roads as well as they used to. Texas also has more wildlife in its countryside than I'm used to; roadkill is everywhere, and during night drives, potential deer, foxes, armadillos, and other animals wait around every turn.

The Sandcrabs won convincingly the night before, beating La Vernia 56-40 to begin the season 2-0. La Vernia scored late against the Calhoun backups, making the final score closer than it needed to be. The win is encouraging for a team everyone expected to be rebuilding after a phenomenal 2011 season.

But it's only a non-district game against an untested team. There are many questions to be answered. The 2011 Sandcrabs went 12-1 and became the first team in Texas history to have four 1,000-yard rushers in the same backfield. The Sandcrabs advanced to the third round of the playoffs before falling to Kerrville Tivy, 50-43, at the

Alamodome. But this is not that team; the Sandcrabs are returning just one offensive starter and five on defense.

Whitaker runs an unconventional program in many ways. There are certain things you expect from big-time Texas programs, and on first glance, Calhoun looks very unimpressive.

The facilities are poor by Texas standards. No turf fields or fancy offices here. Whitaker has made major improvements to the locker room and successfully gotten a spacious new weight room built, but the facilities here will never rival the palaces in larger Texas cities. The organization looks antiquated, as well. Whitaker is more comfortable writing everything out longhand and Xeroxing than using a computer. Practice plans and scouting reports are usually handwritten. After seeing the high-tech, shiny program at Carthage, walking into Calhoun Saturday morning was like leaving the twenty-first century and heading back to 1982. But this *is* a top-notch program by the two measures that matter: the product they put on the field and the fanatical support of their fans.

The offensive staff meets in Whitaker's office and enjoys the film. A win with 56 points scored is fun viewing for offensive coaches. The defensive staff is around the corner in the "theater." The room off the practice gym with raised theater-style seating was built for film watching. The Sandcrab defense was a liability last year, especially defending the pass. Changes were made during the off-season to address this, but the results are inconclusive. This week's game against a quality passing team in Somerset will be the first true test for the secondary and pass defense this season.

At 10:00 the players arrive, and after a brief meeting in the theater they head to the weight room. The weight room has become a big focus for Calhoun and it's a major factor in their success. The emphasis shows today. The fifty players spend forty-five minutes on a thirteen-lift circuit covering all body parts. The team does three sets of eight repetitions including squats, bench, power cleans, leg press, necks, curls, rows, and a football-specific machine that works the whole body. Coaches are stationed around the room, blowing a whistle every few minutes to move the groups from station to station.

Strength is a major part of Whitaker's prescription for success. Being the strongest, fittest team on the field is achievable, while being the most athletic may not be. A new weight room was built in 2006. The building includes a small turf area used for mat drills and poor weather practices and a new state-of-the-art training room. The approach to make strength training a bigger part of the culture at Calhoun has been successful both on the football field and in UIL powerlifting. The Sandcrabs have excelled, winning powerlifting championships with both their boys' and girls' teams.

After lifting, the coaches choose players of the week for last night's game. Those selected are given tiger-striped towels to denote their status. Later, the offense is in Whitaker's office watching film. The mood is still loose. While they played well the previous night, many mistakes must be fixed before district starts in two weeks. Whitaker jokes with fullback Cory Williams. Williams good-naturedly accuses Whitaker of picking on him after he played such an outstanding game.

Recognizing and numbering defensive threats by alignment is key to running the option successfully, and most of the criticism during this session is about recognizing what the opponent's front and movement means for the called play. Whitaker tells me, "It's all about counting one side of the ball and getting in a situation where they don't have enough to cover all the options."

Whitaker is a master at recognizing whether a defense is set up to stop particular plays and calling the right variant to exploit the weakness of any front. This gives him a huge advantage, as few defensive coordinators are anywhere near as schooled in *stopping* the option as he is in running it.

The teaching continues as Whitaker educates the players to recognize defenses using option terminology. He frequently stops the film and quizzes players, "Who is number three in this front? Why are we blocking number two on this play?" The players are sent home at 1:15 and the coaches begin planning for Friday's game, homecoming against Somerset.

As with all aspects of the Calhoun program, the option offense affects how the Sandcrabs scout upcoming opponents. The defensive staff is in the theater, drawing up Somerset formations and plays, reasonably confident of what they'll see Friday night. Coach Claude Bassett is close to Somerset's staff and has a good feel for their personnel and schemes. He tells defensive coordinator Cory McFall and the rest of the defensive staff what to expect out of a particular formation.

On the offensive side, the coaches are often in the dark when trying to figure out how they'll be defended. Somerset has shown a 4-3 look, a 5-3 look, and a 6-2. When scouting, most teams look for games where other teams run similar offenses to determine what to expect. For Calhoun, this method rarely works. The Sandcrabs are usually the only option team on their opponents' schedules, so they're not sure how they'll be defended.

Whitaker and the offensive staff come up with three separate game plans, one for each front they've seen, and will work them against the scout group this week. Calhoun never adds new plays or wrinkles to their offense; this is a complete package and includes ways to attack every defense. They don't adjust their plays; instead, they watch how the defense adjusts, recognize what they're seeing, and plug in the correct formation and play.

The offensive scout meeting breaks up at around 3:00, and those coaches head to the locker room to put award stickers on players' helmets. The varsity locker room is designed to be a place where players want to hang out. A couch and a big-screen TV with a video game console are along one wall. The growth in the number of players claimed the pool table, as they needed more room for lockers. Over in the theater, McFall and his coaches are still filling binders with Somerset plays. I've seen enough and head out to get a look at Port Lavaca. Later I check into my room at the Holiday Inn Express, take a nap, and work on my blog.

Sunday is a day off for most of the staff and players, but Whitaker is in his office, working in a quieter setting. People assume that because the head football coach doesn't teach in Texas, they focus on football 24-7. This isn't quite true. Almost all head coaches are athletic directors, and even during football season, there's no shortage of paperwork and other details. Many head coaches use weekends to get caught up.

Monday, during athletic period, the JV is in the weight room, while the varsity gets its first look at Somerset. With the defense, Bassett familiarizes his players with the Somerset spread package. Sonny Detmer is the coach at Somerset, father of two NFL quarterbacks and grandfather of current Bulldog quarterback Koy Detmer Jr. While coaching at BYU, Bassett recruited Sonny's elder son, Ty, and still has a good relationship with the Detmers.

The heat of Carthage didn't follow me to the Coastal Bend. A nice breeze blows off the water a mile away at 4:00 when after-school practice begins. The offense wears green jerseys, the defense red, and the JV gold. "Green is for go and red is for stop," I'm told by offensive line coach Roger Saenz. The kids at Calhoun are good-natured and polite. They're taught to be respectful. When I attended their scrimmage a few weeks before, each lined up to shake my hand, thanked me for coming, and wished me a safe journey to my next stop. Today, the kids show up looking happy and have the appearance of a group who enjoy themselves.

Like all 4A and 5A programs, the Sandcrabs platoon, keeping separate units and staffs. However, here, all players learn positions on both sides of the ball. There are two reasons: numbers and the option offense. The numbers are strong now, but this wasn't true when Whitaker took over. In 2006, two-way football was necessary due to thin numbers. When I asked Whitaker if he would ever consider teaching players only one side of the ball, he didn't say no, but said it would take a lot of kids. While the problem of numbers has mostly been solved, the option offense makes it necessary to have many kids who can run it.

One possible weakness of this offense is that it puts the quarterback in the line of fire more than many other schemes. In the option, the quarterback is a true running back, often running into the interior. He can't slide to avoid hits. A good option quarterback is a physical player, and where there's toughness, there's a greater possibility of injury. The quarterback is a target in this scheme; if he goes down, the whole offense can fall apart.

Because the quarterback and the ballcarriers are so exposed and the exchange is so important, Whitaker must have many players ready for each backfield position. The 2012 Sandcrabs have four quarterbacks, four fullbacks, and three at each wing. Everybody gets daily repetitions so they'll be ready if called upon. A ten-minute segment during each practice is allocated to teaching all defensive players an offensive position and offensive players a defensive one. Mostly, the Sandcrabs keep entirely separate offensive and defensive units, but it always pays to be prepared.

During the indy periods, all backs work the double and triple option drills they've done since seventh grade. The two-ball drill is performed daily. The quarterback hands a ball to the fullback and pitches a second ball to the wing. The read drill is a second daily routine: coaches with blocking bags stand at various spots and move in different directions for the quarterback to read and make proper decisions off of, either handing the ball, running, or pitching depending on what the "reads" tell him. By the time they reach high school, the backs have done the two-ball drill so many times they can literally do it blindfolded.

On the defensive field, Bassett works with the secondary. There's a lot of walk and talk as he teaches the DBs to align properly to different formations. A disadvantage of the option offense is that it's tough for Calhoun's scout team to give the defense a good look. Passing the ball is almost a trick play for Calhoun. On a big night, the Sandcrabs may put the ball in the air three or four times. Quarterbacks at Calhoun are selected for their running and reading ability, not their arms. So when the JV runs the spread offense used by Somerset, for example, the scouts have trouble giving the secondary any real competition.

The option offense has three potential weaknesses. The first is the vulnerability of the quarterback. The Sandcrabs deal with this by training many to play this position. The second is explosiveness. If an option team ever falls far behind, it's hard to score quickly. The Sandcrabs overcome this by *not* falling far behind very often. The third is that teams who pass so rarely have a tough time simulating the pass when scouting for their defense. The Sandcrabs addressed this by hiring Bassett.

The defensive problem was exposed during the 2011 playoffs in a third-round playoff loss to Kerrville Tivy. As usual, the Sandcrabs put on an offensive show, but lost to the Antlers, 50-43. It had been a great season, but the ending was disappointing. While winning district is always a major goal, many believe this team could have gone further. Giving up 50 points to Tivy showed a flaw the Sandcrabs needed to solve.

Bassett was brought in to teach the Sandcrab DBs to defend the pass. He was formerly the head coach at Robstown. Before that he had been a college assistant, working with Mike Leach at the University of Kentucky and coaching at BYU. His challenge now is finding ways to teach coverage without an effective scout offense.

During team offense, Whitaker usually watches and directs the action from a chair on the filming tower, calling down plays and correcting mistakes. From his tower, Whitaker gets as excited as I'll see him this week. Other coaches tell me that when he's particularly fired up, he'll slam his chair down onto the platform, bouncing it to the ground. By the end of this practice his voice is hoarse from all the corrections he's made. The offense runs two huddles against one defense and Whitaker corrects things with one team as the other runs their play. The most common command today is "START-DOINGUPDOWNS!" each time somebody makes a mistake.

Whitaker formerly ran the option from the I formation, but the Sandcrabs have gone mostly to a double-wing and double-split formation (also known as the flexbone) because in 2001, the players were more suited to line up in the wing than with a tight end. Whitaker likes the double-wing because it's a balanced formation, forcing the defense to come to balance, as well. The double-wing is the most common look for the Sandcrabs, but other formations are employed to put the defense at a "numbers" disadvantage. Unbalanced formations force the defense to adjust, and whatever the defense does *will* be wrong. They'll have enough to stop plays on the overloaded side *or* the short side, but never both.

The option has many variations and the Sandcrabs run most of them: veer option, lead option, zone option, trap option, midline option, and double and triple options are all in the Calhoun playbook. The Sandcrabs use six different blocking schemes to run all the variations of this one play. As with most offenses, balance is one of the goals, only with the option it's not balance between pass and run or even between different sections on the field, but balance between yardage and carries for the four backs. In 2011, the Sandcrabs rushed for a total of 5,738 yards and passed for only 315 but were balanced using their criteria. The quarterback position rushed for 1,621 yards, the fullback for 1,538, and the slot for 2,543. By the standards of this offense, that is very balanced. It worked. The Crabs averaged 46 points during the 2011 season.

The kids are too sloppy today, and Whitaker begins to worry. The starting quarterback, Hunter Boerm, isn't making his reads correctly, and Whitaker wonders about his focus. The coach had gotten a little spoiled having such a veteran backfield last season and a quarterback with exceptional speed. Boerm is strong and has the solid look of a physical runner but will never be able to pull away from pursuit like Joseph Bargas did in 2011.

After practice I meet Coach Whitaker's wife, Kellie. Kellie is everywhere at Calhoun. She teaches physics, coaches girls' powerlifting, runs the booster club, and is very involved in helping her husband build the program. Kellie exudes an energy that makes you think she can juggle all her roles and work twenty-hour days without breaking a sweat. The Whitakers are a team. They work closely together and toward the same goals. The sum is much greater than the parts when these two work together.

Kellie is the daughter of two coaches and a coach herself, so the life of a coach's wife comes naturally to her. This is important. Not all women are suited to being coaches' wives. It takes an independent woman to handle being alone for long periods every fall. During the season, coaching is a seven-day-a-week job. The team is on the coach's mind every waking hour and frequently in his dreams, as well. I was lucky to have found a woman independent enough to handle football season, but I've known many coaches who married women who weren't cut out for the life. Those men either gave up coaching or gave up the marriage.

In Texas, the life is especially tough, as coaching so often requires moving from town to town, chasing the next rung up the ladder. As the common saying goes, "There are a lot more coaches' ex-wives than coaches' wives."

As for their plans, both Whitakers keep an open mind. The coaching profession is volatile; new schools open and good jobs can turn bad with the hiring of a new superintendent or a demographic shift. If a job were offered where the Whitakers feel they have a better shot at winning a championship, it would be worth considering. It's foolish for any coach to rule out anything, but the Whitakers are well taken care of at Calhoun and it would take the perfect situation to make them leave. Kellie tells me she loves the people and support of this town and says it was a great place for their younger two kids. "This place is about as perfect an atmosphere as you could find."

The same basic practice plan is used Monday through Wednesday: two indy periods, then group, with the offensive and defensive lines and skill kids working against each other. Calhoun does a little "good on good" (starters versus starters) work during group but aren't very physical. The main focus is always fundamentals. The offensive line under Coach Saenz is proficient at getting off the ball very low. This scheme has cutback lanes, so the back-side works hard at reaching and cutting the linebackers.

This technique would be illegal in most of the nation's high schools, but it is perfectly fine here. The difference this rule makes in how the game is coached and played is huge. Backs diving into the legs of linebackers, and those linebackers taking on pulls by cutting the legs of the puller, thus spilling counters (clogging the inside, forcing the play to the outside), make the Texas version of the game both faster and lower.

One could argue that it makes Texas football more dangerous, but I don't agree. Yes, offensive players are better at executing the low block, but defenders are also better at taking it on. The second-level cut is so important in this scheme that Saenz doubts they could run the option without it. Sandcrab linemen do an outstanding job of executing this block. An advantage to rarely throwing the ball is that the linemen can use a run-heavy stance with all their weight forward. As a result, the Sandcrab front gets tremendous push when the ball is snapped.

Fundamentals are also stressed on the defensive side. The Sandcrab 3-4 is purposely kept simple, but the players are well schooled at taking on blocks, pursuing the ball, and tackling. With the notable exception of the fullback Williams, few Sandcrabs look like good football players until they're playing football. The linemen aren't big and most of the skill guys aren't very fast, but everyone's strong and well conditioned. They all move with purpose, creating a quickness that overcomes the lack of raw speed.

The weight room and an off-season conditioning program called the Champions Course are the main components in building a Sandcrab football player. For six weeks every summer, all players must attend the Champions Course for four days a week. An hour in the weight room is followed by an hour of conditioning work outside. The workout varies from day to day, getting progressively tougher each week. Tuesday is 40-yard sprint day. The players go from running twenty-five 40-yard sprints in week one to fifty in week six.

This part of the state is absolutely flat, so a few years ago Whitaker asked Boyd to build him a hill. Boyd trucked in the dirt, and "Champions Hill" was built just past the main practice field. The hill is twenty-two feet high and sixty-five yards long, and the Sandcrabs earn varsity jerseys by running it during the spring. The kids at Calhoun live in the weight room during the off-season. Squats of 300 to 400 pounds are not unusual for the smaller skill players, while many of the linemen are putting up 400 to 600 pounds. It's no fluke that the Sandcrabs have had as much success in powerlifting competitions as in football.

After athletic period, I go to lunch with Whitaker, the high school principal (in Texas, it's never just the principal, but the high school or building principal), and an assistant superintendent. We go to a Mexican restaurant and eat fajitas while locals come by and wish Whitaker luck Friday night. I have a good talk with principal Brandon Stiewig. The relationship between the HC/AD and high school principal is different in Texas: both are hired by the superintendent. The principal is in charge of academics, while the AD is responsible for athletics. Texas HC/ADs are responsible for finding and hiring all high school *and* middle school coaches for every sport. The AD and principal work together to find applicants who can coach and fill teaching needs. Most principals let the AD bring in people he wants but retain veto power if a candidate isn't a good fit in the classroom. Stiewig has worked outside of Texas but prefers this arrangement over the way things are done in most other states, where principals oversee everything. In fact, every Texas school administrator I spoke with liked this division of duties.

Football coach is a political position because of public interest. A principal who hires or fires a coach could get the superintendent in trouble, making this a more appropriate decision for those at the top. Sharing responsibilities also allows the high school principal to focus on the classroom and leave parent complaints, paperwork, and other headaches to the AD.

After lunch, Whitaker returns to his office. On Saturday, each player had written out his class schedules. Grade checks are coming soon, and Whitaker assigns each assistant players to check. Kids in danger of falling below a C in any class (Texas state law requires all athletes to have Cs or better in all classes to play) will get extra help from the coaching staff.

Tracking and classroom help is an added benefit for athletes. Programs are judged by the scoreboard, but the perception that only winning matters in places like Port Lavaca is incorrect. The *work* that creates those wins is where important growth occurs. Yes, Port Lavaca started winning and success changed the town, but the people, not the numbers on the scoreboard, are the most important part of the change.

Boyd tells me, "I don't really care about football or basketball . . . what I care about is the kids learning how to be adults and learning what achievement means . . . [Winning] happens because of the ethics and values that you're taught." Phillips, a former Sandcrab who's now the parent of a player, tells me that football has done incredible things for his boy, things having nothing to do with football skills.

"In a group setting you won't find a better way to turn boys into men."

Wednesday's practice starts well, but during the home stretch the kids lose focus. Players forget snap counts and miss exchanges. Whitaker looks ready to blow his top. He yells, "STARTDOING-UPDOWNS!" from the tower too often today. It's the last true practice this week, and he hates to end on a poor note.

The assistants aren't as worried as Whitaker. I have the feeling it's just Whitaker's nature to worry and see every possible pitfall. Thursday, he tells me he's decided practice *wasn't* so bad after all, but I'm sure the worry isn't entirely gone.

After practice, the Sandcrabs perform the first of many pregame rituals leading up to Friday night's game. An important component of Whitaker's program is developing a feeling of family within the team.

"Whit breeds a sense of community that is just unbelievable; these kids love each other," Boyd tells me. Every Wednesday, the Sandcrabs randomly hug each other for several minutes after practice. This exercise must have seemed strange when first implemented, but the kids genuinely enjoy and appreciate it now. They take to it with complete openness. Nobody looks embarrassed or self-conscious— traits I'd expect from awkward teenage boys and reactions that only could have been overcome by a staff that has earned the players' trust.

Thursday during athletic period the two JV squads prepare for the trip to San Antonio for their games with Somerset. The high school is surrounded by thunderheads as the varsity goes outside to do a walk-through. The joke among the players is that Whitaker has the ability to keep the rain off the field.

"Coach Whitaker is God," I'm told by a player. The story is that once, several years before, black clouds were approaching over the cotton fields to the south. The players watched, preparing to scurry off as rain and lightning approached the practice field. Whitaker raised his hands as if to hold the clouds off. The wind changed and the sun came out. Today, Whitaker's magic doesn't work. A downpour soon begins. Everyone heads into the weight room to finish up.

A second pregame ritual is held during the final ten minutes of Thursday's practice. The entire team, including coaches, circle up on the floor. Whitaker calmly talks about expectations for tomorrow, and then the players speak about whatever's on their minds.

The sharing serves two purposes: team unity is built, and the rituals surrounding the game hammer home that this is important, something to take seriously. According to Boyd, during the bad years, "Before the game kids were talking about where the parties were going to be." Winning isn't the most important lesson taught by the game, but in those days, "losing didn't hurt. Losing is supposed to hurt. If it doesn't, winning can't taste as sweet. When these kids lose a game, they're devastated, and that's a good thing. That teaches you to work harder."

After everyone has shared, they finish with a prayer and head to lunch.

This afternoon, Sandcrab Stadium hosts a freshman doubleheader. The lunchtime shower has passed and it's a beautiful late afternoon, with a picturesque sunset behind the visiting stands. First the freshmen B team is taking on the El Campo Bs, then the A team matches up with the Somerset freshmen. Texas schools often have multiple freshman and JV teams. The philosophy of sub-varsity is to give everyone game experience. As numbers rise, teams are added, ensuring playing time. Since individual schools may not have the same number of lower-level teams, creative scheduling is required to give every team a game. Having head coaches who are also ADs aids in this process, as does the policy of using assistant coaches as bus drivers.

This system is superior to where I come from. In my hometown sub-varsity teams vary greatly. Struggling programs have trouble fielding lower-level teams at all, while more affluent and successful ones dress over one hundred players on a single freshman or JV team. The system is unfair on both ends of the spectrum. The kids playing for poor programs cannot be successful playing against deep programs and often become (understandably) demoralized by the lopsided losses. Many quit before really knowing what football is about. The deep programs suffer in this system, as well. They have huge rosters but can't use that many players; fifth-string freshmen rot on the bench until they lose interest and quit.

Having only one or two sub-varsity teams and so many players doesn't allow young players develop. Sometimes, late bloomers are awful freshman players who become stars later. It's impossible to judge how a freshman will look or play after puberty. Many fifth-stringers can be productive if given the opportunity and encouragement to continue playing. In Texas, marginal players are on B or C teams—but who knows where the opportunity to play may lead. It isn't uncommon for even C players to become varsity contributors as juniors or seniors.

Whitaker watches from the press box while getting JV updates from Somerset. He stays up top because his presence on the sideline would distract his freshman coaches.

It turns out to be a good night for the young Sandcrabs. The A team freshmen fall behind 22-0 early but chip away and eventually beat the Somerset squad, 38-35.

The game is an outstanding example of how the option offense can level the playing field. The visiting Bulldogs have much better athletes, but Calhoun's teamwork eventually prevails. Whitaker is excited throughout the game, often yelling from behind the press box glass where he can't be heard below. He's thrilled by the comeback and talks to the freshmen afterward, letting them know how proud he is.

The coaches are looking at a weather website Friday morning as I arrive. Rainstorms surround Port Lavaca. Whitaker is hoping for rain tonight; he's been worried all week about his defense. He thinks a wet field will be an advantage against Somerset's passing game. The offense meets during athletic period to review the plan against each of the three fronts they've prepared for. The defense watches film from last night's JV game, looking for clues of how Sonny and Koy Detmer will attack their 3-4 front.

Whitaker's twenty-five-year-old son, Rusty, came from Pflugerville for a visit. He'd been a quarterback for his father and attributes his success as a computer analyst to values he learned on the field. Rusty tells me that learning to recognize defenses helps him in his job. What he does mostly involves recognizing patterns, and his mind was trained for this by running his father's offense.

The kids are excited about the game but also about the "gallon challenge" taking place in the H-E-B parking lot after the game. It's a local tradition during homecoming week for boys to guzzle a gallon of milk and run a race. Whoever finishes first without throwing up is the winner. Rain has kept some away, but tailgate parties start at lunchtime in the H-E-B lot. All over town, businesses have decorated their windows with "Go Sandcrabs, beat the Bulldogs" and similar messages in black-and-gold paint.

Whitaker is a worrier but he doesn't seem overly stressed. Tonight is a non-district game, really nothing but a test. Calhoun has progressed to where they're always expected to win, and tonight is no different. However, next week has real meaning, when they play district rival Calallen. Whitaker's mindset will be different.

After an enthusiastic pep rally, two buses head to the Wagon Train for a pregame meal. Before eating, the players stand at attention behind their chairs and say the first of many game-day prayers.

From now until the scoreboard clock hits zero, the players go from one routine to the next. The meal is quick, quiet, and businesslike. Then the Crabs head back to the weight room, where they'll spend an hour in the dark quietly meditating. Like naptime in kindergarten, the kids and coaches lie on the mats, mentally preparing for the game.

The sky is spitting rain at Sandcrab Stadium. Kickoff is still two hours away, but already several hundred people wait for the gates to open. Season tickets are sold in Port Lavaca, but with no reserved seating, fans must arrive early to secure any of the 3,000 seats on the home side. By kickoff, three-quarters of the stadium is filled with Sandcrab supporters. The quarter of the stands roped off for Somerset fans is almost empty.

A message is written on a locker room whiteboard: "Focus & Finish. Homecoming 2012! Our team's last chance to improve before district . . . Leaders lead in big games, great players show up in big games. Tonight we need leaders and great players to step up. 48 minutes of hell."

During warm-ups, Whitaker introduces me to Coach Detmer and tells him about my project. Detmer tells me about his coaching career, mostly spent in the San Antonio area. He's a classy and likable guy. Both head coaches are so cordial and look so relaxed, it's easy to forget a game is about to be played. At this early point of the season and for a non-district game, they aren't going to get too nervous. They've both been in this business long enough to know there'll be bigger nights later.

Each position coach gathers his kids to talk before sending them in at the end of warm-ups. Defensive line coach James Weatherwax is a crusty old-timer from Ohio with a quick temper, but he tells his players he loves them.

Back inside, Coach McFall hands out scout sheets for his defense to review. Unlike most coordinators, he doesn't give out a big packet early in the week. He feels packets give the players too much to forget. Instead, he limits the game plan during the week to what players can absorb, gives them a cheat sheet right before kickoff, and then lets them fly.

Number one on the sheet states: "The QB is the best runner and passer we have seen this year. We must look to contain him on all rollouts and look for crossing routes by the TE (#82) and the back out of the backfield (#27 & #1). Hit all receivers crossing your face and hit the QB hard and often. #23 is their fastest receiver but #26 and #82 lead the team in catches and yards. When they are under center, look for blunt, sweep, GT and iso."

With about ten minutes until kickoff, McFall talks to the team. "If anybody has a little bit of doubt going into this game, it's them," he says. "No silly mistakes tonight. It's time to work out the kinks and show what you're made of."

Whitaker is up next, "There are no coaches on the field. It's up to you to deal with the adversity yourselves." He then addresses the offense, reminding them, "If we don't turn the ball over, they can't beat us."

They gather on the floor and kneel for a quick Lord's Prayer as the lights turn off. In the dark now, Whitaker adds to the emotion, talking about focus, as music rises from the speaker brought for this purpose. I recognize *The Ecstasy of Gold* from the scene in *The Good, the Bad and the Ugly* (my favorite movie) where Tuco searches for Arch Stanton's grave. The Metallica version plays as Whitaker finishes and the Sandcrabs hit the field. The soundtrack is replaced by the Calhoun fight song, borrowed from the University of Notre Dame. The band plays as the players rush onto the field.

Whitaker's worries are unfounded; it's a big night for the Sandcrabs. The Bulldog defense doesn't know how to deal with the option and, in particular, Williams. The Sandcrab fullback is the best player on the field and has a huge game, rushing for 255 yards on eleven carries and three touchdowns. Somerset tries all three fronts the Crabs prepared for, but Whitaker calls the right plays to counter each look. The Sandcrabs rush for a total of 550 yards.

The defense is impressive, as well. The plan to contain and pressure the young Somerset quarterback is successful. The Sandcrab front brutalizes Detmer, sacking him five times. Coach Bassett's secondary also plays well, showing the changes he's made may have solved past weaknesses.

The defensive play tonight is a big surprise for me. With a team that doesn't hit much during the week, it's hard to judge physicality. Nothing during the week had given me a clue the Crabs were as intense and physical as they're showing tonight. They are the nicest kids in the world, but play with fury. The Sandcrabs lead 35-6 at the half.

With the game decided, adjustments don't take long, and during halftime, Coach Detmer compliments Whitaker on how the Sandcrabs are playing, clearly impressed by what he's seeing.

Williams caps the night with a remarkable 85-yard touchdown run during the third quarter. The run highlights all three skills a great back needs: agility, speed, and strength. Making a move after hitting the hole, he runs over a tackler before pulling away from pursuit with speed that isn't supposed to exist in South Texas. Williams, just a junior, is being looked at by several D-I schools, and tonight he shows why. Backups get significant playing time in the fourth quarter. The final score is 49-6 Sandcrabs.

After the game, the teams gather and do something that I come to find is fairly common in Texas, but new to me. Both teams gather at the 50-yard line, kneel, and pray together. I've seen this with college teams and with groups of players in the NFL, but never in high school. I've been asked about the religiosity of the Texas game by coaches both within and outside of Texas. The best way I can describe the difference is that programs in Texas are more likely to have a religious aspect and are open about displaying it. This shouldn't come as a surprise. Texas is a very religious state, and several places I visited can rightly be described as the "buckle of the Bible Belt." Church attendance in this state is so much more a part of life than it is in most of the West.

Coach-led prayers are less common in the West. Of the six schools I coached at, three had regular prayers. Texas teams don't all do things the same way. Of the eleven teams I followed, two don't pray at all and the others are all over the spectrum. Several do it only before games, while others make it a big part of their programs.

Do the prayers have any correlation to the moral quality of the program? Not that I could tell. Programs with more prayers are likely to have lower tolerance for profane language, but that's as far as the difference goes. Coaches generally are in the game for the same reason, regardless of religious belief: believing in sportsmanship, in teaching commitment, discipline, teamwork, and positive character traits. That said, seeing two teams pray together minutes after playing a football game is a beautiful gesture, serving to put the game in proper perspective. I wish I could stay for the homecoming festivities, especially the "gallon challenge," but I have a seven-hour drive to Stamford. As with every other stop, I say goodbye to everyone and let Whitaker know I hope to return during the playoffs. This time, though, it doesn't work out.

Calhoun finishes the regular season undefeated, with a record of 9-0, sweeping district 30-4A. Their defense plays well all season, shutting out Calallen the week after my visit and holding all subsequent opponents but Victoria East to three touchdowns or less. Offensively, they again put up big numbers, averaging 43.7 points per game and rushing for 4,830 yards. Unfortunately the Sandcrabs lose fullback Williams to an ACL injury during week seven against Victoria West. Still, they win the bi-district playoff game against Floresville, 48-21.

The Sandcrabs' season ends the following week, however. They fall to Edcouch-Elsa, 36-34, in an upset.

Whitaker is positive about the future of the Sandcrab program. Their returning quarterback, Boerm, is doing well in the weight room and weighs 225: "He's becoming a man."

Whitaker also is excited that the numbers continue to climb. In the aftermath of a surprising 2012 season, 132 upperclassmen have joined off-season workouts. With the freshmen who'll be coming next year, they should have more kids playing football in 2013 than any year since he arrived.

Whatever happens, there won't be any going back to the way things were before success changed this community. Success has been ingrained into the culture; these kids are raised understanding the values that bring victory on the field. Program alumni will carry those traits into other aspects of their lives and teach them to the next generation of Calhoun Sandcrabs, a generation who will never know the embarrassment previous Sandcrabs struggled with. Being a Sandcrab is now something to be proud of, and will be as long as the people of Port Lavaca continue to teach the values that turned around this program.

4

IT'S OUR TIME
Week Four: Stamford Bulldogs

When setting up this trip, it was suggested I consider Stamford. I'd contacted several Texas high school football experts to come up with the right mix of schools. The man who recommended the Bulldogs gave Stamford's location as West Texas.

Not yet having much experience in the state, I looked at the map and found Stamford was forty miles north of Abilene, right in the center of the state. I didn't understand that to Texans, anything twenty miles west of I-35 is considered West Texas.

Geographically, it may not make sense for two-thirds of the state to be considered "West," but demographically and historically there's logic to it. A huge percentage of the state's population lives along the I-35 corridor, running from the Metroplex through Austin to San Antonio. With Houston to the east, far more Texans live along or east of this line than to the west. People perceive themselves to be the center of the universe, and for most Texans, I-35 marks the dividing line between east and west.

During the early years of the republic and state of Texas, this same line roughly marked the frontier between white civilization and the areas controlled by the Plains Indians. The Llano Estacado is a land where coastal plains meet the high plains, stretching to the Rocky Mountains. For much of Texas' history, the land west of this line held far more buffalo than people. After the Civil War, when the area first opened to settlement, small ranching and farming towns, of which Stamford was one, began to dot the region. West Texas is more rural, more wide open; water is scarcer and residents are more spread out than in the rest of the state. The population here continues to decline, as people leave the farms and ranches for jobs in the cities.

I arrive early Saturday morning after an all-night drive from Port Lavaca. Except for a few hours of sleep in a truck stop in Cisco, I'd been driving since I left Sandcrab Stadium the night before. After a night of dodging armadillos, coyotes, and deer on the twisting and dark two-lane highways from the Gulf Coast to "The Big Country," I pull up to the fieldhouse at Stamford High School.

It's 8:50 Saturday morning. The Bulldogs played well the night before, beating Merkel, 36-0, in a game they'd expected to be difficult. This raises their record to 2-1 after a week two loss to top-ranked Munday. The coaches are spread around the two rooms of the office entering data into Hudl. Between plays they swat flies with one of several flyswatters around the cluttered room. In a state full of amazing facilities, Stamford's is nothing special. The fieldhouse is small and cramped, without a separate head coaches' office. Bulldog Stadium is well taken care of but impressive only in its capacity, which far exceeds the population of the city.

With 2A and 1A schools, enrollment is such that participation from nearly every student is required for a program to be successful. At Stamford, participation is outstanding, even by Class A standards. Exactly three boys *aren't* involved with football, and those three were asked to be managers.

In the bigger schools, participation is often for the elite, for gifted boys with higher-than-average work ethic and special players. In small schools, it's about *everybody*—all hands on deck. Stamford isn't a place for specialization. If the school offers a program, the kids are expected to be involved and almost everybody is. It doesn't matter whether a boy is talented or big or strong. Students at Stamford will be on the team and make the most of whatever talent they have.

The difference is also seen in the coaches' office. Instead of the twelve to twenty coaches common in bigger schools, the entire staff consists of seven coaches. With almost the entire male student body to pick from, Stamford has it better than most in the 1A. This morning, five coaches are still watching Merkel film from the night before, while the other two watch Colorado City, this week's opponent.

At 11:00, the players come in for a quick workout and meeting while several assistants continue on their laptops. Head coach Wayne Hutchinson meets his team in the large corrugated shed that serves as the weight room. About forty Bulldog players are here, dressed in tight powder blue Under Armour tops and black shorts.

The workout is quick. Players rotate through a circuit and stand at attention with hands clasped behind their backs after each exercise. Every few minutes, Hutchinson "breaks" them to their next activity with small words of wisdom. Although Stamford doesn't have organized summer lifting, the kids look fit and strong. Most are self-motivated and work out on their own during the summer. Giving the summer off is rare these days. Stamford also avoids the seven-on-seven tournaments that have become all the rage in Texas. Between all the sports, the agricultural program, and academic competitions, Hutchinson wants these kids to have time for themselves before hitting it hard in August.

After lifting, the players have quick meetings, first with offensive coordinator Jeremy West, then with defensive coordinator Mitch McLemore. The coaches give their final impression of the Merkel game before moving on to what they'll face this week from C-City. The kids are out the door at noon to enjoy the rest of the weekend. Saturday is a short day for the coaches, as well; one advantage of the Hudl system is that it allows coaches to scout at home. They will watch and break down film at home before meeting again at 1:00 tomorrow afternoon.

I'm happy to leave early. After my long night on the road, checking into the Stamford Inn and taking a long nap sounds great. My wife is arriving later this afternoon. It's her second visit during my five-month road trip and will be the last time I see her until I get home for a few days during Thanksgiving week. I'm excited about her visit. The "lonely road" is such a cliché that I hate mentioning it, but it's a cliché for a reason.

Stamford has around 3,000 residents. It's a place where, if people don't know everyone, they believe they should. People don't stop here on their way someplace else. If you're here at all, you probably live nearby. As I'm coming out of Stamford Donuts on Highway 6, passing drivers wave hello. Later, the lady working at Dixie Dog tells me it's her birthday and that Mr. Underwood sent her flowers, assuming I know who Mr. Underwood is. It happens that I *have* met Underwood, who runs the funeral home and is a big supporter of the school.

Bulldog Stadium has a listed capacity of 8,000. I'm not sure it's really that big, but even at 5,000, its capacity says something about fan support in this part of the state. Stamford needed a stadium big enough to hold everybody in town *and* from whatever town will be coming in. It's rarely filled, but the home side is usually crowded from goal line to goal line.

It's a West Texas stereotype that everything takes a backseat to the game Friday night. The common criticism is that football is so important that it sucks energy from other "more worthy" pursuits. Maybe places like that still exist, but the four West Texas towns I visit don't fit that image at all. People here always point out other things the community takes pride in and supports: Agriculture Club (Ag Club), track, golf, baseball, basketball, and UIL academic competitions in Austin.

Football holds a special place for Texans, especially in small towns. The game speaks to the people here in ways other activities don't. The boys at Bulldog Stadium fight for Stamford, as they have since Gordon Wood coached them to two state championships in the '50s and even before.

It's easy and common to attribute the support shown by small-town residents to the fact that "there is nothing else to do," but this isn't accurate. People from Stamford do most of what big-city denizens do: watch satellite TV, go to dinner, or drive down to Abilene for a movie. The Metroplex is just 170 miles away, putting the Cowboys, Rangers, Six Flags, and other big-city activities just a few hours away. The traditional local recreations of hunting and fishing also keep these people occupied.

Small towns don't support their school and kids out of boredom but because small-town Texas social life revolves around the high school in a way it doesn't in bigger cities. As with church, school events allow Stamford residents to catch up with neighbors and recognize their kids. It's simply a civic duty to attend community events.

Sunday afternoon, after church, the Stamford coaches meet again to work up a game plan for Colorado City. Before getting to football, however, there's some housekeeping to do.

The coaches discuss details for the junior varsity and junior high games in Colorado City on Thursday. Coaches are assigned to drive the buses and order postgame meals. These seven coaches are the entire football staff for the Stamford Independent School District; they not only coach varsity, but also the freshman, JV, and junior high teams. Half will go to Colorado City. C-City is a 2A school that's slightly bigger than Stamford but has only two high school teams. The freshmen will stay in Stamford and play Clyde. Coaches West and Hutchinson will stay and work with the freshmen since both have boys on the freshmen squad.

Once logistics are worked out, the staff puts the Merkel game to bed. They're happy with the performance, especially the defense. Hutchinson tells them, "That's one of the best games I've seen us play." Personnel adjustments on special teams are discussed before talk turns to this week's opponent, the Colorado City Wolves.

Coach West diagrams the front they're likely to see from the Wolves defense and they move into tweaking the practice schedule to allow time to reach their weekly goals. Up on the left side of the whiteboard are listed the components of Stamford's daily practice plan, broken into five-minute segments. 1A programs don't have the staff or player numbers to platoon. Everyone works both sides of the ball. On Monday and Tuesday, the first twelve five-minute blocks are set aside for the offense, followed by twelve for the defense.

Coach McLemore goes to the whiteboard and lists five defensive keys to stopping C-City. 1) Stop #22- the Wolves running back. 2) Make the QB panic (he does not make good decisions when under pressure). 3) Stay in coverage. 4) QB throws touch passes well, DBs need to work on pass drops. 5) #5 and #32 are the favorite receivers, they throw screens well and all defenders need to work at stopping them.

McLemore is the nephew of Pulitzer Prize-winning author Larry McMurtry, who lives up the road in Archer City. McLemore says that when *The Last Picture Show* came out, Archer City basically disowned McMurtry, finding the book too risqué and critical of the people in a fictitious town loosely based on Archer City. But after *Lonesome Dove* won the Pulitzer, the people of Archer City changed their opinion, forgetting they'd ever had a problem. Hutchinson adds, "It sounds a lot like coaching," with a laugh.

A hunched old man comes into the office and visits awhile, talking to Hutchinson about the Merkel game. He's a local man who finds little ways to show appreciation to the coaches whenever he can. I'm sure his visits are a regular part of the week.

At his desk, Hutchinson exchanges texts with the coach from C-City. The Wolves coach jokingly asks Hutch if this is Stamford's homecoming, saying they're getting a float ready because they might be able to win that competition if not the game.

Despite the joking, Colorado City is a good team; they're 2-1 and play in a higher classification. Stamford, however, is expected to do big things. After losing the state championship to Mason in 2011, the Bulldogs return eight offensive and eight defensive starters, including the preseason pick to be 1A player of the year, quarterback and safety Hagen Hutchinson, the oldest son of Coach Hutchinson. He put up outstanding numbers his junior season, leading the Bulldogs to the finals but injuring his shoulder during the semifinal against Mart. He was made ineffective by his injury when the Bulldogs fell to the Mason Punchers, 62-40, in the state championship. Both major high school football publications in Texas predict a Bulldog return to Cowboys Stadium in 2012.

It's not unusual for coaches to have kids on their teams, but it's even more common in small towns like Stamford where everyone plays. It would be unusual if the kids of the coaches weren't playing. Hutchinson's younger boy is a freshman player. Coach West has two boys in the program, and Coach McLemore's son is a linebacker and running back.

The meeting wraps up at 2:00. After the long weekends I'd watched the previous two weeks in Port Lavaca and Carthage, this is a little surprising. Thinking about it, I realize that while not a lot of time was spent, not a lot was wasted, either. What could be done at home was done at home, and the coaches only met to coordinate their pieces into the overall picture. Efficiency is a big part of the Bulldog philosophy. These coaches don't have as much time to work on specific details as big-school coaches do because kids here do so many things. The staff must make sure every second counts. The other factor that shortens the meetings is that, with only thirty-eight varsity players, many going both ways, the plan can't be as complex as those used by bigger schools with one-way players and coaches.

Each week I drive around whatever town I'm in to get a feel for the place and see how people live. Stamford has nice neighborhoods of older but well-kept homes east and south of the high school. Toward downtown and north of the highway are blocks of abandoned neighborhoods, with weeds filling the yards and growing up through the porches, collapsed roofs, and boarded-up windows. These aren't poor neighborhoods, but empty ones.

During the 1960s Stamford reached a peak of over 5,000 residents. At that time, the city was a rail hub and agricultural center.

When the railroad left, some of the population went with it. Over the years farming has gotten less labor intensive, and the population has declined further.

West Texas is full of small towns like Stamford. Texas is growing fast, but the small towns in West Texas are shrinking. During the first decade of the twenty-first century, Texas added 1,000 new residents a day, but West Texas slowly emptied as children of ranchers and farmers joined new Texans moving to the booming cities of the I-35 corridor.

During the school week, the day starts early for Hutchinson and his staff. Stamford Junior High is just across the practice field, and the seventh- and eighth-grade players come over for first-period athletics with the high school coaches. The high school athletic period takes place just before lunch. McLemore quickly goes over the eleven-page scouting report covering the main points the defense needs to focus on; the same points were on the whiteboard on Sunday.

Stamford runs a 3-3-5 defense. McLemore believes the 3-3 stack is better for stopping the run than the more common 3-4 and 4-3, with three protected linebackers keying the run. Against passing teams, one linebacker may drop, giving the Bulldogs more of a two-safety look.

Stamford runs the zone read spread. They implemented this scheme four years ago after years of running the option. Looking at the kids in the pipeline, Hutchinson saw a lot of good skill kids (backs and receivers) and thought the spread would be a good fit.

With a dual-threat quarterback like Hutchinson, who is dangerous both running and throwing the ball, this offense is very tough to stop. The question was how to implement a completely new offense after years of running something entirely different.

Until recent years, Texas had been much more comfortable with smash-mouth running offenses. "Ten years ago, if you put two receivers on the same side, someone was liable to call you a communist," Hutchinson says, only half joking. Now, most of the state has adopted the spread.

The change really took hold with the hiring of Mike Leach at Texas Tech University up in Lubbock in 2000. When Leach took over, he brought new twists to an old formation. The base package is ten personnel (one back, no tight end, and four split receivers). The formation has been around for many years. It's the same look that run-and-shoot teams used in the '80s. What's different now is how this formation is used. Whereas previously the spread formation relied on a quarterback throwing from the pocket and a limited running game, Leach's philosophy was much more dynamic.

The goal was to force defenses to defend the entire field vertically *and* laterally, creating mismatches by getting the best athletes into open-field situations with defenders. Spreading the defense puts players on "islands" where they'll have to bring down offensive athletes without much help. With the quarterback in a shotgun and using quick screens to the perimeter as sweeps, defenses can't rush too hard or they'll take themselves out of position to stop screens. Because it relies on quickly taking advantage of mismatches, this is a no-huddle system, allowing coaches to attack weaknesses they find after the defense lines up. The running game utilizes the quarterback as a second running back.

The final piece to the scheme is a different type of option than was described in the preceding chapter. The zone read allows the quarterback to hand off the ball or pull it out and run, depending on how an unblocked player reacts, as with the veer. However, in the read, the quarterback can pull the ball and run with the blocking or in the *opposite* direction, away from the blocking. This spreads the area the defense must cover and makes many traditional defensive keys obsolete.

The chess game of football has always been a pendulum between offensive and defensive strategies. Offensive coaches come up with new tricks, and defensive coaches devise new ways to stop them— but the defensive strategy to stop a well-executed spread is still waiting to be discovered.

Like the triple option, the zone read spread gives offenses the ability to make the defense always be wrong in how it defends the field. Unlike the triple option, however, the "options" are spread all over the field. Key the running back, and the quarterback will pull the ball. Key the quarterback, and he'll hand it off. Pressure the QB with the defensive line, and they'll be out of position to stop screens; have them play back, and the QB will have all day to hit receivers.

After his success at Texas Tech, Leach's offense quickly became popular in colleges and high schools. Today, most Texas high schools use some variation of the read option; even many run-oriented attacks have adopted parts of this scheme and implement them within their playbooks. The NFL is actually the last to the party. NFL coaches have forever been afraid of anything that smacks of option football, too scared that their quarterbacks would be susceptible to injury if they were allowed to run the ball. They're just now implementing this scheme that high schools and colleges have used for years. As more young quarterbacks come out of colleges using this scheme, with the skills and physical traits to run it, NFL coaches are being dragged into the twenty-first century of football. With the emergence of Colin Kaepernick with the 49ers, Robert Griffin III with Washington, and Russell Wilson with Seattle, 2012 would prove to be a watershed year for the zone read in the NFL.

Head coach Hal Mumme first hired Leach and then Tony Franklin as offensive coordinators when he was at Kentucky. Recently, Franklin has run the same offense he learned with Leach and Mumme as the offensive coordinator at Louisiana Tech University and at the University of California, Berkeley. Franklin began marketing a package that included drill DVDs, playbooks, a play-calling wristband system, special clinics, and teaching progressions for high school coaches who want to implement this offense. Four years ago, Hutchinson decided to make the switch and bought the package.

Short of replacing a coach, implementing a new offense is the most significant change a program can make. It's not simply drawing up new plays. Blocking schemes, position drills, terminology, adjustments versus different defenses, ways to best use personnel, and a million other little tweaks all must be learned over the course of years, usually through trial and error. Everything needs to fit into a coherent framework, with plays and adjustments for every defensive strategy built in, or the scheme will eventually collapse as defenses learn how to stop it.

I've known coaches whose egos wouldn't allow them to buy a package like Franklin's, preferring to make their changes after attending one-hour sessions at clinics or from reading books. Hutchinson recognized that doing things the right way would save his staff years of learning.

All coaches are thieves; stealing good drills, schemes, and ideas is part of the job. Good coaches aren't afraid to admit it and do whatever's necessary to become experts at what they're teaching. After a season when the Bulldogs attempted to run their old option scheme alongside the spread, Hutch bought in entirely. Stamford is now 100 percent a "Tony Franklin team."

With just seven coaches working with all three high school teams, it's impressive how little standing around there is during after-school practice. The organization is thought out and efficient. Kids and coaches meet in different combinations for each session without much wasted time. During the offensive indy period, Hutchinson takes the quarterbacks, McLemore has the line, and West has the receivers. The three levels work together before the varsity screen session. This is followed by a "good on good" pass-rush drill know as PUP, or pass under pressure, while Lannie Templeton, Joe Walts, and Shawn Speck work with the JV and freshman teams on the practice field. After the pass session, the teams come back together, with the JV running scout for the varsity offense.

One advantage of the spread is that it limits the defensive fronts a team sees.

"We either get a 4-2, 3-2, or 3-3 stack box; anything else and we'll kill them with screens," West tells me.

This makes things much easier for the offensive line, as they don't need to adjust to as many fronts as a team using two-back and/or tight end looks. The no-huddle offense allows more reps in a shorter period of time during practice. It also eliminates having the quarterback recite plays over and over and getting into and out of huddles. This efficiency allows the Bulldogs to average three plays per minute during their team session, getting them through their script very quickly.

After the offense finishes, the entire program breaks into five defensive position groups for ten minutes of individuals before interior run, seven-on-seven, and finally defensive team. Hutchinson keeps the practice on schedule, using a stopwatch that's set to beep every five minutes to move the coaches through the twenty-four segments of today's practice.

After practice, Hutchinson tells his players to "take care of business between their ears." Each student at Stamford is assigned a laptop computer, and players are expected to use them to watch the C-City film on Hudl this week.

Hutchinson made a few stops before landing at Stamford six years ago. He grew up just north of Stamford in Knox City, where he won a state championship as quarterback in 1983. After graduating from Angelo State University, he took coaching jobs at Kermit,

Archer City, Whitewright, and Abilene High before getting his first head job, back at his alma mater. Unfortunately, in 2005, the Class A Greyhounds decided to switch from eleven- to six-man football, a completely different sport, so Hutchinson moved down the road to Stamford. Many small-town coaches prefer the small-town life for raising their kids. The lifestyle here is easy to like; everyone knows and pulls for each other in ways not seen in bigger cities. Jim Astin, a local bank president, tells me, "This is a nice way of life; I always know where my kids are and I know my neighbors."

The success rate at Stamford High School is almost 100 percent. Nobody slips through the cracks and everyone is involved with something. Principal Jim Raughton says that, of the 188 students, all but two take part in at least one extracurricular activity. Stamford isn't a rich town—73 percent of its students come from economically disadvantaged homes—but you'd never know that from how the school runs.

"Here, you're going to play football until December, then you're going to play basketball until March, then you're going to play baseball into June, then you're going to run track in the state track meet," Raughton says. The administration sees finding niches for all students as part of their job. The proof of the effectiveness of this approach is hard to argue: kids at Stamford mostly get As and Bs. Most go to college.

A stereotype of small-town life is that the kids can't wait to get out. At least with the small-town boys I visited, this wasn't the case. They like living in Stamford, Port Lavaca, Carthage, Idalou, Abilene, and Throckmorton. They like being involved in so many school activities and appreciate the support from their communities. Many hope to go to college, then return to their hometowns after graduation. Unfortunately, making a living in small towns is getting harder. It's ironic that these schools do such a good job that many students achieve beyond what their towns can offer them in opportunities. A boy in Throckmorton told me he wanted to become a physical therapist. He'd like to open an office in Throckmorton, but in a town with only 813 residents, it's unlikely he could make a go of it. Most of these kids will end up in Dallas, Houston, San Antonio, or Austin.

Except for a few years in Abilene, Hutchinson has always been a small-town coach. He wonders, however, about the offers Hagen might get if he attended a bigger high school. Colleges don't scout

1A schools as well as schools 3A and above. Hagen has great numbers, and throws and runs beautifully, but colleges question how much his numbers are padded by the level of competition in the 1A. He's gotten offers from a few schools, but not the notice he would get if playing for a bigger school.

Wednesday is a quicker practice. Instead of the twenty-four five-minute segments of Monday and Tuesday, there are only seventeen, eight on offense and eight for defense. It's known as "eight and eight and out the gate." The seventeenth segment is the two-minute offensive session, known in many schools as NASCAR. While any no-huddle offense can move quickly, NASCAR takes it to another level. The Bulldogs only run six plays from NASCAR, signaled directly to all eleven players, allowing the offense get plays off almost immediately after the ball is set.

Thursday there is no after-school practice. During athletic period, Hutchinson addresses a concern. He's upset to find some players had been sending texts the previous night at nearly midnight, meaning they hadn't gotten a full eight hours of sleep.

"We're saying 'It's our time' and I believe we have the guys to make it all the way, but it's not going to be your time if you don't take care of business . . . when two teams are the same on paper, what's going to make the difference? Taking care of the little things," he reminds them.

After school, the coaches who aren't at the JV game in C-City give treatment to banged-up varsity players before coaching the freshmen. Stamford uses two quarterbacks; one is Hutchinson's boy, and the other is Coach West's son Gus. Hutch and West take turns calling the offensive plays, each calling the offense when his boy is taking the snaps.

1A freshman football isn't pretty. With just eighteen players, few are good and many just fill spots. It isn't anybody's fault, but with so few players, there are holes all over the field.

Many of these kids will be completely different once weightlifting, coaching, and puberty take hold. Tonight, however, the football is sloppy. The coaches are teaching fundamentals as much as coaching. The final score is 12-8 Stamford.

Friday morning, after checking out of the Stamford Inn, I meet with Woncile Fowler. She's spent most of her life in Stamford, working at the now-closed movie theater downtown and the drive-in where the Walmart sits today. When I get to the Subway sandwich shop, she's writing out a list of Stamford all-state players from 1952 through 1959, from memory. She thinks the '52 team was the best, but they lost in the semis when most of the team got the flu. The Bulldogs have won four state championships, back-to-back in 1955 and '56 and again in 1958 and '59. From 1951 through 1957, the legendary Gordon Wood was the coach. People outside of Texas probably have never heard of Wood, but his is a household name in Texas football circles. He coached high school ball in the state from 1938 until 1985, spending his last twenty-six years at Brownwood High School; he won a total of nine state championships and compiled a lifetime record of 396-91-15.

Fowler talks about the history of the program. She didn't miss a game for thirty-one straight years, from 1942 through 1973. She misses some now because she has trouble getting around, but she still gets out to Bulldog Stadium often and always listens on the radio. She tells me nothing beats getting out and sitting under the press box with all of her friends on a nice fall evening.

I met people like Fowler in every small town. They demonstrate the importance of the game to people in the community. It isn't really about football, but about having a connection with those who share your life. Supporting the team in a place like Stamford is akin to patriotism in Texas and closely tied to the idea of Texas Pride.

There are three forms of Texas Pride: statewide pride, usually displayed to non-Texans; regional pride, shown to people from other parts of the state; and community pride, seen in places like Stamford. West Texas is made up mostly of small towns, but in most of the West these towns are fairly close. In every direction from Stamford the nearest town is less than an hour away, making local rivalries stronger and strengthening regional connections. Stamford residents have friends and family in Anson, Munday, Haskell, and Abilene. If the Bulldogs bow out of the playoffs early and another local school advances, Stamford residents will support their neighbors and take pride in their success.

For all the support of the community, this isn't a "win at all costs" kind of place. The Bulldogs haven't won a state championship since 1959, and during my week here, I never hear any desperation about ending the drought. If the Bulldogs win state in 2012, the celebration will be long and joyous, but if they come up short, the world won't come to an end. Everyone's excited they made the finals last year; the loss was disappointing, but not to the point where anyone publicly second-guesses coaches or allows it to get out of perspective.

Focusing on just football misses what makes small-town sports unique. Local booster Chico Underwood tells me, "Football is my passion, but we follow everything, basketball, baseball, and all the sports." About the successes he says, "We may not be the best at anything, but when *any* Bulldog team comes to town, they know they [the opponents] better watch out."

Game day in Stamford is a community event. Blue-and-white Stamford flags hang on nearly every business in town. The night before games, mothers decorate the Bulldog locker room. This week, a man-size stuffed bulldog wearing a bloody apron stands in the middle of the locker room, behind a meat grinder with a human hand sticking out of it. Fingers and eyeballs litter the table along with cans of Wolf Brand Chili. A sign on the table holding all this Halloween-style gore says, "Make chili out of the Wolves." Around town, everyone wears Bulldog T-shirts. The few who can't get to Bulldog Stadium tonight will be listening to the game on the radio.

During athletic period, the kids meet in the locker room and begin preparing. Hutchinson lined the field this morning. With only seven coaches and no trainers, coaches have to do many odd jobs, unlike bigger schools that have support staffs of trainers, student-trainers, filmers, and managers. Doing laundry, lining fields, giving medical treatment, monitoring grades, coaching each team—for every sport, from seventh grade through varsity—on top of their teaching schedule are all job requirements for coaches in Stamford.

Being well-rounded is just as important for the students as the coaches. As well as playing quarterback and safety, Hagen Hutchinson also plays basketball and competes in track, baseball, and golf during the spring. Like all Stamford students, he's a member of Stamford's nationally recognized Ag. program. During springtime his activities run "from 6:30 in the morning until the sun goes down on the golf course."

Busy schedules aren't unusual in Stamford. During the spring season, between baseball, track, golf, agricultural competitions, and UIL academic competitions in one-act plays, debate, and academics, "The halls are pretty thin," according to West. With so many teachers acting as coaches and advisors, many days the high school operates on a skeleton crew.

Despite missing so much class time, the students do well on the statewide standardized tests. Raughton tells me, "A professor once told me, 'Grades get in the way of learning.' And I believe that. Do I think testing gets in the way of learning? Yeah, I do."

Stamford doesn't ignore this facet of education. They make adjustments, hold tutorials, and recognize that reaching the state and federal benchmarks is important. But they *don't* allow it to interfere with the real purpose of a comprehensive high school: teaching well-rounded kids.

These who argue more classroom time is necessary for quality academics should come to Stamford. The kids miss a lot of school, but they still achieve. The more they're involved, the closer the connection they have with the school, and the more likely they are to be successful. Involved kids are better students.

It's a nice evening in Stamford. The home stands are jammed a half-hour before game time. The fathers are invited into the locker room for the pregame prayer, led by a local pastor. The mothers shake plastic bottles full of pennies and line the path between the locker room and the inflatable Bulldog.

The Bulldogs go up 13-0 in the first quarter, but Colorado City hangs tough. McLemore's prediction that the Wolves quarterback would make bad decisions when pressured isn't panning out. Number six shows great poise tonight and throws a long touchdown pass right before the half, making the score 13-6. With many players and coaches working both ways in Class A, there isn't time for sideline position meetings. The adjustments come at the half when West meets with the offense and McLemore meets with the defense.

During halftime, a coach mischaracterizes how C-City is defending the GT play (a play where the back-side guard and tackle pull to the play-side). Offensive tackle Roy Alaniz corrects the coach, saying the problem is coming from the linebacker, not the defensive tackle. To their credit, the coaches accept the information and make appropriate adjustments. The Bulldogs are a little flat; Hutchinson tells the team that they're "throwing their suits out there."

The Bulldogs pull away in the fourth quarter, winning 34-14. Hagen Hutchinson is clearly the best player on the field; he has the rare combination of superior ability and a knack for knowing how to use it. Whether using his speed to get to the edge, making a move, or stepping up in the pocket to throw, he has a tremendous football IQ. He always seems to make the right decision.

As good as Hutchinson is, what really makes this team so hard to stop is that unlike many small programs, Stamford can hurt you many ways. The Bulldogs have four outstanding receivers in James Washington, Bo Wimberly, Dalton Mathis, and Isaiah Llewellyn and two solid running backs, with Mario Gonzales providing speed and Ty McLemore bringing strength. If teams focus too much on stopping Hutchinson (something they often must to do to stop him at all), the Bulldogs beat you with their running game or by dumping quick screens to their athletes on the perimeter. Tonight's game isn't pretty, but the Bulldogs are clearly a dangerous team if they can eliminate mistakes.

Hutchinson isn't happy after the game. The Bulldogs looked sluggish, they turned the ball over too often, and it took too long to put away C-City. During the postgame talk, he sounds worried, and takes responsibility for what he's decided was a poor week of practice. After a good win last week, it's clear a little complacency set in. Hutchinson thinks his team slacked off this week and vows that he won't let it happen again.

After the game, I'm invited to the weekly party at Coach McLemore's house. The coaches' families, the superintendent, former coaches, and administrators get together after each home game to watch the local high school highlight show and hopefully celebrate. The event rotates among the coaches' houses, and after a long day, the party breaks up quickly. The gathering is a little somber. Nobody says anything about it, but there's a general sense that things have to improve for the Bulldogs to make a second run at state.

I thank the coaches for being such good hosts and hit the road. I have a 170-mile drive to Fort Worth.

The Stamford Bulldogs improve the following week, beating then-undefeated Class 2A Cisco before running though their district schedule without a loss and winning the District 4-1A title. Their run continues into the playoffs with a convincing win over Tahoka before I catch up with them again for their playoff game against the Quanah Indians in Wichita Falls.

One frustrating thing about Class A football is that, with schools so small, there are bound to be weaknesses; some kids just "fill suits," as Coach Hutch put it. A Division I-type talent like Hagen Hutchinson can attack those weak spots and dominate a game. This happens tonight in Wichita Falls and through the early rounds of the playoffs. Not playing their best football, the Bulldogs still jump up on the Indians 35-8 and cruise to a 48-22 win.

The following week the Bulldogs beat Stratford, 27-7, in Lubbock, setting up a state semifinal matchup with the surprising Italy Gladiators. With only four teams left, all the early-rounders with clear weaknesses are gone. Italy won three playoff games to get here, and when I meet Stamford in Mineral Wells, I see something new: a nervous coaching staff. Nobody says it, but deep down the goal had always been to get back to state with a healthy Hutchinson. Now the Bulldogs are only one step away.

The hours before kickoff are always hardest for coaches; there's nothing to do except count the minutes and worry about things that might have been overlooked. "The hay's in the barn," Coach West says. A little later Hutchinson says, "I have to keep telling myself to enjoy this," looking like a man who isn't enjoying anything at all. During his pregame talk, McLemore tells the team, "I honestly believe you are the best [Class A] defense in the state of Texas." In a few minutes, it would be time to prove it.

Many small-school teams rely on one or two great players, and in Class A, success is often about identifying and shutting down the opponent's main threat. Stamford's defensive game plan centers on containing Gladiator running back Ryheem Walker and quarterback Marvin Cox. The plan is effective. The defense holds Walker to 98 yards; Cox rushes for 108, but much of that is after the game has been decided. During the first half, the defense completely shuts down Italy, holding them to just 86 yards and building a 21-0 lead. After the break what had been a drizzle becomes a monsoon, and the Bulldogs quickly build a 35-0 lead. With the game in the bag, Hutchinson is removed, guaranteeing he won't be lost to a meaningless injury. The stands empty as most tire of sitting in a downpour and attention turns to the clock.

With the game well in hand and the rain falling, I talk with some of the dads manning the inflatable Bulldog head the team runs through before the game. I'm told about "The Blue Crew": after each Bulldog score, these middle school kids run around the field, each carrying a large flag with a single letter, spelling out STAMFORD. I watch as a parent dresses down a kid for jogging instead of running as he circled the field with his flag: "If you're going to do it, then do it right!" The boys and girls call out, "Yes, sir!"

A local who's not a parent tells me proudly about buying enough flags for "The Blue Crew" to spell out STAMFORD, whereas other 1A schools would go with just SHS. One father on the sideline talks excitedly of his son getting the opportunity to play in the state championship two years in a row while he himself never got past the second round with the Bulldogs during the 1980s. Tradition, family, and pride of community are the basis for the support the Bulldogs enjoy. Tonight, the town is excited that they'll again have the opportunity to show off Stamford and the program on the biggest stage in the state.

Late in the fourth quarter, the Gladiators finally get on the board against the Bulldog second string, but the game has long been decided. The Bulldogs win, 41-8.

This was much easier than anybody had anticipated. The Bulldogs look polished and sharp and are peaking at the right time. Maybe it's the anticlimactic way they won, but there's more a sense of relief than jubilation during the postgame celebration. The feeling is one of unfinished business at Cowboys Stadium last year, when they came up short against Mason in the state championship. They've had a year to wonder what might have happened had they been healthy. This time the Bulldogs will play for a state title at as close to 100 percent as possible for a team playing its fifteenth game with just thirty-eight players.

The Bulldogs have a short week to get ready. Until last year, championship game procedure had been the same as earlier rounds. The two teams would connect and agree to a time and a neutral site. The championships were held at venues all over the state, many played at the same time, making it impossible for fans and the significant Texas high school football media to see more than a few games.

In 2011, the UIL decided to have all ten of the eleven-man games played at a central location. For the second straight year, Cowboys Stadium in Arlington will host ten games over four days. This setup allows every championship to be televised and fans to see each game from the same seat. One Stamford assistant complains about it. If two Houston teams meet or somebody from Central Texas meets a team from South or West Texas, the Metroplex doesn't make sense.

This is true, but I doubt the current setup will change anytime soon. Kids are thrilled about playing in big stadiums and it's been popular with the fans. On Thursday, December 20, at 4:00, Stamford will play the middle slot of the first of three tripleheaders for the 1A Division I Championship.

I return to Stamford around lunchtime on Monday. Christmas decorations are mixed with the blue-and-white ribbons tied to every stop sign, mailbox, and light pole. Most businesses will close early Thursday, allowing employees to make it to Arlington by kickoff. Two charter buses have been scheduled to take locals who'd rather not drive to the game. Schools will be closed Thursday but will have a half-day on Friday before the start of Christmas break. The eighteen teams vying for nine remaining Texas championships are the only high schools in the entire nation still playing football.

Hutchinson is going nuts from all the paperwork, interviews, requests for sideline credentials, and phone calls he's getting this week. He says this "is the worst thing about playing in the state game." I feel bad about adding to this burden, but I'm happy to be back and he's as friendly and gracious as ever. The grass on the field is no longer green; there's a chill in the air, and along the horizon, the hazy look of a dust storm.

The only thing between Stamford and its first championship since 1959 are the Mart Panthers from outside Waco. In 2011, the Bulldogs defeated Mart in the semifinals, but nobody is looking past them now. A perennial contender, Mart has five state championships, three since 1999. This isn't a 1A school with obvious shortcomings for Stamford to exploit. Like the Bulldogs, Mart breezed through their four playoff games by an average score of 56-21. Coach Rusty Nail's squad (great name!) is led by sophomore quarterback De'Nerian Thomas. The Stamford staff has high regard for Nail and the Mart program, and are certainly not taking anything for granted. They expect a tough battle.

The staff is confident, though. Film shows Mart is always in man coverage. This is risky against a quarterback who runs as well as Hutchinson. If the receivers run deep routes, taking the secondary with them, it will open a lot of field underneath for him to scramble in.

Practices on Monday and Tuesday are quick and sharp. At this point there's no reason to complicate things, and the Bulldogs look loose but efficient, what a staff hopes for before a championship game. Hutchinson is proud of how his team has played, "having a target on their back every week."

Getting *back* to the championship is, in many ways, tougher than getting there for the first time. Nobody overlooks you, and this is doubly true for a team with a preseason *Dave Campbell's Texas Football* magazine cover boy on the roster, as Hagen Hutchinson was. Winning on Thursday is the ultimate goal, but just getting to this point is a huge accomplishment. They're happy with how the offense looks, and McLemore tells Hutchinson, "If we play like this on Thursday, we're fixin' to kick their ass."

A pep rally is held in the gym Tuesday evening. The stands on one side are packed with Stamford residents rattling noisemakers. The team files in to sit in folding chairs on the floor, the band plays, cheerleaders dance, and a highlight film is shown. Hutchinson sticks to his routine of never speaking at a rally, but has invited the head coach from Abilene High, Steve Warren, to fire up the crowd.

Just forty miles down the road, Abilene is the hub of The Big Country, and neighbors pull for each other unless they're on opposite sides of the field. More importantly, Hutchinson was formerly on Warren's staff at Abilene. Short of winning the championship, there's nothing better for a head coach than having his former assistants be successful. When I had visited Warren a few days earlier, he'd been excited that two of his former coaches were playing for state titles this weekend, Hutchinson at Stamford and Jason Dean at 4A Georgetown.

Warren does a good job revving up the crowd and talking up the coaches, at one point yanking his Abilene black pullover off to show a blue Bulldog T-shirt underneath. The rally breaks up, and after a short pregame practice Wednesday, it's time to head to Arlington.

Thursday morning, fans line both sides of the road to see off the Bulldogs. The line stretches a mile and a half from the town square down Highway 6. Most of these people will make the same drive in a few hours. A phrase often heard in small towns is that thieves would have great pickings on a game night because nobody's home. If ever this were true, it would be accurate this afternoon in Stamford.

I meet the blue-and-white Stamford bus for the team meal at Jason's Deli, just across the street from "Jerry's World," as Cowboys Stadium is commonly called.

Coach West is driving, and as we pull into Cowboys Stadium he comments, "You could pile a lot of hay in there." Pro stadiums are always impressive, but Cowboys Stadium is breathtaking. The outside is all steel and glass and seems to rise forever. It's even more impressive when you enter and see that despite the height above, you're already at the top of the second level, the field far below. From the stands, eyes are naturally drawn to the eighty-yard long high-definition video screen hanging over the field. During a game, it's easy to fall into the habit of watching the action on the screen rather than looking down to the field. At night, the place glows and shines in a way that makes its other nickname make sense: the "Death Star." Just as high school stadiums in Texas put stadiums in the rest of the country to shame, Cowboys Stadium makes other NFL venues seem minor league. For high school kids, the experience of playing here must be both exciting and intimidating.

Stamford's West Texas neighbor and the only team to beat the Bulldogs this season, Munday, is just starting its 1A Division II championship game against Tenaha when we arrive at noon. The players are escorted to the third level to watch and get a feel for the atmosphere. At halftime, the Bulldogs start their pregame routine: taping, position meetings, a short stretch in the tunnel. Many players watch Munday pull away from Tenaha on monitors in two little rooms off the main locker room before taking the field.

In his final pregame talk, Hutchinson tells the squad, "I am so proud to be back here, this is a special time for me, I've got two boys in this program . . . that live under my roof that I'm getting to enjoy this game with . . . but every one of you are my boys. I love every one of you the same because you have committed to this program and you have done everything we've asked you to do for seven years . . . you've believed in us and we've believed in you, and you have done some great things for Stamford, Texas."

His voice rising, Hutchinson speaks of the fundamental skills they'll need to come out on top. He asks them to close their eyes and visualize carrying the ball correctly, reading keys, getting to their drops, and throwing great blocks. Then he talks about toughness.

"Effort and desire, the guy that can endure the most pain, the one that has the most desire in his heart, is going to walk off that field state champions tonight." A major theme for the season was "No Regrets," and he finishes by telling his players that if they can walk off the field tonight without any regrets they will be champions.

Around 10,000 fans are in the lower two levels of the stadium as the game begins. Audra Arendall from the *Stamford Star* tells me that many Munday fans stuck around, trading black Munday shirts for blue Stamford tees to support their West Texas neighbor. Both teams had played the previous year, and in 2011, Stamford fans had done the same thing. Regional pride means a lot in this state and the area is proud of having two teams among the 1A elite.

Mart takes a 6-0 lead on their first offensive play, a 70-yard touchdown pass from Thomas to Quentin Bryant. The Bulldogs come right back on a beautiful pass to Washington in the left corner of the end zone from 9 yards out to go up, 7-6. The lead is short-lived; Mart goes back on top, 14-7, when Thomas scores from 4 yards out after an eleven-play drive. The Panthers extend their lead to 21-7 early in the second quarter on a 6-yard run by running back D'Marcus Cosby.

The first pivotal play comes on the ensuing possession. After a sack and an incomplete pass, the Bulldogs face third-and-22 from their own 25-yard line. It's still early, but the game is in danger of getting away from Stamford. Mart is great on both sides of the ball, and despite having only twenty-eight players, they're a complete team with none of the weaknesses of Stamford's earlier opponents. On offense, Thomas, Cosby, and Bryant give the Panthers three tough weapons, and the Bulldog defense has its hands full. If the Bulldogs don't find a way to convert and lengthen this drive, they could be in big trouble.

Hutchinson lofts a nice touch pass to Llewellyn for the first down. On the tackle, Mart's safety grabs Llewellyn's face mask, tacking on an additional 15 yards, and suddenly the Bulldogs have a fresh set of downs on Mart's 34-yard line. Six plays later, Washington goes high in the air and makes a one-handed grab in the left corner to close the score to 21-13 with 7:46 left in the half. Later that night, Washington's circus catch is featured on ESPN's *SportsCenter*.

The Bulldog defense stiffens and the next two Panther drives falter. Stamford has a chance to score before the intermission but sloppy play stops the Bulldogs at the 10, and at the half they trail, 21-13. Neither team has been in a battle like this for a long time; both are exhausted. Hutchinson spoke about enduring pain during the pregame, and it's clear this ability will be a factor in the outcome.

The "fire everyone up" Knute Rockne halftime speech is mostly a myth. Halftime is a time to rest, assess whatever happened in the first half, fix mistakes, and make adjustments to the game plan; any rah-rah stuff is probably a sign of desperation. The mood is calm and focused in the locker room. There's a confidence among players and coaches that they've weathered the storm and the game is right there for them, as long as they play as they've been coached. Coach McLemore tells the defense, "They couldn't have scripted a better first half, it couldn't have went any better for them, and they're still hanging by a thread . . . everybody wants a ring, everybody talks the talk but it's another thing to beat a good football team at the state finals in Cowboys Stadium. We're fixin' to do that. You're the better team, that's the bottom line."

Halfway through the third quarter, Hutchinson shows why he'd been named AP 1A Player of the Year earlier this week. On a quarterback sweep to the right, he's nearly brought down in the backfield but breaks the tackle and then two more on a 43-yard touchdown run. A slant to Mathis on the two-point conversion ties the game at 21.

The momentum has clearly switched sides and it feels like it's now Stamford's game. Mart is talented, but with so few players and so many playing both ways, they look tired but have a lot of fight left. The hitting is intense considering the fatigue. Both squads play very clean and show respect, helping their opponents up after hard hits. The Panthers burn most of the rest of the third quarter on a thirteen-play drive, retaking the lead, 28-21, with a 1-yard touchdown run by Thomas with 31 seconds remaining in the third.

The Bulldogs come back quickly. On the first play of the fourth quarter Hutchinson completes a 57-yard pass to Wimberly, moving the ball to the Mart 14. Llewellyn scores on a jet sweep from the 8 to tie the score at 28.

It is still anybody's game, but both teams are exhausted. A fifteen-game season is long for schools this size and it's taking its toll tonight. Players are picking themselves off the ground more slowly and taking knees to catch their breath during any break. This kind of battle isn't something seen in the bigger classifications, where personnel groups and separate offensive and defensive units guarantee fresh players. The outcome will come down to who can overcome fatigue and maintain their intensity and execute during the final eleven minutes.

With just over seven minutes remaining, Mart falters. On third-and-1 from Stamford's 42, a bobbled snap by Thomas leads to a sack and a dislocated right shoulder. On their next possession, the Panthers, now playing a backup quarterback, aren't able to move the ball, and after a punt the Bulldogs take possession with 3:08 remaining on the 49-yard line. A face mask penalty moves the ball to the 29, a pass to Llewellyn takes it to the 20. Two Hutchinson runs and a pass to Mathis set up a third-and-6 from the 9-yard line. The ball is snapped with 37 seconds on the clock and Hutchinson takes a QB sweep around the right edge, ducks behind his blockers, and powers into the end zone to give the Bulldogs their first lead of the second half, 35-28.

There's no quit in the Panthers, though. Thomas returns to the game, and with only 26 seconds left, the Panthers take the ball on their own 15-yard line and complete two passes to the Bulldog 35. With time for one last play, Thomas drops back and throws down the middle, attempting to hit Bryant slanting toward the end zone. Hutchinson steps in front, intercepts the pass, and slides to the ground as time expires.

The Stamford side erupts as the Bulldogs begin celebrating their first state championship since 1959.

This game represents the best of what small-school and small-town football is about: two evenly matched teams, both with passionate supporters, fighting through exhaustion in a game that isn't decided until the very last snap.

The joy of the Bulldog players can't hide just how exhausted they are after their toughest battle of the year. Sweat soaks through many jerseys as the kids celebrate.

On the other side, the disappointed Panthers show the class you'd hope to see after such a tough battle, congratulating the victorious Bulldogs. It's a very emotional scene with lots of tears and hugging, a proud moment the entire town shares. The boys in small towns like Stamford don't just play for a school, but for the town itself. In Stamford and other small towns, football is more than just a game; it's a window to show the rest of Texas all that's best about their city. Today Stamford, Texas, showed the rest of the state composure, guts, and toughness and represented themselves as worthy champions.

The Bulldogs never faltered or lost their cool, finding a way to beat a very tough Mart squad. The Panthers played a great game but in the end fell just short. Beating a strong opponent in such a tough battle makes the victory that much sweeter.

Following the awarding of medals to each player, quarterback/ safety Hutchinson is named both offensive *and* defensive player of the game. On offense, he was directly involved with four touchdowns, running for two and passing for two more. He was 22-of-30 in the air, passing for 248 yards and rushing for 132. Defensively, Hutchinson made 16 tackles and ended the game with an interception. This caps an amazing week, as he was named AP 1A Player of the Year on Monday. Football is such a team sport that I hate to single out one player, but his performance was remarkable.

Coach Hutchinson choked up during his interview with Fox Sports Southwest after the game. Winning a state championship in his son's last game and the boy being named offensive and defensive player of the game is something most coaches and fathers can only fantasize about. If that won't bring tears to a man's eyes, nothing will.

Back in the locker room, the celebration continues. Players and coaches pose with the trophy. They shower, dress, take their individualized nameplates for souvenirs, and load buses in the tunnel just outside the door. As I make my rounds congratulating everyone and saying goodbye to the coaches and players, a player approaches coach Ronnie Casey, who is also the basketball coach, and asks if there will be practice the next day. Casey tells the kid to enjoy the football win for a few days and that he'll be in touch over Christmas break. For kids and coaches in Stamford, it never ends, just transitioning from one season to the next.

5

RELOAD MODE
Week Five: Aledo Bearcats

I was often asked about the lineup of teams I'd be following during my trip. Running down the list of schools, I could count on certain responses. People would talk about the outstanding athletes at La Marque and Cedar Hill, they'd mention the toughness of the kids in West Texas, and they'd ask about Aledo . . . after Johnathan Gray. The Aledo running back became a household name throughout the state, leading the Bearcats to three consecutive Class 4A championships. Now, the 2011–2012 Gatorade National Football Player of the Year and Gatorade State Football Player of the Year for Texas has moved to Austin, where he goes on to have an impressive freshman season with the University of Texas Longhorns. So it's not surprising that one of the biggest questions in the state was how the Bearcats would do without Gray in their backfield.

Located just west of Fort Worth, Aledo hasn't quite been swallowed by the suburban sprawl of the Metroplex. That day may come, but as of now, it's still a small town. For a school with such a small enrollment, it has an impressive campus: new, modern, and shiny, drawing its students not only from the city, but also from ranches up to thirty miles away.

This bedroom community has the kind of football facilities that have become typical in the Metroplex. The freshman center has its own weight room and field turf practice field. Adjacent to the stadium is the fieldhouse, with coaches' offices, meeting rooms, a spacious training room with a rehab area, and locker rooms for the varsity and JV teams. The indoor practice facility was built in 2011, with a twenty-eight-rack weight room and 80-yard long football field. The stadium has 9,155 seats, the middle sections with orange seatbacks spelling out AHS in black. A two-story press box sits atop the home stands and can be reached via an elevator. The elevator itself is a bit of a status symbol. A coach at another school told me he knew he'd reached the big time when he got his first job at a high school with a press box elevator.

Just inside the main entrance, at the corner of the east end zone, is an open area of tent-like awnings for other Aledo programs to set up fund-raising tables. The area was designed for the school's other programs to benefit from the huge crowds football attracts. Three marble monuments, each the shape of Texas, commemorate the three state championships this program won in 1998, 2009, and 2010. A fourth monument for their championship in 2011 will be unveiled Friday night before the game.

Aledo has a waiting list for season tickets and the 5,000 seats on the home side are filled most every Friday night. Even on the road, Aledo supporters usually outnumber fans of the home team. On Friday night, 10-year-old cheerleaders from Aledo's youth program have the thrill of coming down to help the varsity cheer squad. The sub-varsity teams at Aledo are always good. Youth football is strong. The goal and focus is always about building toward success during high school. "As a kid, I looked forward to every Friday; it was the highlight of my week," I'm told by senior defensive back Shea Wood.

Aledo is coming off a bye week when I arrive for their first district game of the season against Fort Worth's Arlington Heights. The Bearcats are 2-1, with two good wins but a loss against top-ranked Class 3A Stephenville. With the extra week to get ready, the Bearcat staff is preparing differently this week. Head coach Tim Buchanan doesn't care when the staff gets their weekend prep work done, just as long as it gets done. Defensive coordinator Steve Wood and his staff decided to work on Saturday, while the offensive staff chose Sunday to put together their scouting report.

When I show up on Sunday, Coach Buck, as Buchanan is known to everyone, works in his office, taking care of athletic director business. Several years ago, due to budget issues, Buchanan was given the choice of losing an assistant coach or losing a secretary. He chose to keep his staff complete and now makes do without a secretary. The loss means that even in the middle of the season, there's no shortage of paperwork to keep Buchanan busy. After talking to him about how the season is going, we head into the group coaches' office to eat Railhead food and see how the offensive game plan is coming together.

Railhead Smokehouse is one of Aledo football's best boosters; the restaurant is *the* place to eat in Aledo. Besides having great food, Railhead could double as an Aledo Bearcat Hall of Fame. The walls are covered with Bearcat memorabilia, framed jerseys, posters, and game-action pictures. Railhead hosts the pregame meals and post-game coaches' parties.

The five offensive coaches diagram the defensive look they expect to see against each formation. Offensive line coaches Doug Wheeler and Lee Bishop list running plays they like from each offensive set. Arlington Heights isn't a very good team, but they have one outstanding player. Defensive lineman A'Shawn Robinson is 6-foot-6 and 305 pounds without an ounce of fat on him. He's made a verbal commitment to Texas (he wound up recommitting and signing with the University of Alabama) and swims through opposing offensive linemen as though they aren't there. He'll line up at any spot along the defensive front.

Aledo runs a multiple offense with a lot of two-back sets. They're a spread-gun team, but the power running game is important to their philosophy. The offensive line comes off low and quick; they work under the chutes every day to drill at keeping their pad level down.

As the offensive staff continues to discuss the running game and add more to the board, Buchanan comes in to check on the progress. Buchanan quickly puts an end to the listing, telling the coaches, "That's enough; we can't run all those plays, anyway."

Before going back to his paperwork, Buchanan talks to the offensive line coaches about his son. Caleb Buchanan has recently moved from the defensive side to play center and has had trouble with the snap. Bishop and Wheeler let Coach Buck know Caleb is coming along well. The coaches head out around 5:00.

One of the biggest obstacles Aledo will face in 2012 is their district schedule—not because the schedule is challenging, but rather too soft. In previous years, Aledo had been in a district with schools to the west, a very competitive group including rival and perennial power Stephenville. After redistricting, however, Aledo was put in a new district made primarily of Fort Worth ISD schools. If there's a weakness in the Texas public school athletic system, it's the deterioration of big-city school districts. Dallas, Fort Worth, Austin, and Houston are the four largest districts in the state. Their athletic programs have the minimum all schools in the state have: full-time professional coaches with athletic periods. These minimums would be excellent anywhere else, but not in Texas. What these districts don't have is much support.

Many of these schools have transient and low-income students. They are huge, with levels of bureaucracy separating administration from individual schools. It's a truism that the greater the number of schools the administration oversees, the less those schools are treated as individual, unique places. Numbers and stats become the measuring stick for success. Extracurricular and athletic programs are increasingly sacrificed to focus instead on improving those stats. This is a dynamic I recognize from my experience in Washoe County, Nevada, a district with eighteen high schools. Further hindering these programs, many who care about athletics and well-funded school programs have relocated, moving from the big-city ISDs to places like Aledo, Southlake, and Allen, places with support and well-funded programs.

Because these neglected programs don't have much public or parental interest, superintendents aren't pressured to make them successful. The Fort Worth ISD is one of the few in the state where the hiring of football coaches is not the responsibility of the superintendent's office at all, but is left to high school principals.

It's known within the coaching community where athletics aren't a priority, and many ambitious coaches won't take these jobs. A few, like Mike Jackson from La Marque, gamble with their careers. Jackson took a Houston ISD job at Chavez and had success. Coaches willing to take a chance may go to a place like Chavez for a short time, build a resume, then leave for a job with better pay and support. It's a huge risk for an aspiring coach; if the team loses, he'll probably never get another head coaching job.

One of the saddest things I saw in Texas was the first-round play-off game between La Marque and Furr High School from the Houston ISD. The game was played just a few miles from Furr and about forty-five miles from La Marque. La Marque brought a crowd of around 2,000 for a game they expected to win handily. (The Cougars won 54-0, with the clock running the entire second half.) Furr had a crowd of sixty. Furr's marching band had about twenty members, and there were only three coaches on the sideline. Furr had won six games in a district made up of other Houston schools. I can't imagine what the losing teams looked like.

Great *teams* occasionally spring from places with lack of support, but over the long term, good *programs* can't survive where people don't care about them. I'm sure a lot of good people work in the big ISDs, but they fight uphill battles.

Texans often asked me what high school football looks like elsewhere. I always point to big-city ISDs. This is where Texas is headed if the great support most of the state enjoys ever disappears.

Aledo won't have many tough games during district play. The real challenge will be getting through the regular season and going into the playoffs sharp. The success of this season will largely depend on how the Bearcats play during the six weeks of playoffs.

The Bearcats practice in the morning. Before sunrise, I drive west from Fort Worth on Interstate 30. I avoid most of the Metroplex traffic; it's headed the other way at this hour. It's still dark as I pull up to the Aledo fieldhouse.

Practice at Aledo starts at 7:20. With athletic period scheduled during first period, this gives the Bearcats almost two hours before they hit the showers and get ready for class. They started early practices a few years ago when they moved to the new artificial turf stadium and no longer had to worry about morning dew ruining footballs.

Mornings have several advantages. The Bearcats avoid early-season heat. Even on the hottest days, it's pleasant at this hour. This schedule also allows flexibility after school; lifting, watching game and practice film, working on special teams, and polishing rough spots are all done. After school is also when the sub-varsity practices.

Football practices often take on the personality of the head coach. Buchanan is professional and relaxed, and this is the vibe of mornings at Bearcat Stadium. Position groups stretch in little circles around their coaches while the coaches discuss details of the game plan or any other needs. Buchanan strolls from group to group, an insulated coffee cup in hand, checking attendance. Aledo is one of two programs I cover who practice to music. During stretching the songs are soft and mellow, the type of music you'd like to wake up to. With the sun rising over the far end zone, the feeling is relaxed and loose as a buzzer marks the start of the first timed segment at 7:35.

The morning is meticulously scheduled. On offense, nine minutes are assigned for individuals, then a two-minute water break, outside hull for nine minutes, another two-minute water break, then inside team for nine, another twelve-minute team session, eight minutes of red zone, and ten minutes of crossover, letting the few defensive players who contribute on offense work on their skills. To mark the time, the scoreboard has been programmed to count down each segment.

Aledo has very good numbers. Between 180 and 240 kids from freshman through varsity play football in this school of 1,344 students. This morning about 120 are here. Varsity players wear white jerseys and have orange Aledo "As" on their helmets, along with four small Texas outlines denoting Bearcat state championships; the JV kids are in black and have no helmet decals. During inside run, the varsity runs two separate offensive units against two JV defensive scout teams. Across midfield, at the same time, the starting defense works against two JV offensive groups. One offense runs a play while the other huddles and reads the next play from a binder held by one of the coaches. The huge number of JV players gives the varsity many reps in a short time.

Stationed around the field are twelve student-trainers with caddies of six water bottles. Above the field, near the press box, two students film the activities, one focused on the offensive end of the field and one on the defense.

On the track, the basketball and cross-country teams go through their workouts with their coaches. Aledo, like all larger schools, has separate athletic periods for each sport.

Buchanan doesn't coach a position but instead roams the field, walking between the offense and defense, watching drills and occasionally pulling out a player to talk with.

The relaxed atmosphere slowly becomes more intense this morning. The music gets faster as the pace quickens. Teachers know kids tend to be more focused during morning hours; this is another benefit to Aledo's system. This morning, the intensity never turns to screwing around at the end of the day or sluggishness in the hot sun.

At 9:02, Buchanan gathers the team and says a few words about what to expect this week, and then everyone runs off to the showers to get ready for the school day. Yes, the kids actually do shower, something rarely seen with kids who go home after practice instead of to classes. In the office, coaches quickly change from coaching gear into school clothes and head across the parking lot to teach their second-period classes.

At 3:00, players and coaches return to the fieldhouse. Today players are with individual coaches watching practice film from the morning. I watch some of the freshman practice, about sixty players with three full-time freshman coaches and three varsity coaches. After film, the varsity squad goes outside for special teams and JV goes to the weight room. Buchanan runs special teams practice while Bishop works behind the end zone with the offensive line, reviewing blocking assignments. Afterward, it's the varsity's turn in the weight room. The JV runs offense and defense on the indoor field. The workout ends around 5:25, and finally, Monday is over.

The motto for this season's program and practice gear is "Reload Mode." After losing a player like Gray, this motto makes sense, but people forget just how much of a team sport football is. This mindset also forgets that the system that encouraged Gray to come here had begun years before Gray arrived.

When Buchanan was hired at Aledo, he took over a very different program and built it into one of the state's showcases. With exceptional facilities and a winning tradition, this is the kind of high-profile job coaches line up to interview for, but this wasn't true in 1993. First fielding a team in 1946, Aledo was a small Class A school into the 1970s. By the time Buchanan arrived, it was a 3A program playing at the old campus across town. The facilities were poor and the football team had only been to the playoffs once since 1977. "Rebuild Mode" might have been a fitting motto for those Bearcats.

The first priority was attracting numbers. During Buchanan's first year, only seventeen kids enrolled in football athletic period. The first season saw a total of eighty-one players suited up, just twenty-six on the varsity. The 1993 Bearcats finished just 2-8. This would be the first and only time a Buchanan team would finish with a losing record. In '94, the Bearcats were 6-3-1. Two years later the Bearcats made their first playoff appearance, and they haven't missed since, reaching the postseason sixteen straight times.

In 1998, Aledo defeated Cuero, 14-7, for the 3A Division I state title. Three consecutive Class 4A championships in 2009, 2010, and 2011 followed. During nineteen seasons at Aledo, Buchanan has a lifetime record of 201-51-3, a playoff record of 54-12, and four state championships.

"Coach Buchanan is not just a tremendous football coach . . . but he's an outstanding athletic director," says Aledo principal Dan

Peterson. "He gets the big picture; he's committed to all the sports. He is about what's best for students. It's not just about football; he's going to make sure he takes care of all of those athletes and he's going to do what's best for kids. He's not lost perspective of that and I don't believe he ever will."

As Aledo transformed from a ranching town to a bedroom community for neighboring Fort Worth, new housing developments raised enrollment and brought the school to the 4A classification in 2002. The town had outgrown the old campus, but the new property was built without athletic facilities. It took two bond issues before the fieldhouse, indoor practice facility, and stadium were added. With newfound success and top-notch facilities, the Bearcat athletic program became a power on the west edge of the Metroplex. Plans for more housing developments east of town are in the works. Growth will continue to increase Aledo's numbers, and most likely move the school into Class 5A within a few years.

During the early weeks, the Bearcat defense has carried them while the inexperienced offense finds its feet. Aledo returns only two players on offense. A player like Gray can't be replaced, but Buchanan has built a system bigger than any one player—a program based on teamwork and sound football principles. Having superior individual athletes always makes the job easier, but it's the system, the support from the community, and the numbers within the program that have kept the Bearcats among the elite programs despite the loss of Gray.

Tuesday morning is a repeat of Monday. A receiver shows up late, and Buchanan pulls him aside and jokes that he's afraid of Arlington Heights. The tardy player will have extra running to do after practice. For ten minutes this morning, the offensive line works live pass pro against the starting defensive line. The defensive front isn't big but *is* startlingly quick. Bishop tells me the philosophy here is to put their best athlete at quarterback, then the next eleven on defense before filling the offensive positions. Watching the defense today, the payoff is obvious. All eleven players fly around the field. I'm seeing more of this; a few years ago, it was common to see big, gap-plugging defensive linemen. With the spread offense replacing so many power-running offenses, it's become rarer to see those huge defenders. Speed and agility have become more important than size. This ten-minute session is the only time all week that offensive and defensive starters work directly against each other.

During the afternoon, the kids watch more film in six different offices; in the offensive line meeting, Wheeler and Bishop show the big Arlington Heights defensive tackle.

"If you get beat, get beat fighting," Wheeler tells the boys. Aledo's offensive line is made up of nice, hardworking kids, and the coaches worry that they're a little too nice, wishing this unit had a nasty streak.

A strength of Aledo's offense is the physical play of the line. The starting five linemen are relatively small, but they're quick, get off the ball well, and have wonderful technique. Wheeler and Bishop do an outstanding job with this unit. I never learn who's senior between the two. It doesn't matter. They work well together, often splitting the line into smaller groups to give more individual attention.

During the Gray years, the line was much bigger but not as quick. I never had the chance to see Gray play, but nobody can put up numbers like his without an outstanding front.

Coach Bishop came to Texas from Mississippi. When he first began coaching, he looked for jobs in his home state. Desegregation in Mississippi caused many white students to leave the public school system for private schools. As a result, Mississippians who can afford private school tuition don't have a stake in public education. Unsurprisingly, Mississippi is near the bottom in educational funding.

It's tough for teachers and coaches to earn a living at private schools. Even in states with poor public education, public schools still pay better than most private schools, leaving teachers with two bad options: either make a living at a neglected public school or scrape by at a private one.

Bishop knew coaches in Texas and made a visit to the Metroplex. Like me, he was amazed by what he saw. For anyone interested in a career as a high school coach, there's no better place than Texas. Bishop doesn't see himself ever returning to Mississippi.

He doesn't like everything about Texas, though. The summer season has gotten too involved, with mandatory weight training and seven-on-seven tournaments. "When I started, summer was just about whose turn it was to open the weight room and let the kids in to lift," he tells me.

Summer was a time for kids to just be kids. Now for a program to be successful, it must go all year. This trend toward year-round football troubles many coaches.

After watching film, the Bearcats move outside. The running backs are given "water balls" to carry during their sprints. These are footballs filled with water, heavy enough that the backs are forced to carry them correctly, covering the points and keeping them high and tight.

Buchanan tells the team that Heights has some "dangerous players" who can cause problems. I notice he doesn't say they're a good team. Coaches need to choose words carefully when playing inferior opponents. You never want to overlook anyone or show so little respect that you come out flat. At the same time, making out every opponent to be the second coming of the '65 Green Bay Packers is also a problem. Looking at film, it's clear Aledo is much stronger than Arlington Heights and should win handily, but to say so just isn't done.

Given its football success, people might be surprised that Aledo is a well-rounded school, often finishing toward the top of the Lone Star Cup standings, a UIL competition that combines athletic and academic competitions and rewards schools that excel most broadly. Principal Peterson tells me "Whether it's Tuesday night on the volleyball court or Friday night on the football field, to see everybody rally around those kids . . . it's really been a fun experience for me to be around."

The band has as much standing and clout around campus as the football program. The Bearcat Regiment has 250 members, its own booster club that raised $156,000 last year, and a better website than the football program. They're a regular contender for UIL band championships.

Aledo excels in sports other than football. The softball and golf teams have won multiple state championships. Baseball, tennis, and soccer are also very competitive. In academics, Aledo has won UIL championships in literary criticism, social studies, and current issues and events. As was true at Stamford, the administration encourages involvement in extracurricular activities and athletics. Peterson estimates that 75 percent of the students are involved in extracurricular activities, either athletics, arts, or UIL academics. These are great numbers for a 4A program. Aledo is another example of a school that proves outstanding extracurriculars *promote* academics.

Like many coaches in Texas, Buchanan spent the early part of his career moving from job to job. Growing up in Killeen, he was lucky to have gone through a high school program playing for the same coach. When he began coaching, he learned his experience was an exception in this state. During his first five years in the job he made five moves, working his way up the ladder and bouncing around North and Central Texas.

After those five seasons, Buchanan decided he didn't particularly enjoy the moving and planned to settle down. He got the opportunity when he got his head job at Aledo. Aledo was lucky to have hired a man who preferred to build and stay, rather than jump to a "better" program whenever he gets an offer. This hadn't been a blue-chip job when he took it. Even now, aspects make the position less cushy than it looks. Assistant pay isn't competitive with other schools in the area, making it difficult for Buchanan to keep coaches. He's the only HC/AD I met who doesn't have a secretary. There is no dedicated football booster club and the kids at Aledo have to fund-raise, something I rarely saw in Texas.

Not that there isn't a lot to work with. The school has an affluent demographic, making fund-raising easier. Buchanan is well respected and liked. Coaches in most of the country would be thrilled to have a fraction of what Aledo has. The players lack for nothing, as is true of almost all high school programs in the state. Texas student-athletes rarely pay a dime to participate. Practice gear is assigned and laundered daily, and practice and game shoes are usually given to every player. Insurance and activity fees are often covered.

But with four state championships and the record he's compiled, Buchanan could find a better-paying job elsewhere, with a secretary, a football booster club, and other perks.

"I was so worried when my kids were growing up that Buck would leave," former Bearcat parent Bruce Franz tells me. Coaches who've won championships are in high demand, and there's no shortage of ISDs in Texas that will pay to bring in a proven winner. He's chosen to stay because Aledo is a nice place to live and he wanted stability for his family.

A big part of any practice week is repetition. Practices are designed to progressively drill aspects of a game plan throughout the week. Monday through Wednesday practices are usually pretty similar, each day becoming more polished as the game plan is digested.

On Wednesday morning I talk with several student-trainers. One feature of big-school Texas programs is the support personnel around the field. Each Class 3A and above school in Texas has two full-time trainers. But with so many students involved with athletics, even this isn't enough. Most schools offer a sports medicine program, teaching students the fundamentals of training. Aledo has sixteen student-trainers. All take a sports medicine class during their sophomore year and are required to take first aid and CPR to qualify. During practice, they spread around, toting water bottles and wearing fanny packs with first aid kits, tape, and portable AED units (heart defibrillators). On game nights, most taping is done by student-trainers, and they're on the sideline helping with whatever comes up.

Most schools outside the state have nothing like the trainer programs of Texas schools. I talk to several girls (most, but not all, of the student-trainers are female) about the program. One tells me she plans on going into medicine and sees this as a good starting point. As well as learning valuable skills, most like having a role in the school's athletic program and enjoy the work.

Since athletic periods are held throughout the day, trainers are available during every school period, as well as before and after school. The student-trainers and at least one adult trainer attend every practice, athletic period, and event. In Nevada, athletic trainers are part time and spread very thin. It's hit or miss whether a trainer is around when needed. Coaches are responsible for many training jobs. As a head coach, making sure water was available was my responsibility. Most Texas coaches never have to worry about such things; it's the trainers' job. In the smaller schools in Texas, trainers aren't usually on site but are contracted from private firms to work game nights and a few days a week, while coaches usually double as trainers for routine needs.

If they haven't traveled and seen for themselves, Texas trainers are amazed to hear their counterparts in other states aren't full-time employees. They wonder about liability should an athlete get hurt. To them, it sounds like a reckless system that invites poor treatment. More trainers lead to better safety, and fewer trainers to more danger. Concussion management is one area where the Texas system has an edge over less organized states.

The biggest football controversy to non-football people during 2012 was the danger of concussions. Stories about Junior Seau—the former NFL linebacker who committed suicide and was found to have suffered brain damage caused by repeated concussions during his football career—and other NFL players who've suffered debilitating brain damage led some to questions of whether football is just too dangerous. It can't be argued that the game is without its risks, but comparing the NFL with the high school game is like comparing the impact from a Volkswagen Bug to that of a Mack Truck. NFL players today are much stronger and faster, the collisions much more severe. Including preseason, their regular season is twenty-one weeks long. Many continue to wear older helmets because they're comfortable in them. Pretending that what the biggest, strongest, and fastest players in the world endure has anything to do with the game played by seventeen-year-old boys isn't reasonable.

Texas has taken strides to protect student-athletes. In 2011, the legislature passed HB 2038, known as Natasha's Law. The law requires players showing concussion symptoms to stay out of contact for seven days before beginning a five-day progression and returning to the field.

Any coach, trainer, or medical professional can start the ball rolling. Once the process starts it cannot be cut short. The athlete isn't allowed to return until cleared by a medical professional. No law, however, can eliminate every risk involved with playing football. Abilene High had three football concussions during 2012, but also four from gymnastics, three from volleyball, and five from girls' basketball. Cedar Hill had five from football but also five from girls' soccer. La Marque had zero football concussions in 2012 after three the previous year. The risks are real but must be put into perspective and weighed against the benefits.

How can you even begin to measure the positive results from playing high school football? How many of these kids would have dropped out of school entirely if not for their love of the game? How many become more successful due to the discipline, commitment, toughness, self-sacrifice, and delayed gratification they learned through the long hours, weeks, and years preparing to play a handful of games? How many friendships were formed? How much value is there in being a part of the glue that connects a kid to his town and school in a way few other things can? How do you measure the effect on a community and student body of having a team to rally around?

Football will never be completely safe. That's one of the reasons players' careers are so short. Players in quality programs spend thousands of hours preparing to play a handful of varsity games. During all those years, they're mentored, with their academic and behavioral progress followed by coaches who care about them; they're taught discipline, commitment, to organize time and exercise the body. During these years, they aren't at home playing video games or out getting into trouble without consequence. Athletes are statistically more likely to graduate, and have higher grade point averages and test scores. They are brought into the very fabric of the school and community.

Basketball, band, and other activities get many of the same results without the dangers, but high school football reaches a larger cross-section of boys than any other activity. Football is a no-cut sport almost everywhere. Any boy willing to follow the requirements and submit to the demands is welcome on the team. While team members aren't guaranteed playing time, the fifth-string scout player receives many of the real-world benefits the starting quarterback gets, because the truly important things taught aren't the ability to block and tackle, but rather the responsibility, discipline, toughness, and commitment.

It's easy to point at the dangers of concussions and other injuries and call for football to be eliminated, and if we were just talking about the games, this argument might be valid. Although it's the only thing most people see, the game is the *least* important part. It's just a test, a reward and celebration for the years of preparation that got the players to that point. Those who don't value athletics never get this. The positives of playing football are found in the *process* of preparation. The game itself is only special because of the work before kickoff.

Using the morning allows the Bearcats to do more with their Thursday practice. While the JV is inside trying on game uniforms, the Bearcat varsity has a short special teams workout on the game field. With so few kids outside, things are loose and relaxed; the game plan is in place, and now everything is more about getting the mind right than preparing the body or learning the plan. Today, there aren't any meetings after school, as the staff is busy with the two freshman teams playing at Arlington Heights and the two JV squads in Bearcat Stadium.

Friday morning the players can sleep in. Athletic period is still held, but the varsity is told to be in the fieldhouse by 8:30. Buchanan talks to the kids about how what makes them successful on the field will lead to successes in their lives. Commitment, work ethic, toughness, and sacrifice make good football players and also good men. He reminds them not to take Arlington Heights lightly.

Again I notice that Buchanan is careful never to describe Heights as a good team. They have a few good players, absolutely—Robinson is the real deal on defense—but football is a team game, and the teamwork of eleven kids, all in the right places, all with a common purpose, easily overcomes a few great players. The success of Gray's Aledo teams may seem to have rested on the shoulders of just one man, but even he had to rely on twenty-one other starters. This team needs to be much more about twenty-two good players becoming something great when they pull together.

After school lets out at 3:00, the countdown begins. Among other items, boosters have brought a giant cookie decorated like the field at Bearcat Stadium. With nothing to do for the next few hours, the ritual of watching the clock and trying to fill empty time before warm-ups is the hardest part of the week for coaches.

Most often they aren't nervous; it's too early for that. This is just a purgatory between the preparation and the payoff to come.

Every staff has its own way to kill time. At Aledo the coaches gossip about people they know from past jobs and former Bearcat coaches who've moved on, and watch YouTube videos on their laptops. One of the coaches puts on a scene from the movie *Tombstone*. Judging by the fact that everyone knows every word, I'm guessing it's a weekly tradition.

"Run you cur!!! And tell the other curs the law is coming. YOU TELL 'EM I'M COMING AND HELL'S COMING WITH ME!!!! YOU HEAR?!!! HELL'S!! COMING!!! WITH!!! ME!!!" During my later stops, two other programs use this scene to motivate their kids.

Buchanan has taken the team for their pregame meal at Railhead. He brings back boxed meals for the kids who couldn't make it due to their class schedule. Somehow they are two meals short and Buchanan makes a phone call to get more delivered.

The weather is threatening early in the afternoon. Everything west of Aledo is drenched and the sky opens up around 4:00. It's the type of rain you don't go out in if you have a choice. The parking lot between the fieldhouse and the indoor practice facility is quickly flooded as the early arrivers wait out the downpour in their cars.

According to the schedule taped on the door, the players are due to arrive at 3:55 for the 7:30 game. Taping will begin at 4:30, group meetings are at 5:20, and offensive and defensive unit meetings are at 5:30. During the offensive line meeting, Bishop tells his group, "I truly believe we can be great. We're not there yet, but we can get there and we need to. We *have* to get better." After each coordinator says some words to his units and Coach Buchanan addresses the team, the Bearcats are ready to warm up.

By the time the first groups go outside at 6:28, the rain has slowed to a heavy mist. The artificial turf is damp, but there will be no more rain tonight. Buchanan is loose and in a good mood, standing in front of the fieldhouse talking to early-arriving fans. One supporter tells Coach Buck how much he hated not having a game to watch during Aledo's bye week last Friday. Another says that not playing is better than losing. Buck responds, "I'd rather play and lose than not play at all. At least we have a chance of winning if we play."

Arlington Heights takes the field as the Bearcat players stand outside. It isn't hard to find the star of this team. Robinson, number eleven, towers above every other Yellowjacket player, six-foot-six and a lean 305. He looks like a man among middle school kids. I overhear one Bearcat player say, "He's not so big." A teammate responds, "Bullshit!"

About forty-five minutes before kickoff, the Bearcat Regiment begin their long, slow march on the track around the field, banging drums as they pass first in front of the few Yellowjacket fans around the far curve and then past the home stands.

Buchanan, for whatever reason, is not a fan of the inflatable tunnels every team runs through coming out of the locker room before the game. I've noticed that almost every team in Texas has an elaborate procedure for taking the field. The inflatable tunnel is just part of it. The cheerleaders and drill team girls line in parallel rows by the tunnel exit. A group of boys bearing flags that spell out the team's nickname wait, as well. The band plays the fight song as the team busts out of the tunnel to run between twin lines of dancing cheerleaders; led by the flag boys, they sprint the length of the field. Most players run to the far end zone and take a knee for a private prayer before heading to the sideline. The whole production reminds me that in Texas, football is just a part of the picture. The fans that have filled the home side of the stands are here just as much for the cheerleaders and band members as for the game.

Texas high school football games just have a different feel than prep games in most of the country. Between the elaborate entrance sequences, the bands, and the postgame alma mater recognition, it's almost a college atmosphere. The very sound is different; one quirk of using the NCAA rulebook is that, unlike the high school book, it allows bands to continue playing during the action. As the teams move up and down the field, a steady din of rhythmic tunes accompanies the play, and the cheerleaders and spirit squad continue dancing—activities that, in most states, are confined to halftime and other breaks.

Of the schools I cover, Aledo has the largest and most thoroughly organized marching band. I'm not qualified to comment on their ability as musicians, but based on the awards they've won, it's an excellent band. At 250 members, the Bearcat Regiment is respectably large but hardly unusual. Up in the opposite corner of the Metroplex, Allen High School boasts of a band with 600 members.

In general, bands in Texas are almost as serious as football. Unlike where I've coached, the bands are not merely a diversion at the game to lend atmosphere, but an important part of the experience. Usually visiting teams take their bands on the road. During the game, one of the two bands plays almost continually, taking turns depending on which team has the ball. Because both perform at the intermission, Texas halftimes are twenty-eight minutes long, and often that isn't enough. During the 2012 season, I often saw teams wait five to ten minutes while bands finished routines, something that would cause a delay of game flag in California or Nevada.

As expected, the Yellowjackets are no match for the Bearcats. Number eleven is as advertised. He makes some plays, but he can't be everywhere. The Bearcat offensive line is effective slowing him down with double teams. Quarterback Pate Davis throws well, finishing the night 14-of-16 with 227 yards passing, throwing for three touchdowns and running for a fourth despite being pulled halfway through the third quarter.

The Bearcat defense is impressive; they're not big, but their quickness and violence overwhelms the Jackets. During the first half Heights doesn't cross midfield and has only one first down. By halftime the score is 35-0 and the second half is given to the backups.

The second string scores 10 more points after the break and the Bearcats go up 45-0 before Robinson finally makes an impact on the scoreboard, blocking a punt that trickles out of the back of the end zone for a safety, the Yellowjackets' only points of the night. Final score: 45-2 Aledo.

After the game, the Bearcat Regiment puts on a concert under the scoreboard for those who have remained. The band concert probably kept many of the fans at the stadium through a long second half, even though the game had been decided.

At the coaches' party after the game, the families gather at the Railhead to eat BBQ and enjoy the win before getting to work on their next opponent. I have a drive to Abilene. I eat a little before heading out. As with all the programs I visit, the coaches and people of Aledo have been very nice and take deserved pride in the program they've built. It was a fun and interesting week, but the level of competition this school plays against is somehow depressing. I came to Texas to see programs like Aledo, but not games like I watched tonight; I felt sorry for the Yellowjackets. Football is not a pretty thing when one team is so much better than the other. Mismatches like this are part of what I traveled 2,000 miles to escape. It's a shame to see a non-Texas-like program lining up against one that works so hard and does everything the right way.

Aledo can't be blamed for being in a district full of schools from an ISD that isn't committed to success. He never says so, but I sense from Buchanan some frustration over this cupcake district schedule. Buchanan is a competitor and would rather play more worthy opponents, even if it means a few losses. The consolation is that no matter how easy the district season is, real competition awaits once the playoffs begin.

The Bearcats breeze through their district schedule without a loss. They allow only 25 points in their six District 7-4A games, beating their opponents by an average of 49-4. The Aledo Bearcats claim their seventh straight district title.

I catch up with Aledo the weekend before their first-round playoff game against Cleburne, sitting with Coach Buchanan and asking about the likelihood of a fourth straight championship. By now, I'm learning it takes three things to make a run deep into the playoffs: luck, good football, and a favorable draw. Of the three, the only aspect a team can control is the football.

Luck involves staying healthy and getting a few calls and bounces along the way. Playing good football is self-explanatory. The draw is the system the UIL uses to determine where to place each squad in the sixty-four-team bracket. Where a team is placed determines its route through the playoffs. Several coaches who've won championships acknowledged to me that their draw was a factor, giving them an easier path than other, less fortunate teams.

A poor draw may make the road to the championship almost impossible. The brackets are set up so a team must advance within their region before playing teams from other parts of the state. Region 1 is made up of West Texas schools, Region 2 is mostly the Metroplex, Region 3 is East Texas, and Region 4 is South Texas. If the top ten teams in a classification all happen to be from Region 2, they'll have to run a gantlet while good teams from Regions 3 and 4 coast along a much easier path. The toughest game in the playoffs for an eventual champion may take place in the early rounds for schools who have good competition in nearby districts.

When I meet with Buchanan on Saturday morning, he's worried about Aledo's draw. The top four finishers in each Class 4A district qualify for the playoffs, but they compete in two separate brackets based on the enrollment of each qualifier within the district, Division I for the larger schools, Division II for the smaller. Playoff qualifiers with the top two enrollments go D-I and the lower two go D-II. Aledo has the fifth-largest enrollment of the eight teams in District 7-4A, meaning that more often than not, Aledo plays in the Division II bracket. In 2012, however, two of the three schools with *smaller* enrollments than Aledo qualified for the playoffs while the three *largest* schools finished at the bottom, putting the Bearcats in the big-school bracket. To make matters worse, Aledo's position sets up a potential second-round matchup with the top-ranked team in the Class 4A, a school that played in the 5A a year before, Denton Guyer. If you're thoroughly confused by now, just know that Texas playoff seeding, like life, isn't always fair and the Bearcats have been dealt a poor hand.

Buchanan tells me this may be the difference between competing for a championship and an early exit. He lets me know he's also worried about potential rust; the Bearcats only played one decent opponent in the past seven weeks. Good regular-season opponents shine a light on a team's weaknesses and allow them to fix mistakes before the games become "win or go home."

The Bearcats easily win their bi-district game with Cleburne, defeating the Yellowjackets 45-7. Buchanan tells his boys before kickoff, "Play like you're supposed to and this game will be over at halftime." He's correct. Aledo dominates every aspect, recovering five turnovers in the first half and building a 31-0 halftime lead. In the second half the Bearcats go up 45-0 before Cleburne scores in the final minutes.

It's cold and windy at the Northwest ISD Stadium in the Fort Worth suburb of Justin the day after Thanksgiving when the Bearcats take on Denton Guyer. Guyer is the top-ranked team in Class 4A. They're led at quarterback by University of Texas verbal commit Jerrod Heard.

During the 2012 regular season I was on the sideline and in the pregame locker room for eleven games. During the postseason I added seventeen more. I was probably in more playoff locker rooms than any man in the state of Texas. It was a great opportunity few ever get to compare teams' preparation. By now, I could sense the mood in the room. Most often, coaches acted confident, talking about who and where they'd be playing in the following round, as if this game were a foregone conclusion. Wins didn't always follow those shows of confidence, but usually teams expected to win. Twice during the season, however, I caught a different pregame vibe, and both times the outcome was a loss.

It isn't as though the coaches expect to lose. It's more a message coming across that losing is a distinct possibility. When talking about the future, the answers aren't "when we win" but "if we win." Good coaches never lie to themselves about the situation they face. Optimism is great, but coaches must be realistic, as well. I don't know if this attitude helps cause the loss or if the coaches simply scouted well enough to know trouble is coming, but the feeling is unmistakable. Aledo's staff knows this could be a long afternoon.

Guyer scores on their first drive, then it's three-and-out for Aledo, another Wildcat score, another Bearcat three-and-out, followed by a quick Guyer strike, and the score is 21-0. The Bearcats have had just six offensive plays and are down by three touchdowns at the end of the first quarter.

About halfway through the second quarter, Aledo gets on the board with a 15-yard touchdown pass to Willie Gibson to make the score 21-7 at the half.

The Bearcat offense looks tentative and sluggish. The Bearcat defensive front has trouble figuring out the Wildcat quarterback, Heard. Big and strong and running the zone read, Heard is the type of quarterback the scheme is built for. The quick Aledo front has hesitated on the rush, worried about losing contain and letting Heard scramble for big gains. This gives Heard time to find receivers.

Gray is in the locker room at the half, his Texas Longhorns having played on Thanksgiving the day before. The Bearcats trail by only two scores, and one big play can change the game. Yet there is a feeling in the locker room that today is not going to end well. The coaches make adjustments with typical professionalism, but I see the resignation from the players. As they leave the locker room I overhear one tell another, "Well, this is the last half of the season."

With the wind behind them, Aledo has a window to climb back into the game early in the third quarter. A defensive stop by the Bearcats sets up a Wildcat punt from the end zone; Aledo scores a safety when Guyer covers up a bad snap in the end zone. The free kick gives the Bearcats the ball in good field position, trailing 21-9. A touchdown will pull the Bearcats within a score. On third down an Aledo receiver gets behind the secondary on a post route, but the ball is overthrown and the window slams shut.

The Bearcats punt and Guyer drives the field. A 7-yard touchdown run makes the score 28-9. The Bearcats' nineteen-game playoff winning streak comes to an end as Guyer goes on to a 42-30 victory.

It's a frustrating end. Guyer was the better team today, but Aledo didn't play well. Buchanan tells the papers as much after the game, "I'm never ashamed of losing. The problem was how we lost—dropping the football early, not playing a good game offensively."

Denton Guyer wins the state championship four weeks later, beating Georgetown 48-37. A team doesn't need a Johnathan Gray or a Jerrod Heard to win the big game. Those types of players simply allow them to win without always playing great football. Without the best player on the field, however, a squad needs to play better *team* football than the opponent. During most of the season the Bearcats did that; today, they made too many mistakes.

To whatever degree a 9-2 season can be called disappointing, this was a tough year for Aledo. That in itself says a lot about how far this program has come during Buchanan's tenure. Players come and go every few years, but the system that allows this program to stay successful has been in place since the early 1990s. As long Aledo keeps valuing excellence and supporting the program, as long as the coaching staff keeps teaching the skills, character, and discipline that have brought this program to the top of Texas football, "Reload Mode" may mean "poor" seasons of 9-2 and district championships. During the up years, the Aledo Bearcats will have opportunities to add a fifth championship monument behind the end zone at Bearcat Stadium.

6

ABILENE'S FINEST HOUR

Week Six: Abilene Eagles

"100% American, but on 10-5-12 I detest red and blue."

—Caption written on the back of T-shirts worn
by Abilene High supporters on game day of the Cooper game.

West Texas is the birthplace of Texas football culture. Businesses close on Friday nights. Populations of entire towns caravan hundreds of miles across the prairies and plains to follow their boys. Here high school football is not just something done during fall weekends; it's a way of life. This fervor has been adopted in parts of the Metroplex as well as suburban Houston, Austin, and San Antonio, but the foundation and much of the history of Texas football culture is in West Texas.

The tradition of West Texas football stretches back nearly one hundred years, across this huge swath of the state. Places like Odessa, Sweetwater, Midland, Brownwood, Breckenridge, Lubbock, Amarillo, and Stamford have all contributed to the tradition. In the big-school ranks, West Texas football has been encapsulated by schools in what's known as the Little Southwest Conference (LSWC).

Due to biannual UIL redistricting, the Little Southwest Conference has come, gone, and come again, with teams dropping out and joining. Breckenridge and Sweetwater were once members, eventually dropping to lower classifications. The schools in Lubbock and Amarillo have played in this conference from time to time; other years, they've formed separate districts. The charter members and core of the Little Southwest Conference are the big schools in Odessa, Midland, San Angelo, and Abilene.

In recent years District 2-5A has been the home of the LSWC. Besides winning, the Little Southwest Conference is known for its hard-nosed style of play. Made up entirely of towns that traditionally rely on ranching, the oil field, and farming, this district plays a brand of football befitting the character of their part of the state. They win with discipline and determination, often against more athletic programs. From its early days through the turn of this century, the Little Southwest Conference may have been the toughest district in the country, with teams from Odessa, Midland, and San Angelo winning multiple championships.

Besides the play, history, and success of this district, another defining characteristic of the Little Southwest Conference are the distances. The eighty-seven miles from Abilene to San Angelo is a "short" trip by LSWC standards. The conference stretches west to east 170 miles from Abilene to Odessa and north to south 307 miles from Amarillo to San Angelo. No other big-school district in the state comes close to covering the real estate of the Little Southwest Conference.

Abilene High is the first Class 5A program I visit, and initially the school and kids in this highly ranked program are disappointing. The campus isn't impressive: several practice fields, a small turf room about 20 yards long and 10 yards wide, and a humble fieldhouse containing the coaches' offices. Little touches, however, offer reminders of the tradition of this place. A bell sits on a low table in the foyer of Chuck Moser Field House, the trophy traditionally given to LSWC champions. On the wall are photos of each Eagle state championship team; some are old black-and-whites from the leather helmet era. Finally, above the bell is a picture showing three hands, one black, one brown, and one white, holding a football high in the air; head coach Steve Warren says this picture means the most to him, and that it best exemplifies how this program has found success.

The weight room is dark and cramped. The equipment has seen better days. Warren doesn't mind that the facilities aren't on par with many other Texas schools. He talks about a visit to a school trying to hire him away a few years back. "I could tell there wasn't a lot of work going on there," he said of the shiny, clean weight room. "At Abilene High we have rusty bars and it smells like work . . . that's what a weight room should be like."

Abilene itself doesn't look like it's changed much in fifty years. The downtown blocks are clean and well maintained, but there's none of the bustle and new construction seen in other Texas cities.

In a state defined by the growth of its cities and the drain of the rural population, Abilene has remained remarkably steady. In 1990, Abilene had a population of 106,000; today, 118,000 people call the city home.

Despite its small population, Abilene is home to three Christian colleges: McMurry University, Hardin-Simmons University, and Abilene Christian University. Abilene is a God-fearing place with a church for every one hundred residents. The religious, social, and political conservatism of West Texas is well known, but whatever negative stereotypes may be associated with these belief systems, these values fit here.

The politics and religion of these people serve the community well. West Texans I met were sincere, hardworking, and honest. Making outsiders like me feel welcome is important in this part of the state. After my first visit in April, I always look forward to return trips to The Big Country.

The noteworthy first impression from looking at Abilene High players is just how *average* they look. No physical specimens here. During my first visit, I'd thought I was watching a JV squad, but that quickly changed once I saw the players move. There is no blinding speed here, but these kids *all* move very well. The tempo of everything is fast, and practice organization is a joy to watch. Everything is efficient and well thought out. Without athletes, organization and execution are the keys to success.

Just as with the high schools, seventh- and eighth-graders have athletic period with on-campus coaches. Sometimes prospective players begin training in sixth grade, taking pre-athletics instead of regular physical education. The hiring of the middle school staff is usually done by the varsity coach so middle schools conform to the varsity level. Varsity players begin learning schemes, terminology, drills, and techniques during seventh grade.

I'd made the relatively short drive from Aledo the night before, so I show up at 8:00 Saturday morning well rested. The 35-6 victory over San Angelo Central raises the Eagles' record to 5-0, 3-0 in district play, and they are ranked fifth in the state.

The coaches use three separate rooms to watch film of the Central game. The mood is about as you'd expect for a staff that has just won its fifth straight game. It poured rain the night before, but the Eagles hung onto the ball and didn't let the weather affect performance.

At 10:00, the players arrive for their workout. They first head to the small turf room to stretch and do some light agilities. Usually Saturday's workout is outside, but the rain is still falling. The corrugated roof leaks in several places as Warren runs this part of practice. There's no dress code this morning. The kids wear whatever they put on when they rolled out of bed.

After warm-ups, the team heads to the weight room. At Abilene, Saturday is the heavy day during the season. The players work in pairs and complete a circuit that includes bench, parallel squats, overhead squats, kettlebell squats, box step-ups, V-ups with medicine balls, and dumbbell inclines. Defensive coordinator Mike Fullen blows a whistle at timed intervals as other assistants space themselves around the room.

By five weeks in, I'm getting used to the intensity of the workouts in Texas. A byproduct of the athletic period system is that it allows so many coaches to supervise the weight room. In my years teaching weights, athletes and non-athletes usually shared the same classes. Also, I was often the only coach watching forty to fifty-five kids.

It's impressive to see how hard kids work when each coach is responsible for only a handful of motivated athletes. Not only is there no sitting, there's also hardly any standing. When the whistle blows, kids hustle to the next station as they've been trained to do since seventh grade.

At 11:30, the players split into position groups and watch film of last night's game. After forty-five minutes, Warren holds a team meeting in the portable classroom behind the weight room. On the walls murals and game shots show important moments in Eagle history. Helmet stickers are issued, and Warren gives a brief talk about what to expect this week.

The players leave and the coaches get back to work. It's time to put Central away and begin preparing for one of the state's biggest rivalry games, Abilene High versus Abilene Cooper.

A two-school city rivalry game is nothing unique. The Little Southwest Conference has three such games: Odessa versus Odessa Permian, Midland versus Midland Lee, and Abilene High versus Abilene Cooper. The history between Abilene and Cooper, however, makes this game special for reasons beyond the field. This season both teams are expected to compete for the district title.

In previous decades, the power of the Little Southwest Conference was in Odessa, with the Permian Panthers winning six state championships between 1965 and 1991. The power moved a few miles east during the '90s, with Midland Lee claiming titles in three consecutive years from 1998 to 2000.

More recently, though, the strength of the district has been in Abilene. Not only is Abilene High a perennial power, having made the playoffs thirteen straight years, but Cooper has been outstanding, as well. Cooper comes into the game with a 4-1 record. The usual bragging rights will be on the line, but the game could decide the championship, as well.

Today's meeting isn't a formal one. Warren lets the coaches work at their own pace on Saturday, but most of the staff is here watching Cooper film.

By early afternoon I'm starting to nod off. After my drive from Aledo, I hadn't gotten to bed until around 2:00 in the morning, and sitting in a dark room watching film has its limits. I take off and head back to my home for the week: the Super 8 Abilene South.

The main weekend staff meeting is held on Sunday at 2:00, leaving the coaches time to go to church with their families. When I arrive, coaches cut pictures of Cooper's defensive players from a game program and paste them to a poster board along with heights and weights. Other coaches input date into Hudl. On the offensive side of the office, a whiteboard has every Eagle formation drawn up in boxes against the 3-4 look they expect from Cooper.

Warren starts the meeting by asking the coaches to look for things needing improvement. A 5-0 start can make a team complacent, giving the impression it will be smooth sailing the rest of the way. Players must always look to improve; there's still a lot of football to be played.

"Both staffs [offensive and defensive] need to brainstorm about things we may be overlooking," Warren says.

Grades are the next topic. The six-week grade check is approaching. The coaches don't expect any varsity issues, but a few JV and freshman players are on the bubble. Players at Abilene High turn in a weekly grade sheet to a coach during the entire school year. The staff has a handle on when problems begin to develop and can step in immediately.

Several coaches monitor what's going on in the outside world while they work. One computer screen has the gamecast of the Texans-Titans game running. Another has the pitch-by-pitch update of the Rangers-Twins game in Arlington.

The special teams scout is next on the agenda. Abilene assigns various coaches to scout particular special teams units. Each unit has a different form, with "look for" boxes for the responsible coach to fill in.

The kickoff form has boxes listing the starters, best returners, best blockers, and anybody who is poor with the ball. Each coach takes a turn discussing their assigned unit as Warren gathers the forms to put into a packet for the players.

Shortly after 3:00, the coaches break out into their positions. The next three hours are spent watching film and discussing plays, fronts, stunts, and formations.

This is the sixth time I've watched a weekend scout in Texas, and I've seen enough to know when I've seen enough. Watching professionals go about their jobs is rarely a spectator sport.

What's happening *is* important. Friday night, coaches often have only seconds to make adjustments; a coach must have a feel for everything he may see. Coaches need to recognize what's happening through the chaos on the field and know the adjustments by heart. Long hours spent tediously learning every nuance of the opponent are the only way to see the patterns. All the staring and thinking is necessary, but not much fun to watch. The staff finishes around 6:00, and it's home to see their families and watch more film on Hudl.

The Abilene Eagles may be the most historically significant program in Texas. The "Warbirds" are the only team to win state championships during three separate eras, taking titles in 1923, 1928, 1931, 1954, 1955, 1956, and 2009. With 644 victories since 1912, Abilene is seventh on the Class 5A list of total wins. From 1954 until the state semifinal of 1957, the Eagles didn't lose a single game, compiling forty-nine straight wins and setting a Texas record that stood until Class 2A Celina broke it in 2001. The *Dallas Morning News* declared the '50s team the "Team of the Century." Although more than fifty years have passed, many members from those championship teams still live in Abilene.

Just south of downtown on Butternut Street is the Athletic Supply sporting goods store. For many years, it's been a meeting place for coaches, officials, and administrators from throughout the region. Abilene is the biggest city in the west-central part of the state, the heart of what is known as The Big Country, and is surrounded by dozens of small towns. Since the store was built in 1952, the

A sign on the Cougar practice field reminds players of the school's football tradition.

Carthage coaches in front of the new scoreboard, the biggest high school scoreboard in the nation.

The Carthage offensive staff discusses second-half adjustments.

Head coach Richard Whitaker teaches the intricacies of his option to players at Calhoun High in Port Lavaca.

Coaches Whitaker and Sonny Detmer gather Sandcrabs and Bulldogs for a prayer following their game in Port Lavaca.

Empty storefronts in the Stamford town square.

The Stamford Bulldogs celebrate following their state championship game at Cowboys Stadium in Arlington.

Aledo JV players meet in their indoor facility after school.

8:00 the morning of the Crosstown Showdown. The Abilene High gym is filled to the rafters for the annual "Black Out" pep rally.

Abilene High offensive line coach Tommy Martinez talks to his players during the Cooper game at Shotwell Stadium.

Sign at the main intersection in Throckmorton announces homecoming week events.

A house across from Throckmorton High commemorates the 2011 state championship team.

A pep rally in Throckmorton. The Greyhound band includes many football players and cheerleaders.

First-half action between the Throckmorton Greyhounds and the Bryson Cowboys.

Halftime in the Throckmorton locker room.

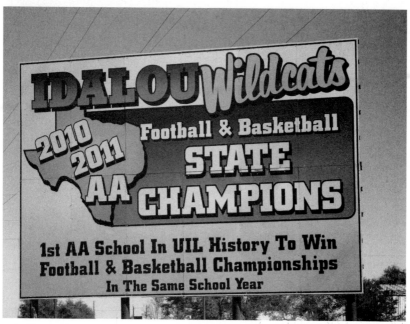

A billboard by State Highway 82 reminds travelers of recent Wildcat history.

Head coach Don Long talks to his team before the Denver City game.

The Wildcats ready to emerge from their tunnel before playing Denver City.

Head coach Craig Chessher addresses the Stony Point Tigers after a tough loss to Westwood.

The Harlingen Cardinals in the weight room during athletic period. Every rep is synchronized and called out: "One, sir! Two, sir! . . ."

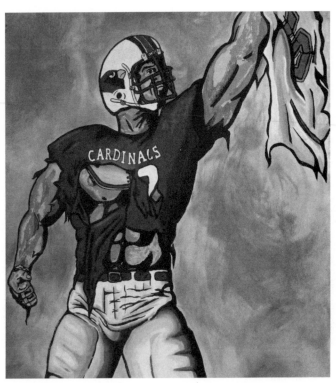

Artwork in the hallway of the Harlingen fieldhouse. The jersey in the Cardinal's fist belongs to Harlingen-South.

Harlingen head coach Manny Gomez and Nathan Prado with the Bird Bowl trophy after defeating Harlingen-South.

Cedar Hill coaches await the second half of the semifinal versus Austin Westlake.

Lots of hardware! Trophies for each of Cedar Hill's 2012 playoff victories.

Cedar Hill offensive coordinator Steven Lemley meets with players prior to the state game at Cowboys Stadium.

The Cedar Hill Longhorns ready to take the field before the championship game.

No smiles for silver: the Cedar Hill Longhorns reluctantly pose with their runner-up awards after losing to Katy in the state final.

"Straphouse" (slang for a place selling jockstraps) as it's commonly known was the place where coaches met to exchange game film on Saturday mornings.

Nobody meets to trade film anymore, but the tradition remains. It was probably sometime in the 1960s that it became a hangout for old coaches.

These days, a group of retired coaches, superintendents, officials, and players meets in a room in the back every weekday morning to drink coffee and "solve the world's problems." On the walls are sports page clippings, black-and-white photos, and a giant map of Texas with orange dots marking state champions over the years.

Warren told me there was a ton of Big Country high school football knowledge to be found here but warned I'd better have thick skin and be ready for some ribbing. When I introduce myself, the men in the room good-naturedly tell me that they know the answers for *anything* I might ask, but that I better have specific questions or I'm wasting their time. They introduced me to David Bourland, quarterback and defensive back on the 1954 and 1955 championship teams. It's been over half a century since he wore black and gold, but he has strong memories of those teams.

Bourland is tall and lean. In his well-used white cowboy hat and boots, he looks like a Texas legend should. He retired in Abilene and his pickup is full of Merle Haggard CDs and spit cups for his leaf tobacco. He happily tells me about his time with the Eagles. He talks about Chuck Moser, the hall of fame coach who rebuilt the program after taking over in 1953.

"He was ahead of his time," Bourland says. Moser would hold flashcards of defenses up for two seconds, training his quarterback to read quickly. He put together detailed scouting reports before this became common. Long before the state implemented a "no pass, no play" policy, Moser required his players to fill out weekly grade checks and would hold kids out if they weren't up to his educational requirements.

Bourland tells me about playing against future Oklahoma and Miami Dolphins great Wahoo McDaniel, the best West Texas player of his time. I recognize the name from my childhood. After retiring from football, McDaniel made his living as a pro wrestler.

The Eagles had tremendous support, with special trains taking thousands of fans to playoff games in Houston, El Paso, San Antonio, and Dallas. Fair Park Stadium, with 10,000 seats, was often too small for everyone who wanted to see the top team in the state.

During Bourland's time the Eagles won three straight championships, not losing a single game for almost three years. The win streak ended at forty-nine games in the state semifinal of 1957. The score was tied, but the Eagles lost on penetrations to Highland Park at the Cotton Bowl in Dallas. In those years, tie games were determined by "penetrations," the number of times a team moved the ball inside its opponent's 20-yard line.

The Eagles remained competitive during the rest of the 1950s, but '56 would be their last championship for many years. In fact, 1959 would mark the last playoff appearance for the Eagles until the final year of the twentieth century.

In 1959 a new stadium south of town replaced Fair Park, the Eagles' home since the 1920s. What was to become Shotwell Stadium (named after P.E. Shotwell, Abilene High's first championship coach) holds 15,000 fans, putting it on par with others in the Little Southwest Conference. More importantly, in 1960 Abilene became a two-high school town with the opening of Cooper High School.

At 7:15 on Monday morning, the team meets in their portable classroom to review scouting reports for the Cooper game. The offensive and defensive players get separate packets.

Pages one through three are the same in both packets. There's a cover page with several motivational quotes: "The fight is won or lost far away from witnesses—behind the lines, in the gym, and out there on the road, long before I dance under those lights." — Muhammad Ali.

The second page has a message from Warren, a few paragraphs congratulating the team on their play against San Angelo Central and an overview of what to expect this week. Finally, there's some advice on dealing with pressure: "Everything that surrounds this week should be fun for you guys. I want you to enjoy the week and do not let anything from outside our family take away our focus on the task at hand and that is going 4-0 in district play, nothing more and nothing less. This game is important because it is the next one and not because of who we are playing."

Warren reads this page word for word and expands on the themes, telling the players not to sacrifice self-control for intensity.

"You can't get in the place where you're thinking, 'I'M GOING TO KILL HIM!!' when it comes to Cooper."

The meeting is only about fifteen minutes long; the tone is set and the kids head to class.

Athletic period is just before lunch at Abilene. On Monday the JV is in the weight room with three coaches, while the other nine are on the practice field walking through the three scouts (offense, defense, and special teams.) Monday is also the weekly booster club meeting, and halfway through athletics, Warren and I leave to attend the luncheon.

About fifteen men and women are at Joe Allen's Corral. A BBQ buffet lunch has been catered in, and Warren makes the rounds as everyone eats. Warren introduces me to his wife, Carol, and more people than I can keep straight.

The booster club president leads a prayer and talks about the blessing of the rain they've had during a drought year, saying that nobody even minded standing in it during the game.

Warren gets up and talks about the sub-varsity results before showing highlights from Friday night. After film, the floor is opened for the boosters to ask questions.

"Is the Sims boy [on Cooper] kin to Kerry and Darnel?"

"Did you wear your lucky socks?"

"What can you tell us about Cooper's defense?"

Warren answers the questions, and the meeting breaks up.

Several boosters introduce themselves. Al Pickett, the host of a local call-in radio show who's written several books about the Abilene Eagles, says hello and gives me copies of his books. I meet Bobby Johnson, a former coach at AHS and big supporter of the program. Before returning to school, Warren drives by Shotwell Stadium. Tickets go on sale for the Cooper game at 5:30, and already at 1:30 several dozen people are lined up. By 5:30, hundreds will be waiting on both the Abilene High and Cooper side of the stadium.

Because of the rain, the practice fields are wet and Warren decides to practice at Shotwell. It's 4:00 by the time the kids get bused there and begin warm-ups. The Eagles wear full pads today, and an athletic trainer uses an air horn to signal the end of each segment.

The Eagles mix static stretches with agilities to begin practice, doing quick toe or hamstring stretches between agility movements. It's an efficient beginning to practice, as there is no sitting around, and it sets a good tempo from the start.

From there, both the JV and varsity offensive teams, wearing white jerseys, run a series of screen passes versus air. In eight minutes, each offensive unit will run through exactly twenty-eight passes.

The "blackshirts," as the defensive players are known, are on the other side of the 50. Except for a short session of one-on-one pass rush, the two units are entirely separate. Abilene only uses a segment timer for individual periods. Warren had noticed that too many players focused on the clock instead of their assignments and turns it off when running team scripts.

Screen period, inside hull, and pass hull will be done when the script is completed, not based on any clock. Instead of the sixteen or twenty-four segments, Abilene uses only six today. As with all Monday practices, today is about learning the relevant position points from the scout. With so many coaches, it would waste time to go over the entire report together.

More than 240 of around 2,000 students play football at Abilene. This is a small Class 5A program, the smallest school in the district, but participation is exceptional. In addition to fifty-four varsity players, the Eagles field two JV and three freshman squads. Numbers here were not always so high. When Warren took over, Abilene High was a very different place.

This morning, I walk the main campus with Warren, who talks to everyone he happens to pass. He asks about families, tells jokes, and answers a few questions about the San Angelo and Cooper games.

An important part of being a good head coach is the ability to get everyone on board by being personable and making a good impression. This part of the job is natural to Warren. He generally likes people; he's happy and positive. By nature, Warren is not a boisterous, emotional man, but he's good-natured with a sense of humor. He makes people feel comfortable and has close relationships with his staff. During games he's relaxed and low-key. At the Texas High School Coaches Association conference in July, Warren was elected as president for the 2013 season, a strong indication of the respect he's earned within the coaching community.

After graduating from Angelo State University in 1984, Warren began his coaching career there as a graduate assistant. He got his first high school job in the Metroplex, coaching at Grapevine for two years, before heading back to West Texas and coaching at Sweetwater. His first head job was at Wall in 1987. He then moved on to defensive coordinator at Rockwall from 1989 to 1991. Afterward he spent two seasons as head coach at Rotan before landing at Abilene High in 1994.

Warren came to Abilene as defensive coordinator for Gary Gaines when Gaines took the head job for the Eagles. Readers may recognize Gaines as the coach made famous by the book *Friday Night Lights*. He had two stints as the head coach at Odessa Permian, including the year documented by that book. After leaving Permian the first time, he coached linebackers at Texas Tech before returning to the Little Southwest Conference to take over a struggling Abilene High program.

The glory days at Abilene High were long gone by the time Gaines arrived in the mid-1990s. The newer Southside school, Cooper, had become the dominant program in the city.

Although Abilene High hadn't made the playoffs since 1959, this stat is somewhat misleading. The LSWC was often the toughest district in the state, and during many of those years, only the district champion made the playoffs.

"It wasn't like they never won, they just couldn't get out of district," Pickett tells me. Locals hoped the hiring of a big-name coach like Gaines would bring new life to the program. It didn't. After two seasons and just four wins, Gaines left for a job with district rival San Angelo Central.

Gaines' move was a surprise to Warren, who happened to be in San Angelo working his summer job as a house painter when he was told to call his wife. This was before cell phones, and his first thought was of a family emergency. He came down off the ladder and was assured everyone was fine, but was told to hurry back to Abilene. Gaines had just resigned and the superintendent wanted to announce Warren as the new head coach.

It was early summer, and this isn't the way coaching changes are normally handled. Usually openings are filled during the winter, allowing time for a smooth transition. This late, there couldn't be a lengthy search and interview process, and Abilene's superintendent wanted someone in quickly.

Initially the superintendent offered Warren the job of interim head coach. As much as he wanted the job, Warren wasn't willing to take it with the "interim" title attached.

"Give me the job and fire me if you don't like the way it's going," he said. The administration decided to take him up on the proposal.

A firing wouldn't happen anytime soon. Improvement was immediate. During Warren's first season, the Eagles posted their first winning record in almost a decade, finishing 5-4. The following season Abilene improved again, finishing 6-3.

When asked what made the difference, Warren credits a positive attitude.

"Previously coaches came here and talked about improving. I came in and announced that I expected to win."

The watershed moment came after a disappointing 1998 season, where the Eagles took a step backward after two winning seasons and finished 4-6. The program had shown promise but hadn't gotten over the hump. Things could have gone many ways. Would the school board show faith that the program was moving in the right direction? Or would they use this losing season as an excuse to go in a "new direction," a polite euphemism used when a coach is fired?

In a meeting with the superintendent, Warren asked to make changes to his staff. Warren didn't see eye to eye with five of his coaches. According to Warren, they weren't bad coaches, but they didn't have his outlook or philosophy. Administration allowed the changes and let Warren bring in his people.

The move served to cement in place the new direction. It assured Warren had the support and trust of the administration, and it showed the community that Warren intended to stay and continue rebuilding Abilene High.

In 1999 the Eagles finished 8-2, making the playoffs for the first time in forty years. Ending the drought was one thing, but the roll continued for AHS, which won three playoff games before falling to South Grand Prairie in the quarterfinals.

There would be no going back. Since 1999, Abilene High has made the playoffs thirteen straight years.

Abilene High has come to epitomize the type of football the Little Southwest Conference has played for generations, but good coaching and hard work can take a program only so far. A foundation must be in place. Before Warren's arrival, significant changes contributed to building a foundation for him to build upon.

Tuesday is media day. During the season, Warren sets this morning aside for interviews with the local press. Abilene is a perfect storm for media attention. As outstanding as support for high school football is statewide, West Texas is where it's most ingrained. The facilities aren't as shiny or new as those along the I-35 corridor, but the support is the best in Texas.

Abilene High usually has more fans than the home team for games one hundred miles away in DFW. With 118,000 residents, it's also the perfect size for media attention: big enough to have its own newspaper, radio stations, and network TV affiliates, but small enough for each of its three schools to get a lot of exposure. Coach Hugh Sandifer at Wylie, coach Todd Moebes at Cooper, and Coach Warren each have weekly television programs where they show highlights and discuss previous and upcoming games.

At 7:30 Tuesday morning, players watch Cooper film before school. During athletic period, the JV pads up and works their offensive and defensive units while the varsity is in the weight room for the second time this week. The workout takes about twenty minutes, then it's outside for offensive and defensive "walk and talks," still going over game-plan adjustments.

During the afternoon, I talk with offensive line coach Tommy Martinez. Today is his forty-ninth birthday. He grew up in Abilene and played for the Eagles during some bad years. He started coaching at Lincoln Middle School, eventually moving to Abilene High as a freshman coach. He was promoted to tight ends coach before finally becoming the offensive line coach in 2005.

Abilene High is different from many other big schools I visited. The staff is pretty evenly divided between ambitious coaches from all over the state and others, like Martinez, who've risen within the Abilene High system. Warren is proud that seven former assistants have moved to head jobs, but he also puts a premium on promoting from within.

"There are two types of coaches," he says. "Those who are happy to find a niche and stay in it, and the ambitious ones who are looking to move up the ladder. I guess I fall into the second category."

Offensive coordinator Del Van Cox has been with Warren from the start. He's never been interested in dealing with the headaches that come with a head job. Secondary coach Adam Verble had college experience at Angelo State and UNLV before landing at Abilene High in 2008. He wanted to live in this part of the state and "felt a calling to work with high school kids." He falls into the ambitious category but really likes working in Abilene. Warren has put together a great a mix of steady coaches happy in their roles and ambitious ones injecting new ideas into the system before getting head jobs themselves. The football atmosphere is so exceptional, it's easy to see how attractive coaching at Abilene High would be.

Before practice, I sit with two supporters, Johnson and Rob Cunningham. Johnson was born in Odessa but eventually married and settled in Abilene. He's a former assistant coach at Abilene High. He raised his family here, and his three children graduated from AHS. Now Johnson helps with the summer seven-on-seven teams and radio broadcasts.

The UIL doesn't allow coaches to be involved with seven-on-seven teams, so experienced and knowledgeable men like Johnson are a big plus. Supporters who do a hundred little things are common in West Texas. It gives these programs an edge over places with less support.

The fields at Abilene have dried enough for the Eagles to stay on campus today. The format, however, is exactly the same. It's the same used by the JV and freshman teams, as well as teams from both of the middle schools that feed Abilene High. This consistency throughout the program makes the transition smooth for kids coming up, as future Eagles will learn the drills, terminology, and tactics long before arriving on the high school campus.

Last week I saw water balls at Aledo. Today I see another new running back drill. During individual period, running backs coach Ryan Lewis pokes at each of his players with what appears to be a giant Q-tip. Coach Lewis tries to knock the ball loose as each player runs agilities while holding a ball. The giant Q-Tip is just a stick with foam rubber taped on one end. It's a nice reminder for the backs to keep the ball high and tight.

On defense, I see another equipment modification for the tackling and stripping circuit: balls with ropes attached through the laces, so the player being stripped can recover the ball quickly to be stripped again.

Each day after practice, the coaches return to the office to watch practice film. They may not see anything new, but in a sport as fast and with as many moving parts as football, even the most experienced coaches can overlook mistakes that could cost them the game on Friday. Many times I've walked off the practice field feeling it had been a good day until I realize from watching film just how many things need fixing. Each day, Abilene High coaches make sure they saw what they thought they saw. Anything needing more attention will be shown to the players, either during before-school film sessions or athletic period.

Abilene High has played Cooper fifty-one times since 1961. Cooper leads the series 31-19-1, but the Eagles have had the recent edge, winning seven of the last eight. The series has had good games, but also quite a few blowouts. Cooper won every game, for example, between 1965 and 1981 and held the Eagles to just six total points in their five meetings between 1972 and 1976. What's made this rivalry special hasn't always been the play on the field but the history of Abilene and the relationship between the two high schools.

"Abilene was a divided city; it was the haves and have-nots," Johnson says. Abilene has always been split by the train tracks running east to west along old Highway 80. The tracks separated the city not only geographically, but also increasingly racially and economically. As the town grew, the older Northside became poorer and mostly Hispanic and black. South of the tracks was more affluent and whiter, with bigger, newer homes. Cooper was built far from the tracks in what was, in 1960, the southern edge of town. Many believe it was put there specifically to keep it as far away from the "darker" side of town as possible.

So far, this is a common story, one seen wherever changing demographics have led the affluent to "protect" their kids by building schools far from the influence of the poor. This isn't limited to Texas or the South. The story of what happened here struck me because of my experience at one of these dispossessed schools.

When I started teaching at Hug High in 1994, it was a lower-middle-class school. Reno wasn't a very diverse town, but by local standards, Hug was the minority school. Though the school's makeup was probably 70 percent white, it had a reputation of being tough and dangerous.

In actuality, it was a good school, full of quality teachers and competitive academic and athletic programs. The stigma didn't become a problem until two new schools were built and the district was rezoned.

A new high school was built in Hug's most stable neighborhood. More than half of Hug's students came from that neighborhood, and those students were zoned to attend the new school.

Adjacent to Hug's zone was a very overcrowded McQueen High School. Since easing overcrowding was the reason the new schools were built, it would have been logical to take some McQueen neighborhoods and send them to Hug, relieving overcrowding at McQueen and creating two quality schools.

Unfortunately, the Washoe County School Board didn't have the will to face the backlash they expected from sending McQueen kids to the "ghetto" school. There was little political pressure from the Hug community to make sure the school was treated right, and the district silenced the little pushback it did get. When Rollins Stallworth, Hug's football coach, was quoted by the local newspaper unfavorably comparing what was happening to the "separate but equal" clause upheld by *Plessy v. Ferguson,* he was reprimanded by the district. Hug's principal was trying to move up the administrative ladder and didn't want to make waves. The district quickly and quietly implemented a rezoning plan that stripped Hug of its better neighborhoods.

In 2000, the new school opened and Hug became the school the city always thought it *had* been. Enrollment dropped by nearly half. The new student body was almost entirely economically disadvantaged and near 80 percent minority. We didn't have students for Advanced Placement (AP) or honors programs, and with the exception of football, track, basketball, and soccer, extracurricular activities were gutted.

English teacher Paul Kibala had to adjust to the new reality of the school.

"I had to change how I taught. In fact—I hate to admit it—I passed students that I would not have in the past because if I did not our numbers [pass rates and graduation] would have been worse. Have I compromised my professionalism? . . . I don't know. What I do know is that if half of my students were failing, my job would have been in jeopardy." By their approach to rezoning, the Washoe County School District (WCSD) had in effect created an inner-city, segregated school.

Once the results of the rezoning were clear, the district took actions to mitigate the damage, at least when it came to public perception. Rather than righting the wrong, however, the WCSD resorted to educational gimmickry.

Hug would hire a community favorite as the new principal; Hug would become a "model school"; Hug would implement a "House" system; Hug would hire another principal to appeal to the local media, never once acknowledging the real cause of the problem or the only real solution to it, rezoning. For all the different approaches tried, Hug remains what it became in 2000: a struggling inner-city school without the resources or support to be successful. The football program had a committed and experienced staff and kept things rolling for a time. But most of the coaches eventually left, and the wheels quickly fell off. Hug's numbers are just as out of whack as ever, but rezoning still simply cannot be discussed in Washoe County.

While the process was much slower, Abilene High was in similar danger. Betty Davis, a school board member during the move, said, "Abilene High was headed to inner-city status if we didn't do something now. Why in the world would you let that happen in a town that's only twenty minutes across?" The question was whether the school board and people in Abilene would have courage that those in Reno did not.

After Cooper opened, the Southside school gradually became more dominant. The imbalance could be seen in the records of the football teams, but also by socioeconomic and performance levels. Cooper had become what Abilene High had been from its founding through the 1950s: the showcase of the Abilene ISD, the place to go for serious athletes and scholars.

Real estate agents contributed to the problem, steering new residents to the Cooper zone, claiming their children would get a better education and ensuring themselves a bigger commission for selling higher-priced homes. As with Hug before the rezoning, I'm told that Abilene High was never as bad as its reputation, but it had become a tough place.

Johnson, a coach during that time, said, "Two weeks wouldn't go by without a call coming down to the fieldhouse during lunch to come break up fights in the cafeteria." Many of the school's programs were still doing well, but perception becomes reality, and if actions hadn't been taken, things might have slipped to the point where there'd be no coming back. Some members of the school board and a new superintendent decided to take action.

Abilene ISD had hired a new superintendent the previous year, Charles Hundley. Abilene High's principal, Jennifer Raney, says Hundley is "an amazing man. He cared about everyone and had the force of personality to convince others."

Would the rezoning of the Abilene ISD during the early '90s have been possible without a man like Hundley and a well-meaning school board? I don't know, but rezoning like this is certainly not the norm. However it was accomplished, it significantly changed the city of Abilene.

In 1990, Abilene was growing and a committee was created to make recommendations on new facilities. Made up of board members and community leaders, the group came back with a proposal to build four new elementary schools and one new middle school. They also recommended something be done to "balance" the city's two high schools.

That this suggestion came from an independent committee and not from a political body lent legitimacy to the issue. After bonds to build the new schools passed in 1990, the school board considered the zoning of Abilene High and Cooper. The timing and situation were perfect. If Abilene High continued to falter, the pushback against rezoning would grow. The issue needed to be addressed, and the right school board and superintendent were in place.

A rezoning committee was created and new zoning lines were drawn. The new lines no longer used the train tracks to determine zoning, but equally divided Abilene's population racially and socio-economically.

"It wasn't about athletics; Cooper got some good athletes that would have gone to Abilene High. It was much more about parent involvement," Pickett tells me.

Families had bought their homes, built their lives around, and been attached to their schools for thirty years. Telling people in the prosperous Southside to send their children to a faded Abilene High wasn't going to be easy. Interest was such that the committee meetings were moved to a high school auditorium. The discussion was often heated—every zoning line was debated and progress was slow—but gradually the plan came together. Over time, Davis saw the mood in the room shift until a slight majority approved of the proposal.

Before voting, though, the board decided that the decision must be unanimous. A neighbor warned Davis that she would never be elected again if she voted for the proposal. That six of the seven board members came from the Southside made unanimity unlikely, but when the plan was finally voted on, it passed 7-0 and the room erupted into cheers.

The change would go into effect for the 1991 school year. It would be gradual, as current high school and middle school students were allowed to remain where they'd been, and younger siblings of Cooper and Abilene High students could also stay at the family's current school. Both schools hired personnel specifically to help students adjust.

The rezoning was validated by the community shortly after the vote, when three board members who'd approved the change came up for reelection. Rezoning opponents put up candidates specifically chosen to overturn the decision, but even in districts where former Cooper kids were now being sent to Abilene High, incumbents were reelected. There would be no going back, as controversial as the move had been. In the end the rezoning worked, because supporters and opponents alike decided they *wanted* it to work.

The change was and remains a bitter pill for some in Abilene. Friendships were ruined; others made the topic off-limits for discussion to maintain civility. Some families moved to the Wylie High School zone rather than send their children to Abilene High. A Cooper supporter tells me the rezoning was corrupt, that it was designed to put all the money into the Abilene High zone. Others spoke of a selfish goal by the school board to return their flagship school to glory.

However, another resident told me that the rezoning had "saved" the Northside, that the slide was not just about the school itself, but that that whole part of town had been at risk if the reputation of AHS had been allowed to continue dropping property values. The Abilene High-Cooper football game has been the stage for much of the bad blood between the schools, but over the years, rezoning has become more of a fact of life and less of a political football. What anger still exists is increasingly among the older generation. The kids and coaches have moved past the "issue."

Statistically, the rezoning effectively balanced the schools. According to the *Texas Tribune*, in 2010 Abilene High was 47 percent white, 38 percent Hispanic, and 12 percent black; Cooper was 53 percent white, 27 percent Hispanic, and 14 percent black. Abilene High and Cooper each had 48 percent of their students qualify as economically disadvantaged.

For all the drama the rezoning created, the last number points out something important. The Abilene ISD no longer has an "affluent" school. This is not a rich town, and both schools now accurately represent the population. The following numbers show that it has worked: Abilene High's completion rate was 90 percent while Cooper's was 93 percent, and the two schools are within a percentage point in both TAKS and ACT testing. In 2006 the city of Abilene was ranked by *Business Outlook Magazine* as seventeenth best in the country for public education.

Raney, Abilene High's principal, attended Cooper and her children are Cougar alumni. She attributes the success of the rezoning to the moral authority of Superintendent Hundley, "There was just no question, that's what we were going to do, it was good for kids, it was good for schools . . . he had a vision and he knew how to get there . . . he pretty much brought everyone into his dream for the district . . . he truly loved the people of Abilene, and because people understood that . . . he could make that hard decision and everybody followed it."

Current Abilene High quarterback Evin Abbe talks about the environment at his school.

"A lot of kids who come through here come from bad homes. When they come here they feel like they're at home and they're here with their family . . . and don't worry about all that outside stuff." I'm sure many Cooper Cougars could say the same about their school.

Athletically, the move clearly helped Abilene High, but Cooper has remained successful, as well. Since the rezoning, Cooper has won state tennis championships in 1993, '94, and '95. Baseball played for a state title in 1993. Football made it to the state championship game in 1996 and has won nine district championships. The program is strong, now reaching the playoffs each of the past five years.

Having seen what happens when inequities are ignored, I can't help but view what the people of Abilene did as courageous in recognizing a problem and having the strength to solve it. Cunningham said, "We still look back and wonder how he [Hundley] could have done it."

It would have been easy for Abilene to let the slow slide of one of its schools continue. The result of the resolve shown by the superintendent, school board, and people of Abilene is the creation of two strong high schools and the opportunity for all children of Abilene to succeed. Davis summed it up, "The story is really about Abilene, I think. It was her finest hour."

After the game plan is implemented on Monday and Tuesday, Wednesday at Abilene High is about creating a positive attitude. Before school at 7:30, the players meet for film. The defense is told that jet motion by the Cooper slot is a decoy when the motion is toward the boundary. When the motion is toward the wide side of the field, the force player must be ready for the jet sweep. The Eagle defense doesn't use many automatic stunts to deal with these tendencies. Coach Fullen's philosophy is to make sure his unit is aligned properly and rely on superior technique to do the job. That said, giving the players a feel for the opponent's offense and what it might do is always an advantage.

During athletic period, the JV is working offensive and defensive units. The varsity offense runs plays versus air, and the defense walks through adjustments. About halfway through they change gears and work special teams.

Every Wednesday, the offensive coaches meet to determine the third-down script for the upcoming game. They choose specific plays for third-and-1, third-and-2–3, third-and-4–6, third-and-7–10, and third-and-10-plus. On most staffs this would be done by the offensive coordinator, but Warren judges third-down plays critical enough to warrant input from everyone. The meeting also makes it more likely the staff will be on the same page if something doesn't work out.

Wednesday's after-school session is shorter than the sessions on Monday and Tuesday. Instead of eight timed segments there are four. Abbe is starting to stand out at quarterback. While he's not a natural runner, he has an accurate arm. I don't see him throw a poor pass all week. Screens, posts, hitches, and deep routes all are on the money, keeping the team sessions humming and letting the offense quickly work through play scripts.

After practice, Martinez tells me my hotel is by the best Mexican restaurant in town, Enrique's. This is about the tenth restaurant in Abilene recommended to me and points out several themes of my trip. Wherever I went, coaches were quick to suggest great places to eat. As different as the regions of Texas are, one thing Texans have in common is a love for Mexican food. My weakness for the cuisine was a big cause of the seventeen pounds I gained over five months. Enrique's was excellent, as was Daddy Sam's BBQ in Carthage, Salt Lick Bar-B-Que and Round Rock Donuts in Round Rock, and Pepe's Mexican Restaurant in Harlingen.

After decades of futility, Abilene High returned to the national map in 2009. It had been ten years since the Eagles had started winning again, but a state championship had not come and many were questioning whether the Little Southwest Conference's championship years were in the past. West Texas hadn't won a big-school championship since Midland Lee took the Class 5A title in 2000.

In 2009, the Little Southwest Conference wasn't intact. Instead of being with other West Texas schools, Abilene High moved to a district that included weak Fort Worth ISD schools. The situation was similar to the one discussed in the previous chapter. Abilene High cruised though their district schedule mostly untested and entered the playoffs with a perfect 9-0 record.

As in Aledo, the playoff draw was uneven. A team's bracket position has a lot to do with its odds of surviving the tournament. The Abilene High Eagles would have their season decided by what happened during the third round, when they would match up against the undefeated, third-ranked team in the country, the Cedar Hill Longhorns. After easy wins for AHS against Arlington Lamar and El Paso Coronado in bi-district and area, the game was on.

The pivotal point came early in the fourth quarter with Abilene leading, 27-17. A Cedar Hill receiver caught a screen and seemed headed for a score before being pushed out of bounds on the 1-yard line (Cedar Hill supporters swear, to this day, that he scored). The Eagle defense held the Longhorns on four straight plays and took over on downs at their own 5.

The game effectively ended one play later when Eagle back Herschel Sims took a direct snap to the right 95 yards for a touchdown to put the Eagles up 34-17. The goal-line stand and big run created a 14-point swing. The Eagles added one more score and shocked the Longhorns, 41-17. A linebacker on the 2009 team tells me, "After that win, I knew we had a good shot at winning state."

Warren talks about the mood the following practice after the big win, "I knew when I saw them on Monday after that game, I expected them to be celebrating, but they were ready to go back to work."

After beating Arlington Bowie in the quarterfinals and Klein in the semis, the Eagles were set to face the Katy Tigers for the state championship at the Alamodome in San Antonio. One morning that week Warren found this letter on his desk, which sums up the relationship between West Texas communities and their teams better than I could:

To Coach Warren, Coaching Staff, Trainers and Abilene High School Football team of 2009,

This note is being written as a Thank You to the team, and as a letter of support, encouragement, and well wishes.

We, the Abilene High Eagle Football Fans, have experienced a great thrill following the team!!! This season has been a real doozie!

We believe in your skill, your character, and your determination! Watching you work together has been great!

We are your loyal fans. We are your Moms and your Dads. We are your Nanas and your Granddads; we are your Aunties, your Uncles and your extended families. We are your knucklehead brothers and your sisters who want to date your friends and teammates!!

We are your neighbors today, and your neighbors who lived down the street years ago when you were little. (Well at least younger! Y'all were never little!!) We babysat you when you were toddlers! We are the co-workers of your father, and the lady who does your mother's hair. We hear about you all the time! We shuffle our work schedule so we can leave work early to see you play. We are the fans who secretly listen to the radio while we are at work when we can't get off work. We are the Eagle fans who are now fighting for the United States Military and are stationed in a hot sandy place. Some of us are your age who graduated last year, some of us, many years ago. We are also listening in on the games.

We are your teachers who push you to be outstanding students as well as athletes. We are the teachers who taught your parents and pushed them to do great things. Some of us even taught your grandparents! We are the fans who are also Eagles who walked the same halls as you and sat in the same desks that you sat in today (and I do mean the same exact desks.)

We are the fans who were also high school boys who are now older boys that also played football at Abilene high. We wore the Eagle uniforms proudly, and we also wore your number. Some of us played on teams that have been where you're headed on Saturday! We cherish the guys we played with and the coaches who molded us, and the fans who supported us in 1956!

We are the fans who you see at the fast food joints. We are seeing you at the gas stations and at the mall. We are the fans who installed your sound systems. We are the ones who gave you gum at church to keep you quiet when you were a little kid. We are your kindergarten teachers and the first kid you ever sat by in school.

We are the little kids who come out on the field after a game and are hoping to see you and have you autograph our football programs that we take everywhere. We want to be just like you. We are the mothers of those young boys who pray for your safety, and for our boys as they grow and aspire to follow in your footsteps.

We are the fans who don't have kids; so when we cheer for you, you are our kids.

We are the fans whose children graduated from Abilene High School years ago and are now grown. We are the fans who never went to Abilene High but love the tradition and camaraderie. We are the fans who are Doctors and Nurses, who follow your career and keep you healthy. Although we like it best when we don't actually see you very often.

We are the fans who are reporters and photographers who get so excited watching you play and talking about your great receptions that we drop our pens.

We are the guys who played on last year's team and the year before that, and the many years before that. You watched us and supported us and we are behind you all the way!

We can see from the stands that y'all enjoy a great band of brotherhood among the team! Just remember, if you keep doing what you've been doing, you're gonna keep getting what you've been getting!

So from all your fans, we believe in you, and Congratulations to you on a great season! Finish strong and claim your prize in San Antonio! It's been a great ride!

Sincerely,
Your Fan

Katy's coaches couldn't have seen linebacker Boo Barrientes as a threat when they watched film preparing for the 2009 title game. At 5-foot-6, 160 pounds, Barrientes hardly had the physique of a Class 5A linebacker, although those numbers are typical for athletes the Eagles regularly turn into outstanding players.

He had a troubled childhood, getting involved with gangs and drugs at an early age. Playing football as a freshman didn't immediately turn him around, either. After making varsity during his junior year, he was demoted to JV for disciplinary issues. He briefly quit, but returned and finally embraced the lessons the coaching staff was teaching. "Football and my mom changed my life, and saved my life," Barrientes said in *Brother's Keeper*, Pickett's book about the 2009 championship season. "Coach Warren did, too. He gave me a lot of chances . . . I don't meet a lot of good people in my life, but that's one good guy. If I was in his shoes I would have kicked me out a long time ago, but he never gave up on me."

The Abilene High Eagles completed their perfect season in 2009, defeating the Katy Tigers, 28-17, in front of 30,000 fans in San Antonio. Barrientes was named defensive MVP of the game.

Barrientes is now an assistant manager at a restaurant in Abilene and told me the whole coaching staff deserves credit for his growth; Warren, Fullen, Verble and Lewis were all instrumental in his progress. When asked what might have happened to him without football, he said, "I had a younger brother and an older brother who both went the other way and are in jail. I was smart, but without football I could have ended up there, too."

Maybe the most damaging misperception about "big-time" high school football is that winning is all that matters. While an excellently written book with a great story, *Friday Night Lights* perpetuated this stereotype. Chronicling the 1988 season at Permian High School in Odessa, *Friday Night Lights* is a story of racism, kids sacrificing their bodies and futures for the "greater good" of Permian football, and the sadness of high school glory being the pinnacle of kids' lives. The corruption of Permian football was exemplified by the treatment of Boobie Miles, a talented black running back who was tossed aside when a knee injury made him expendable.

I wasn't at Permian in 1988 and won't attempt to defend its program, but I'd guess that Permian of 1988 had players like Barrientes, too. Maybe things have changed in the twenty-five years since that book was written, but as fanatical as the fans are in this part of the state, I saw nothing like the excesses described in that book. Barrientes much better reflects West Texas football than Boobie Miles.

Warren summed up the motivation for most coaches when speaking about the growth he saw in Barrientes. "That is why I coach, when you get right down to it. When you can give a kid like Boo a chance to be successful and he finally gets it, it is very rewarding."

On Thursday, the football day starts with athletic period. There are no before-school films, and the after-school session consists of meetings. The varsity goes through its "play the game" drill, running through personnel groups and special teams units, attempting to simulate a game pace and training players to stay alert. Several defensive coaches get a jump on next week, labeling film from Midland Lee, next week's opponent. The offensive coaches hold a quick game-plan meeting.

After school, the varsity meets in the portable classroom to set the tone for tomorrow. Warren asks them to "play the game faster than you've ever played it before . . . don't let anything detract away from what we're going to do . . . we can be a great football team if we keep preparing mentally." He also tells them, "You aren't going to suddenly be more athletic . . . at this point all improvement has to come from your mind and how you mentally prepare."

This is the normal Thursday afternoon routine. After Warren speaks, the players watch a special teams highlight film, then the kids have a private meeting with team chaplain Chad Mitchell. Every season, Mitchell gives each team a theme to keep in their consciousness. This year the theme is "ohana," a Hawaiian word that's literally translated to "family," but emphasizes that family members stick together, and in a team context, no one gets left behind. Each player wears a black rubber bracelet inscribed with this word to remind him of this sentiment.

Abilene High's three freshman teams play at the Lee Complex Thursday afternoon and the JV teams are at Shotwell. I watch the C and B freshman squads before heading over to Shotwell to catch the JV A game.

With so many games at the same time, the staff is spread out. At the Lee Complex a group of coaches catches up with some of Cooper's staff as they wait for the A game to begin. For all the talk about bad blood between these programs, I haven't heard or seen any real animosity. Later on at Shotwell, as the JV A team puts the Cougars away, Coach Martinez, an AHS grad, excitedly tells me how much he loves defeating the Cougars. They may not hate each other, but there is nothing as sweet as beating a crosstown rival.

Game day at Abilene High starts early during Cooper week. I attended many pep rallies, but the annual "Black Out" on the morning of the "Battle at Shotwell" is, by far, the most impressive. Except for a twenty by twenty square in the middle of the basketball court, Abilene High's gym is packed floor to rafters with black-clad families and Eagle supporters of all ages. After the lights shut off, the cheerleaders perform, lit only by the glow sticks they wear. The fans have thousands of additional glow sticks, and as the rally comes to a conclusion, the points of light are thrown around the gym for an amazing climax.

During athletic period, the offense walks through plays one last time, while the defense listens to Fullen in the classroom.

"We're not getting our due respect," he tells his unit. "They think they've seen fast; they aren't ready for what we're bringing tonight.

I want them, when they come off the field, to say, 'Oh my God, they're fast!' God have mercy on them, because we're not going to! Don't test the water to see if it's hot or cold, just jump the hell in!"

The offense comes in for a devotional. The pastor tells the team, "The difference between good and great is unity. Individualism keeps good from becoming great. If you care about the guy in the locker next to you more than you care about yourself, there is no way the good team over there can beat the great team in this room."

Starting around 3:00, the coaches meet to kill time in the field-house before the kids arrive around 5:00. The talk turns to the best gangster movies of all time, and soon the coaches are quoting *The Godfather*, "Luca Brasi sleeps with the fishes." The Texas Rangers are in the process of blowing a huge lead in the AL West and missing the playoffs, and that is discussed, as well. People in this part of the state don't use a lot of profanity, even when talking about the Rangers' collapse; a drawn out "Golly!" with three or four syllables is the most common expletive.

At 5:20, the players quickly meet with their coaches before boarding buses for the ten-minute drive to Shotwell Stadium. The tailgating has begun when we pull up two hours before kickoff. An hour later the stadium is half full. There's a definite buzz. Beyond being a huge rivalry game, the Little Southwest Conference title may be on the line. Cooper looks big; their offensive line must have fifty pounds per man on the Eagle defensive front. Speed is going be the key, as Fullen had said hours earlier. Both student sections are completely full of kids who stand the entire game. The black-clad Eagles, with gold helmets, and the Cougars, in white and blue with red trim, head to the locker room.

The public address announcer proudly brags about Abilene city football: "No town plays harder, tackles better, blocks better than these two teams. Not Odessa, or Midland or Lubbock or San Angelo, but Abilene, Texas."

This is a small town, but this game is as big as can be. Senior defensive back Conlan Aguirre told me, "We don't have a professional team, like a Dallas Cowboys or anything, so I guess high school football is like our professional . . . Every kid dreams of playing in front of thousands of people like NFL or college players, and we get to do that, in some sense we get to live the dream. Abilene High and Shotwell . . . is the closest you can get to living the dream."

He's right—the atmosphere is electric.

For the next three hours, Abilene might end at the edge of Shotwell Stadium for all the attention 15,000 here give the outside world. Nothing beyond this narrowly lit world matters. The pride of Abilene is on the line, and as silly a concept as it may seem from a distance, nothing feels more important than the game under the lights of Shotwell.

At this point of my trip I'm a little frustrated that I haven't yet seen a compelling football game. Tonight the frustration ends. The 2012 Crosstown Showdown is the type of game that will be remembered forever by those who were there.

Sometimes when the setting, stakes, and action are right, a football game becomes larger than life, a beautiful struggle where passion, training, and intensity come together perfectly. Every football fan probably has a list of games fitting this description. These games may or may not be well known, but have elements that create something magical. When I was thirteen years old, I was at Candlestick Park for the 1981 NFC Championship game when the 49ers beat the Cowboys with "The Catch." In 1988, I was there when the University of Nevada beat the Boise State Broncos in triple overtime during the Division I-AA playoffs. I was a coach at Hug High School when we knocked off McQueen, 19-16, for the Northern Nevada championship in 2005. I witnessed a second Nevada-Boise classic when the Wolf Pack ended the Broncos' BCS dreams with an upset, overtime win in 2010. The game between Abilene High and Cooper on this night in 2012 joins my list, and probably the lists of most who were lucky enough to be at Shotwell.

The Cooper Cougars jump ahead, taking a 7-0 lead after an eleven-play drive when quarterback Lorenzo Joe scores on a 12-yard run. The Eagle offense struggles; Abilene moves the ball well but fumbles away two first-quarter drives. The Cougars are stopped deep in their own territory on their third possession. At this point the Cougars make one of their few mistakes of the night, a bad snap on a punt attempt that's recovered by the Eagles in the end zone, tying the score at 7-7.

Early in the second quarter the Eagles take a 14-7 lead on a 4-yard pass from Abbe to Keevan Lucas. Just before the half, however, Cooper scores on a 28-yard pass to Anthony Pierson to climb within a point, 14-13. The point after touchdown (PAT) kick is blocked, and Abilene High leads by 1 going into the half.

Cooper is good; Joe is throwing well and always a threat on the ground. The Cooper defense is flying around as hard as the Eagles. Anything could happen in the second half, but this game just feels like it's going down to the wire.

Both Abilene High and Cooper have big bands with long routines. The 28-minute halftime isn't enough, and players and coaches wait on the sideline as the Cooper band finishes. Warren strolls over to talk.

"This game is always like this," he says, as though talking about something unconnected to him. I don't know what's going through his head, but I'm more nervous than he looks. His cool in the face of what must be tremendous pressure is impressive.

The Eagles score on the opening drive of the second half, getting into the end zone on a 3-yard run by Marcell Porter to extend their lead to 21-13. Any hope that the Eagles may pull away after the intermission is quickly dispelled as the Cougars put together a drive of their own, converting twice on third down, once when a Cougar receiver makes an acrobatic catch along the far sideline, dragging his toe inside the boundary to keep the drive alive. Cooper scores on a 17-yard slant over the middle to KaShawn Brown. It's 21-20 Eagles with 2:38 in the third.

Between the third and fourth quarters the game stops, helmets are removed, and everyone stands to sing *God Bless America*. I'm told that this ritual began this year for all games at Shotwell.

Early in the final period, neither team can get anything going. Abilene drives but stalls at the 10, and the Eagles kick a 22-yard field goal to make it 24-20 with 5:13 left.

My gut tells me that the failure to score a touchdown may come back to haunt the Eagles. The Cougars won't go away, and with just a 4-point lead, Cooper has plenty of time to score a go-ahead touchdown. Sure enough, the Cougars once again rise to the challenge, driving ten plays and taking their first lead since the first quarter on a 2-yard run by Xavier McCann to make the score 27-24 with just 2:17 left.

For the final two minutes, nobody sits. One big play or small mistake will determine the outcome; with so little time left, whatever happens will be decisive and irreversible. The game will be decided by this battle between the Eagle offense and Cougar defense.

One trait of a successful team is confidence that they'll find a way to win. Even when things look bleak, when all the evidence shows they should be beaten, deep down a team like Abilene High expects to find a way to come out on top. Success breeds success; luck favors those with faith. Quality teams have a knack for winning games they should probably lose.

Cooper has outplayed the Eagles tonight and the momentum is on the far sideline, but Abilene High has been here before. Johnson told me that back in the bad old days, Abilene High teams were often beaten before they took the field. Warren and this team are never beaten as long as there's a second on the clock.

Starting on their own 28-yard line, the Eagles move the ball to the Cooper 20, where they use their last timeout facing a third-and-2 with 33 seconds remaining. A pass to the sideline moves the chains and gives the Eagles the ball on the Cougar 10. A 3-yard run by Porter puts the ball on the 7, but the clock is running and Abbe spikes the ball to the ground, stopping the clock with 11 seconds remaining.

Everyone playing has spent years working for this moment; everything hinges on this one play. Just one more stop and Cooper will have a clear path to a district championship. The noise from the packed stands is loud as 15,000 Abilenians roar and stomp their feet, aware of the importance of this snap.

Abbe rolls right, falling backward, and a Cooper linebacker knocks him to the ground just as he releases the ball. Porter, out of the backfield, has no one to block. He heads to the goal line and turns. Number eight for Cooper, covering the Eagle slot, steps in front of Porter to intercept the pass, but the ball deflects off his hands and somehow finds Porter's chest. It's an Eagle touchdown with 3 seconds remaining. Abilene High wins, 31-27.

The Eagle sideline surges onto the field and the home crowd erupts, but Cooper's response to the heartbreaking loss is just as impressive as the last-second win. The Cougars stand at attention while the Eagles celebrate and the band plays the alma mater. Cooper quotes in the paper Saturday don't bemoan bad luck or make excuses. Joe, the losing quarterback, said, "Man, we worked so hard . . . But it was a good game all around. It was just a great game . . . After the game, we're all friends, both teams played very well."

Whatever lingering anger exists between these two schools was clearly not part of what happened tonight. It's an overused sports cliché about it being a shame that either team lost, but tonight I feel that about the Cooper Cougars. Except for the bad snap, they played nearly a perfect game, showed tremendous character and fight, and fell with their dignity intact. If this game is a showcase of the best of Abilene, both programs represent their city and West Texas values admirably.

The Crosstown Showdown was effectively for the district championship, as the teams finish one and two in District 2-5A. Neither Abilene High nor Cooper loses again in Little Southwest Conference play. After winning their bi-district game against El Paso Americas, the Cooper Cougars are upset by Arlington in the second round, finishing their season 9-3.

Abilene High finishes the regular season ranked fifth in the state with a record of 10-0. The Eagles open the postseason with a 34-15 victory over El Paso Montwood in bi-district. Arlington Lamar is next. The Vikings make it a game early, trailing by only one at the intermission. The game seesaws through three quarters, but the Eagles pull away for a 53-34 win, setting up a matchup with undefeated Waco Midway.

I'm in Abilene for a few days during Midway week. The coaches seem happy and confident. It's been a good ride and making it this far is an accomplishment. The quality of the teams in the 5A means that anyone can beat anyone. There are no dogs left. Coach Warren lets his team know that if they can get by Midway, they'll have as good a chance as anyone.

Injuries are a concern. The Eagles' best receiver, Lucas, blew out his ACL the week after the Cooper game against Midland Lee. Against Lamar, safety Nate Kittley pulled a hamstring. It's almost impossible to stay completely healthy through a seventeen-week championship run, so how a team deals with injuries has a huge impact on success during the playoffs.

This game would also come down to the final minute. With Abilene High leading 31-27 and Midway facing fourth-and-20 from their own 10 with less than a minute to go, the Eagles are one play away from advancing. Midway completes a pass over the middle for 31 yards. Three plays later, the Panthers win the game, 34-31, on a 10-yard score with 12 seconds remaining.

As Cooper was earlier, Abilene High is gracious and classy in defeat. "Our guys gave tremendous effort," Warren said. "Those guys made one more play than we did. We made a lot of plays and gave ourselves a chance to win the game. We just didn't get it done today."

Abilene High has developed to where it's consistently among the elite of the state. Any given year, the stars may align and another title will come. Unfortunately for the Eagles, West Texas wouldn't be represented in the Class 5A Division II title game this year.

Cooper and Abilene High each have their supporters, but in the end they're all Abilenians. Where this was once a town divided by economics, race, and railroad tracks, today it's one city with three proud programs. Kids grow up unaware of the old divisions that once separated their town. The older generation is simply proud their town is home of great football and schools. The old resentments still live, but they die a little as each graduating class further erodes the wall once separating the residents of Abilene.

7

MERCY RULE

Week Seven: Throckmorton Greyhounds

"You are not born a winner, nor are you born a loser. You are what you think you are, nothing more and nothing less."

—Quote from Mike Reed's book.

My first indication that Throckmorton would be different came when I contacted head coach Mike Reed. I asked about the weekend meeting schedule. Reed told me the kids and coaches were off until Monday. The fundamental skills are the same. The ingredients for success are, as well: proficiency in blocking, tackling, passing, catching, kicking, and running with the ball. But six-man football is a very different game.

After ten weeks of running from town to town, usually traveling over dark, winding roads in the middle of the night, a weekend off where I could sleep late on Saturday and Sunday before making the leisurely seventy-mile drive up from Abilene was welcome. But weekends are the toughest part of my routine. I'm tired of living in motels and eating most meals out of a bag, and December 22 seems a long way off. The football part of this journey is fascinating. As long as I'm working I forget the bad parts and stop counting down the days. It's the weekends when loneliness hits hardest.

I tell myself it's only five months, thinking about tougher ordeals common to soldiers at war and sailors at sea, who are gone for years at a time. Early on I'd exercise, but now I've mostly given it up. I do laundry, work on my blog, and spend a lot of time wishing I were home. I love traveling; I enjoy driving and seeing new things. Texas is a great place to ramble, with beautiful back roads, interesting scenery, and always something new around the next bend.

Motels are OK in small doses, but I long ago overdosed on them. I miss my wife, my daughter, my baby granddaughter, and my dogs. The permanent road trip is a brutal way to live.

Besides having the extra day in my room, the unusual weekend schedule also tells me I can forget what I knew about football preparation when it comes to the six-man game. This game has its own patterns and tempos. How the Throckmorton Greyhounds prepare can't be measured using eleven-man standards. This is a different world. Six-man is generally played in rural towns in the plains, from Canada through Wyoming and Montana and down to Texas. In the Lone Star State, West Texas is home to the sport.

As I traveled though Texas, people spoke of the six-man game as though it were some exotic animal, mysterious and hard to find.

"I've heard about it," people often said. "Someday before I die, I'd like to see a six-man game."

The game itself is elusive because it's often over so fast. Whenever a team goes up by 45 points, the game immediately ends. Defensive coordinator Blayne Davis tells me a good defensive stand is forcing the opponent to run five plays to score. More commonly a touchdown drive is two or three plays long, and with the mercy rule many games are over by halftime. During the past two seasons the Greyhounds played a total of nine complete games, with twenty ending early due to the mercy rule.

There is some truth to the claim that six-man is difficult to find, at least for suburbanites outside of West Texas. The six-man game is played almost exclusively in very small towns, not Abilene small or even Stamford small, but towns with only one stoplight—towns like Throckmorton, a crossroad of two-lane highways connecting four slightly larger small towns, with a blinking red light strung up where the highways intersect.

Throckmorton sits in a valley where State Highway 183 and State Highway 380 meet. The low hills surrounding it are covered with thickets of mesquite and prickly pear. Going north on 183 takes you to Seymour, south to Albany. Going west on 380 leads to Haskell and east to Newcastle. On one corner is the courthouse with a sign on the lawn proclaiming Throckmorton as the home of Dallas Cowboys great Bob Lilly. The town has two restaurants, two convenience stores, a small grocery store, a bar open on weekends, and, luckily for me, a motel. The Double T Lodge is small, but it's clean and the owners are friendly. Throckmorton High School is a few blocks northwest of the intersection. The elementary and middle schools are steps away; all three schools share the gym and teachers, too, including Reed, the head football coach.

Texas high schools with fewer than one hundred students can choose to play six-man or be placed in Class 1A Division II, playing eleven-man football. Throckmorton had played eleven-man since 1916 with some success, advancing to the state finals in 1986. In recent years, numbers dropped to where they could no longer compete at that level. The school switched in 2004, and success was immediate. The Greyhounds advanced to the state semifinal, losing to eventual champion Richland Springs. The following year, Throckmorton won its first state championship, beating Turkey Valley, 68-22.

Sheriff John Riley, a lifelong Throckmorton resident, was part of the committee that made the decision to switch. He has had two sons in the program.

"It took about three games for the town to get excited about the change, but after that first season, everybody thought we should have made the switch sooner."

The weather has turned cold and foggy this week. For the first time this season, I'm wearing jeans and a jacket instead of shorts. When I arrive on Monday, Reed is in the weight room with about twenty middle school kids during athletic period. The weight room is in the school's brick gym building, connected to Reed's office above five rows of basketball bleachers. The weight room is small, with mix-and-match equipment, but the Greyhounds make good use of it. The players are working a challenging circuit that will pay off when these "Pups" play for the big team.

Throckmorton has only sixty-three students and seven teachers, so the young football coach not only is the HC/AD but also teaches a full load of classes. In addition to running football, Reed is a basketball assistant and head track coach and teaches physical education to students from kindergarten through high school.

Reed's house is just across the street from the school; his wife, Michelle, also teaches and coaches basketball here. The arrangement gives Reed the opportunity to teach his son and daughter, both of whom attend the elementary school. Babysitters are never needed and the coaches don't choose between family and work, as those in bigger schools do.

Throckmorton is 5-1 this season. On Friday night, they played Windthorst, an eleven-man team in a "first of its kind" half six-man, half eleven-man game. Throckmorton hadn't played eleven-man football since 2003. They are a six-man powerhouse, and one problem successful programs have is difficulty scheduling non-district games. Windthorst is a successful Class A program and has the same problem. The combo experiment was the best game either school could find. The Greyhounds played surprisingly well for kids who had never lined up in an eleven-man formation, trailing just 7-0 at the half before dominating the six-man half and winning 46-21.

How exactly is six-man football different?

- 15 yards for a first down instead of 10.
- Conversions are switched; one point is awarded for getting the ball into the end zone from scrimmage, and two points are awarded for kicking it through the uprights.
- All six offensive players are eligible to catch passes. Because this means the whole defense must be in coverage, an exchange is required before the ballcarrier can run (no QB runs or scrambles). In some six-man offenses, the tailback is effectively the quarterback, with the nominal quarterback pitching him the ball and allowing the tailback to either throw or run.
- The playing field is only 80 yards long and more narrow than an eleven-man field, with just 13 yards from the hash mark to the sideline.

Game play is different. With so much field for the defense to cover, six eligible receivers, and so few defenders, scoring is very quick. Davis tells me that the goal of his defense is to force the offense to run seven plays to score, counting on the offense to make a mistake somewhere along the way.

A well-executed offense will score no matter the quality of the defense. As the best basketball defense gives up baskets from time to time, six-man football defenses give up touchdowns. Scores can reach triple digits, and it's rare for a winning team to score under 50 points. The basketball comparison is apt. A six-man football defense, more than anything, resembles a violent form of zone defense in basketball.

So much open field results in several consequences. Each defensive player is exposed and can be isolated, often creating mismatches where weak defenders are exploited. Small schools usually have at least one weak defender, giving the superior team a tremendous advantage. Games between solid teams and those with weaknesses often become lopsided quickly, so the game has a mercy rule. Since the Greyhounds began playing six-man in 2004, as many games have ended early as have gone four quarters.

The type of player who does well at this game is often different, as well. Good six-man players must be proficient at *all* football skills. On offense, everyone must block, catch, and carry the ball. On defense, everyone must be able to tackle, shed blockers, and drop into coverage. With rosters sometimes in the single digits, most six-man players play both offense and defense, and many never leave the field. Big linemen aren't effective here; this version of football favors mid-size players with the endurance and speed to work in the open field. Big players in Throckmorton have an incentive to slim down if they want to play.

It's homecoming week, and Throckmorton is preparing for the Bryson Cowboys. The Greyhound staff doesn't expect much of a test. According to Coach Reed, six-man football success has a greater correlation between talent and winning. Sometimes opponents simply don't have the horses to play with a better team. Reed believes this will be one of those games; Bryson has obvious weaknesses the Greyhounds will take advantage of.

I'm not sure if it's a six-man thing or a Reed thing, but Reed does something unthinkable to most coaches. He acknowledges this game will be a cakewalk and cuts the practice schedule. Coaches *always* preach a philosophy of never letting the opponent dictate preparation. Quality teams strive to prepare the same way every week, regardless of the opponent's talent.

Reed breaks that tradition this week. Practices are shortened, adding up to just a few hours between now and Friday night. On Wednesday, there'll be no practice at all, something unheard of for an eleven-man team during game week. Because he wants his team to problem solve, the scouting report is basic for Bryson. In fact, Reed purposely withholds information about the Cowboys, testing the defense's ability to adjust. Reed knows forcing his team to think and problem solve will be important when the Greyhounds face tougher teams during the playoffs.

Reed's philosophy includes getting the most from the least during practice. Every moment on the field is well thought out and efficient, covering every fundamental football skill. Tempo is part of the equation, as well. Players are often on the clock during team drills, and each player gets many reps in a short time.

A remarkable thing I saw during this trip was how different philosophies can lead to the same place. Given his success, only a fool would argue that Reed's approach is a bad one. Though only thirty-four, he has a long pedigree in the six-man game. He began coaching with his mentor, six-man hall of famer Nelson Campbell, while still in college at Tarleton State. He spent four years at Gordon, then two as an assistant at Strawn, winning a championship there before getting his first head job at Rule. At Rule, Reed took the Bobcats to the state finals in 2006 and 2007.

Since coming to Throckmorton in 2008, his record is 48-5 and he's advanced to two additional championships, winning a state title in 2011. As a head coach, Reed has a lifetime record of 123-17, making the championships four times. He's also working on a book for six-man coaches, describing his philosophy and giving advice on the X's and O's.

While some of Reed's methods seem questionable at first, I quickly learn that he does everything for specific reasons. There's nothing careless about his approach. He knows what he's doing and why he's doing it.

With only three coaches and players who work on every skill, practice is broken up by activity rather than position. Reed takes half the kids and works on blocking technique on the sled, while assistants Jason Blankenship and Davis do the same drills with the rest of the players.

Greyhound Stadium probably looks the same now as when the school started playing football in 1916. The grass field sits below the school building. Getting to field level from the locker room means climbing down four tiers of crumbling cement bleachers on the visitor side. On the home side, a modest steel press box sits atop steel bleachers emblazoned with a purple silhouette of a greyhound in full stride (just like the emblem on the side of a Greyhound bus). The lights are on old-style tripod standards installed during another era. Like every stadium in Texas, a small 24-second scoreboard is near each goal post, something you don't see in other states, where time is kept by officials on the field.

Reed is very energetic when teaching football. He yells a lot but the yelling isn't critical, it's enthusiastic. Football is emotional and Reed isn't afraid to show his passion.

Eleven of twenty players must leave early today for a band competition in Archer City. Sharing athletes here actually means sharing them during the season, and band is important. When Reed spoke of the time commitment taking his football players, he wasn't complaining but rather bragging with obvious pride.

Today I meet the high school principal at Throckmorton, Troy Batts. Two years ago he came from Olney, a slightly larger town thirty miles northeast of Throckmorton, and took a pay cut to make the move. He felt like this was a better place for his three kids.

"It's almost like moving back to the fifties," he tells me. Kids in Throckmorton come from supportive families who were brought up right, with fantastic work ethics hammered home by doing chores and from living in a community where everyone has a role in supporting children.

The dress code at the school is '50s-like. No piercings for the boys; girls may have piercings only in their ears. No visible tattoos, boys' hair off the collar, no facial hair, and no unnatural hair colors. Batts tells me he hasn't had a problem enforcing these standards. The kids here are very respectful. In two years, there's only been one fight.

Close by and of similar size, Olney is very different. Subsidized housing had the town actively recruiting poor people from bigger cities. The new residents wouldn't find jobs in Olney, but the city got money for everyone it brought in. It may've been a good deal for the city, but it didn't make the school a good place to work. According to Batts, coming to town under such pretenses gave the kids an "entitlement attitude" that doesn't exist in Throckmorton. He says, "Society as a whole kind of pushes that, but here the kids are raised with the expectation that they are going to work and earn whatever they get."

Superintendent Clay Tarpley compares Throckmorton to Mayberry from *The Andy Griffith Show*. As good as things are, he worries about the future of public education in Texas. He puts much of the blame on politics in Austin. "The state legislature only meets once every two years, and the way things are, that's a good thing."

In recent years Republican politicians have strongly pushed a voucher system in the state, which would essentially compensate families for sending their children to private schools by letting them use tax dollars to pay private school tuition rather than supporting public schools.

"Our budget has been cut twelve percent during the last two years," says Tarpley. Many worry it will get worse if the voucher system is approved.

"If it happens the way they're talking about, a kid can go from public school to private school and take his money with him . . . that's going to hurt your athletics and fine arts programs, that's what's going to get cut," Tarpley tells me. He's also worried the legislature will disband the UIL, paving the way for private and public schools to compete together.

Texas has completely separate private and public school leagues (with two exceptions; Dallas Jesuit and Strake Jesuit in Houston successfully petitioned to join the UIL). The Texas system is also unique in that public schools generally dominate athletics. "Texas Football Culture" is strictly a public school phenomenon. Private schools don't get the attention, get the crowds, or have the prestige of public schools on the gridiron.

Texas coaches worry about Texas becoming like California, Louisiana, New Jersey, and other states where private schools compete directly with public schools because the former have an advantage in recruiting and funding.

"Private schools don't have to follow the same rules," many coaches tell me. No zoning boundaries prevent private schools from building all-star teams, and private schools aren't required to enforce the "no pass, no play" eligibility rules. Private school coaches are often off-campus volunteers. Allowing part-time coaches into the UIL would erode the standing the coaching profession holds in this state.

As the legislature has become more Republican, the voucher movement continues to gain support. With Rick Perry in the governor's mansion, Tarpley worries that it's just a matter of time before vouchers gut public education.

Batts outlines the average week for a Throckmorton football player/band member in the fall. On Monday, he shows up at 7:15 for agriculture, attends classes from 8:00 until 3:30, and then goes to football practice. Tuesday is an 8:00–3:30 class schedule, with football practice until 6:00 and then band practice from 6:00–8:30. Wednesday is longer: Future Farmers of America (FFA) at 6:15 in the morning, classes, then more FFA from 3:30–4:30, followed by football from 4:30–6:30. Thursday includes classes and JV games; Friday, varsity games, along with halftime and after-game band performances. Batts says sixty-one of sixty-three students are involved in something extracurricular. Most are in more than one.

The spring is even busier, between track, tennis, golf, agricultural judging, and UIL academic competitions. Many kids only get to school once a week. This busy routine doesn't seem to hurt achievement. Last year sixteen of eighteen graduating seniors left for college; the two who stayed have good jobs on ranches.

The staff doesn't ask much from the players this week, but what's expected must be done correctly. During practice today, the offense tries to complete twenty straight passes without a drop. Reed has quarterback Bryson Oliver calling plays based on where the JV scout defense lines up. This lets Reed know the plays Oliver is most comfortable with, useful knowledge when putting together a game plan.

During practice, "demerits" are compiled for each dropped ball, missed assignment, or other mistake. After practice, Coach Davis has the players run a hill for each demerit.

Tuesday morning, the middle school team is outside, wearing full pads and white helmets with the Greyhound outline (varsity helmets have a capital "T" inside a silhouette of Texas). "Pups" is written on the front of the practice jerseys. The Pups haven't been good early this season. Going into this week, they have a 1-1 record.

After-school practice today is the toughest this week. Form tackling is a focus during indy periods. Open-field tackling is the most important defensive skill in six-man football, even more important than in the eleven-man game. Players in eleven-man focus as much on turning ballcarriers back into the defense as tackling. In six-man ball, each defender has so much grass to defend that he's often on his own making a tackle.

Davis tells me, "Sooner or later it'll come down to one-on-one situations, and when it does we need to make the plays." If the offense finds an opposing player who's a poor tackler, a game can quickly get out of hand. In football, defensive weakness is attacked specifically; when a good team finds a defender to go after, the defense is almost helpless. Trying to help one weak link opens up a gaping hole somewhere else. All six players on defense must pull their weight.

During offense, cones are set up 13 yards on either side of the ball. Thirteen yards is the distance from the hash mark to the sideline. This drill essentially makes both sides the "short" side of the field. Reed wants to make sure his players are adept at running into the boundary.

The Greyhounds have the right-size kids: big, but not so big that they're slow. The best two players, receiver/defensive end Gary Farquhar and running back/defensive end Levi Taylor, are tall, strong-looking boys. Farquhar, who will end up signing with Midwestern State in Wichita Falls, is 6-foot-5 and 195 pounds, and Taylor is 6-foot-2 and 185. Both look like they could run marathons.

The players are in outstanding condition. Throckmorton football players resemble elite wrestlers. The weight room is thrown together, but the workouts are well thought out. Bigger schools may have two or three kids rotate through the same exercise; Throckmorton players each work through their circuit individually, completing ten to twenty stations at one or two minutes a pop, the intervals timed by music playing on the stereo. There's no hiding or time to rest.

Their technique is outstanding, almost vicious. Six-man players are smaller but probably more violent than eleven-man players. With so much space, players often are at full speed during collisions. Imagine a game made up entirely of kickoffs, with players throwing their bodies into each other while running full out, and you get the idea. Throckmorton players are especially good at throwing crushing downfield cut blocks, laying out and sometimes taking half the defense to the ground on the same play.

The ruthless play belies the nature of the boys. To me they seem like the typical West Texas boys I met in Stamford and Abilene. "Yes, sir" is the common response to almost anything, and they are polite and generous.

My first visit to Throckmorton exemplifies the best of West Texas hospitality. I was just starting my circuit, trying to see one preseason practice with each of my teams. On a Friday afternoon the first week of practice, I'd just finished watching the morning workout in Carthage. Deciding to head west, I called Reed to ask about practice the following day. He said the Greyhounds would celebrate the beginning of the season as they'd done for several years.

This evening the Greyhounds would practice at 7:00, take a few hours off, and return for a BBQ and midnight practice, marking the first moments a Texas football team is allowed to wear pads. It's a big event in Throckmorton, with a ceremony and fireworks.

Reed offered to find me a place to stay. My GPS showed 317 miles between me and Throckmorton, about six hours. I decided to go for it.

Reed arranged a place for me at the bunkhouse of the R.A. Brown Ranch. After practice, Lanham Brown, one of his players, led me down the dusty dirt road from the highway to his family's home. I returned to town after dropping off my suitcase for the BBQ.

That midnight was my first view of six-man. Maybe one hundred people watched from the stands. The team held a torch-lit ceremony commemorating the new season before the lights came on and practice began. I was impressed by the speed of the contact drills and by the insects attracted to the lights. Big, noisy bugs buzzed into my ears and mouth; others hopped along the ground. Thankfully when I return during the season, the insects are gone. At about 2:00, I headed to the ranch for a few hours sleep. During this quick visit I never met the elder Browns, but Reed arranged for me to use the bunkhouse again in October. I chose to stay at the motel instead to be closer to the school, but the offer to an almost complete stranger made me feel very welcome even before I arrived.

I learn that the generous, humble, and coachable character, however, was taught. The values are absolutely here, but kids are kids, and if coaches aren't diligent, young men make poor decisions. A few years ago the Greyhounds stumbled character-wise, forcing the coaches to analyze the lessons they were teaching.

From the outside the 2010 team looked successful, but five players were caught drinking during the summer and Reed suspended them for four games.

From a football standpoint the move worked. The team finished the season 15-1, losing in the state championship to Garden City, but the coaches weren't satisfied. It wasn't about winning. It had to do with the more important but less recognized task of building boys into men. Reed wasn't happy with how that senior class left.

"We failed that group," Reed told me. After the season he, Blankenship, and Davis sat down and devised new rules and policies so this wouldn't happen again.

The new rules were enacted to prevent the drama of the 2010 season from reoccurring. Each player would have responsibilities: laundry, cleaning the locker room, helping line the field, or other odd jobs. Seniors would no longer dump their jobs on freshmen. Seniority wouldn't be an excuse for seniors to set themselves above their teammates. The players would learn nobody was above a share drudgery, and that good teammates are selfless.

They would not let outside influences affect decisions within the team.

Finally, and most importantly, they'd always coach as though it was their last year. Throckmorton is a pressure job. Expectations are high and opinions are everywhere. Coaches who worry about maintaining popularity risk letting their authority be undermined. Decisions on what's best for the team can't be influenced by politics or popularity. The "final year" mind-set allowed coaches to do what's right without worrying about blowback.

In 2011, with both discipline and upfront character lessons being practiced, the Greyhounds went undefeated, beating Borden County for the state championship.

Tuesday night there's a big BBQ at the Brown Ranch before the bull auction on Wednesday. Yes, it's just as it sounds, and it's a big deal in town. Brown Ranch breeding bulls are well regarded, and ranchers have come from all over the West to bid on the livestock.

Reed has volunteered to help, so Wednesday the varsity is off. Muddy pickups with horse trailers fill a field next to the house when I arrive for dinner. I finally meet Mrs. Brown and thank her for the use of her bunkhouse. The bulls are corralled in pens. Ranchers and cowboys walk between them, assessing the animals. In the barn, bleachers are set up and bulls are shown on a big screen for the ranchers to bid on. Others bid via an Internet feed. The star attraction is a Red Angus bull that sells for $70,000.

At the school, Davis and Blankenship prepare for their JV game Thursday while the varsity lifts on their own. Again, I don't know if losing a practice day is a Reed thing, a six-man thing, or a small-town thing. I'm guessing canceling practice for a bull sale says more about the realities of small-town life than Reed's philosophy or the weakness of the opponent. Kids and coaches in small schools absolutely can't specialize; they must do many things at once. Everyone makes sacrifices. Ranches and farms have chores to be done, and those responsibilities don't disappear because it's football season. Taking a whole practice day off during a game week just isn't something that happens in bigger schools. In Throckmorton, it's just how it is.

This multitasking extends to the coaching staff. The three coaches at Throckmorton, like all small-town coaches, fill many roles. Besides being the defensive coordinator, Davis is the varsity basketball coach, head junior high coach and head golf coach, teaches PE, and has principal duties at the elementary school. Blankenship is the JV football coach, head girls' track coach, and head tennis coach, and teaches history and PE.

On Thursday the middle school and JV teams play, but before heading out, JV players run scout for the varsity. With only ten varsity kids, there's no way to hold practice without JV help.

During school, I watch a middle school girls' athletic period class taught by Blankenship and Michelle Reed. After basketball drills, the girls run across the gym at timed intervals. If they don't make the time, they continue running. All make the intervals except for one girl. She's a bigger girl and tries repeatedly, but just isn't in very good condition.

She begins to cry. She collapses, but the coaches tell her to get up and keep running. Finally, she's the only one left. I'm expecting the coaches to have mercy on her, to give her more time or just allow that she's done enough, but they calmly watch her, stick to their guns, and send her again and again.

Finally, with teammates encouraging her, she makes the time. Things in Throckmorton may look laid-back, but expectations and responsibilities *will* be met. These are tough people who are taught early to pull their weight.

Thursday evening Reed invites me to dinner with his family in Albany. It's "all you can eat" shrimp night at the Beehive, a well-known restaurant that draws people from surrounding towns. Reed tells me about his work schedule, and I realize how family-friendly life is in places like Throckmorton. Every teacher and school employee here works with their own children every day, not just during their high school years but from kindergarten through graduation. This is an opportunity I never had in Reno with my daughter. Even if she had gone to my high school, it's unlikely she would have been in my weights classes.

Reed and his wife were both at Rule when the superintendent set up a playpen in the corner of the gym and watched their young kids so the Reeds could coach. This type of arrangement is common in small towns.

At 3:00 on game day, the pep rally in the gym is forty-five minutes long. The band performance is fun. Among the thirty members are two cheerleaders and five football players. There's no limit on what the kids are involved with. The football players perform a little skit. A mascot in a Greyhound costume hypes up the crowd, and all the little girls help the cheerleaders lead cheers. The crowd may be modest, but most of the 800-odd residents of Throckmorton will be at the game tonight, and many locals have come to the rally, as well.

After the rally, the kids are off until 5:00 and the coaches head home for a little rest. The maintenance crew puts the finishing touches on the field; a huge purple "T" is painted at midfield. Purple flags are lashed to the back of the home stands; a table for selling old yearbooks is set up, as well as another for a fund-raising raffle, offering five-dollar tickets to win a Remington shotgun.

About 5:30, the ten varsity Greyhounds, dressed in shorts and neon green shirts with their names and numbers, stretch in the corner of the end zone. It's strange to realize that this tiny group is the entire squad. As the players warm up, coaches play a game of punt, pass, and kick. Starting from the goal line, the purpose of this game is to get the ball as close to the far goal line with a punt, a pass, and a kick without letting the ball cross into the end zone. Some Abilene High coaches played that same game the week before, but this is the first I've seen it on game day.

Probably because so many six-man games end at the half, the homecoming festivities at Throckmorton take place before kickoff. For pregame entertainment, a biplane does tricks above the field. In the locker room under the gym, players not involved with the festivities sit in front of their purple lockers. A large "T" is imprinted into the purple matting on the floor. The kids are taped and ready to go, pink tape spatting on the shoes for breast cancer awareness month. A few kids and coaches sit in the visiting stands, watching the king and queen competitions and debating which boy and girl would win. Four of the five king candidates are players, but the fifth, an exchange student from Germany, wins the crown. The players and coaches are so casual, it feels more like the preparation for baseball than any football game I've ever seen.

Bryson has brought twelve players, including a few who look like offensive linemen—not an advantage when playing defense. The Cowboys didn't bring many fans. I'm told that Throckmorton often outnumbers the home team's crowd on the road. Greyhound Stadium has a capacity of 2,000, and the home stands are full. With fewer than 1,000 people, there can't be too many Throckmortonians elsewhere tonight.

Bryson's game plan is clear. The Cowboys use their big linemen to pound the ball and slow down the game. The strategy works well early. After the opening kickoff, the Cowboys run nearly five minutes off the clock and take an 8-0 lead. The Greyhound answer is immediate. They score on a 50-yard run by Rawlin Morrell to tie the score on their first offensive play. Bryson has another long drive, taking a lead with just 1:36 left in the first. T'Rock scores two plays later, making it 16-14. During the first quarter the Greyhounds run exactly three offensive plays.

During the second quarter, however, the Greyhounds figure out Bryson's run game and begin getting stops. The Cowboy offense is one-dimensional. Once T'Rock takes away the inside run, Bryson has no answer. The Greyhound offense, however, is varied. T'Rock has multiple plays and formations, and they score almost at will.

Throckmorton gets into the end zone three times on six plays to take a 38-16 lead. Bryson answers with a trap play for a touchdown to make it 38-22, but quickly the Greyhounds score three more TDs, putting the game within one score of the mercy rule with 33 seconds remaining in the half. The score is 60-22. Throckmorton has scored nine touchdowns on only fifteen offensive plays. A penalty on the last play of the half prevents another score, which would have ended the game before the intermission.

Bryson is frustrated and starts to show it, taking a few cheap shots after the whistle. The halftime discussion has nothing to do with football, but consists of Reed reminding his kids to protect themselves, keep their eyes open, and not do anything stupid in retaliation.

"Don't egg someone on when you're dealing with a ticking time bomb," Reed tells his squad as the coaches relax and drink Dr Peppers.

If Throckmorton scores first in the second half the game will end, but for the first time tonight, a Greyhound drive stalls. The Cowboys prolong the game with a TD, closing the score to 60-29 late in the third. A long run by Morrell, a turnover, and another score during the first minute of the fourth quarter and it's official: at 74-29, the mercy rule goes into effect. Game over.

Six-man is an interesting sport, but its lack of drama is disappointing. Scoring is so fast and weaknesses are so easy to exploit that the better team usually dominates. Very few six-man games are competitive throughout.

After the game, the marching band holds another performance. Most of Throckmorton has remained to support their band as they support their team. I wish I could stay and see Saturday's homecoming parade, but my schedule doesn't allow it.

I've enjoyed my week in Throckmorton. Except for people who live in places like this, few ever have a reason to do more than stop for gas or a meal in a "one stoplight" town. That makes it easy to attach all sorts of stereotypes to these places and the people who live in them.

I saw no bored kids who want nothing more than to escape small-town close-mindedness and move to the big city. Nor did I see ignorant, backward rednecks who say things like, "You don't belong here," to outsiders. Everyone was nice, loved their town, and was proud to show it to a visitor. I have to get on the road, though. I'm driving to Lubbock, another long, late-night drive. I thank everyone and hit the dark two-lane highway west.

Throckmorton opens the playoffs with a win over Rotan. I speak to Reed the following week and he tells me the second-round game against undefeated Water Valley will be the best of the playoffs. The Wildcats have played four full quarters only twice, winning eight times by the mercy rule. After watching Aledo that afternoon in Fort Worth, I drive to Early, Texas, hoping to see the second half. I make it just before the second half begins, but the game is nearly over. As good as Water Valley is, the Wildcats can't stand up to the Greyhounds. At the half the score is 46-8. The Greyhounds end the game, 62-16, in the third.

Throckmorton follows this unexpected blowout with wins over Rankin and Valley to give them a shot at a second straight title. This is the fifth championship appearance for Reed (two at Rule and three with the Greyhounds), and it's the fourth title game for Throckmorton since 2005.

The six-man championship games are the only two not played at Cowboys Stadium in 2012. Shotwell Stadium in Abilene is more centrally located for most six-man schools. Throckmorton is playing the Abbott Panthers for the six-man D-1 title. Once again, I can make it for the second half after driving from a 5A semifinal that afternoon in Waco.

Again, I arrive just as the first half ends, and Throckmorton leads, 40-24. It's a chilly night, but there's a crowd of maybe 5,000. Looking around, I see as much gear from other six-man schools as for Throckmorton or Abbott. State championships in Abilene are a gathering spot for the whole six-man community.

During the third quarter, the Greyhounds put the game away, scoring three straight touchdowns. A 69-yard run by Taylor is followed by a 49-yard pass from Oliver to Trinity Haggard, then a pass from Taylor to Hayden Farquhar to go up 64-30. After Throckmorton scores early in the fourth to come within 2 points of ending it, Abbott stalls, using timeouts as the 24-second clock is about to expire. They can't win, but at least Abbott saves some dignity by avoiding the mercy rule. The final score is 72-30 Greyhounds, a second straight state championship for Throckmorton.

Maybe it has to do with winning a second straight title in an anticlimactic way, but I don't see the jubilation I'd see the following week with Stamford's championship. There's hugging and handshakes, but it looks more like relief in doing what they were supposed to than anything else. All season they'd been the favorite to repeat, and this championship is a validation. In football, teams often get what they deserve, and the Throckmorton Greyhounds have earned their place as an elite program in the six-man football world, not only winning, but also doing it the right way, with hard work and humility.

8

KISS A FAT DOG

Week Eight: Idalou Wildcats

My last West Texas stop is Idalou, a bedroom community ten miles north of Lubbock. West Texas is so big that it's subdivided into smaller regions. I've just come from The Big Country, as the area around Abilene is known. West Texas also includes the "Permian Basin" (Odessa and Midland), "Far West Texas" (El Paso), the Panhandle, and something called "Texhoma," though *that* might be more properly placed in North Texas (boundary lines between regions can be somewhat fuzzy and are often disputed by locals). The area around Lubbock is known as the "South Plains" and it's mostly farming land. Hundreds of giant windmills stand above the horizon, capturing wind from the "northers" the area is known for.

This week, I arrive at the corrugated building behind the scoreboard that serves as the Wildcats' fieldhouse at 8:00. It's the same basic Saturday routine I've seen at every eleven-man program, but here I find some notable differences.

In many ways Idalou football is unapologetically a throwback. Head coach Don Long has been here twenty-two years, and most of his eight coaches are veterans, as well. The Wildcats are coming off a 35-7 win over District 3-2A opponent Brownfield. They've had a good first half of their season, going 4-2, with their two losses against good Class 3A opponents.

How this staff watches film is the first time machine moment for me. Idalou coaches sit in a dark office, watching the Brownfield film projected on a pulled-down screen. Coaches have watched film like this since forever, but these days, most staffs split into smaller groups or individually watch relevant parts of the film on laptops or iPads. Not at Idalou. This is a small, tight staff and they see no reason to improve on a method of scouting that has served so many so well for so long.

The next notable thing happens after the players arrive at 10:00. It's typical for players to go through a quick workout after a game. I've seen some intense workouts, but I'm not sure any matched the weight session at Idalou.

Assistant coach Jeff Lofton leads the players though the circuit while four other coaches with clipboards monitor the action. Today's circuit consists of hang cleans, hex bar deadlifts, bench press, and parallel squats intermixed with various core exercises. The kids literally run after each set as though they're getting paid by the rep. In five minutes they're drenched in sweat and panting, but continue to move at this feverish pace for another fifteen minutes.

This is a 2A program and the players aren't especially big, but they're very strong. Long brags on what a good job Lofton, a 1997 Idalou grad, does in the weight room.

These kids have been building to this intensity for many years. Coach Lofton starts with these boys in sixth grade, where he teaches weight room expectations and lifting technique in pre-athletics for future Wildcats. In middle school athletic period, he continues building this foundation. By the time the kids are in high school, this pace and tempo is the only way they know how to lift. It's an impressive workout to watch.

Afterward, the players head into the locker room to watch last night's film. This is done old-school style, as well; the whole team watches together. Assistant coaches are spread around the room, quietly teaching their kids while Long runs the tape back and forth.

A disadvantage of watching film together is that it takes longer, with everybody waiting while each position is critiqued. The Wildcats played well the previous night. Their I formation ground attack ran over Brownfield's defense and the offensive line looked dominant. Film continues until about noon before the coaches give out helmet award stickers for last night's game and send the players home. Long tells his assistants to get lunch and be ready to go to work on Denver City at 1:00.

Long is a funny guy. He likes to joke and find things to laugh about. While watching Denver City film, he keeps up a running commentary, both on important things relating to the game and on little things he finds. They begin watching a Denver City assistant on the sideline who's related by marriage to Lofton. Lofton's in-law is demonstrative, often throwing his hat when something goes against the Mustangs. Long and his staff good-naturedly laugh about the display. Lofton says the clips will be part of the family's Thanksgiving entertainment.

Denver City should be a good test for the Wildcats. With a record of 4-2, the Mustangs are probably the Wildcats' biggest challenger for a district title this season. The coaches expect a good game from Denver City, something they haven't had lately. Film and scouting report creation continues until 6:00. But by now, I've decided there's only so much time I can spend watching coaches watch film. I take off around 2:00, in time to get to the Texas Tech-West Virginia game back in Lubbock.

I'm staying in the "Hub City," Lubbock's nickname marking it as the largest city in West Texas and hub of the region. Every local highway converges on Lubbock like spokes on a wheel. There isn't a hotel in Idalou, or many businesses at all, just a Dixie Dog, a Sonic Drive-In, and several other fast-food chains. A few convenience stores line State Highway 82, but that's it. The town consists of nice suburban ranch houses with Texas stars hanging above the garages. A nearly deserted downtown main street is located near a water tower with "State Champions" painted on the side. Cotton fields surround the town.

Idalou is the textbook definition of a bedroom community. At one time, farming was a huge part of the economy. Today, maybe half the residents have been drawn here for the school system and its proximity to Lubbock.

The dividing line of big- and small-school Texas football is between 3A and 2A. 3As and above are only differentiated by the number of quality programs in their level. In 2A and smaller, however, the game is different. Fewer coaches do more, players play both sides of the ball, and huge percentages of students participate. Idalou High has about 300 students, and like Throckmorton and Stamford, the elementary school and middle schools are very close. Also as with other small schools, each high school coach has responsibilities with younger kids. Idalou has five football teams (seventh grade, eighth grade, freshman, JV, and varsity), and the eight high school coaches have responsibilities with every lower team.

When I show up late Monday morning, middle school and freshman athletic periods are in session. Idalou has a good freshman turnout. Thirty-two freshmen play football and work alongside the middle school kids during athletics. The JV has thirty-four players and the varsity thirty-seven, adding up to a grand total of 103 high school players. Not bad for a school with only 300 students.

After freshman athletic period, the varsity and JV are up. Long, acting as offensive coordinator, and defensive coordinator Mark Turner meet with the varsity inside, going over the scouting reports while the JV performs the same lifting workout the varsity did Saturday. The rest of the staff helps Lofton supervise the workout.

The scouting reports are simple; the Wildcat approach to both offense and defense is straightforward: line up correctly and win with better skills and strength. There is only one defensive automatic, a coverage based on the back-set of the Mustangs.

After the meeting, the varsity players head out for an offensive field chalk followed by special teams and offensive individuals. The varsity wears green practice jerseys and helmets; the JV has white helmets and jerseys. When the entire program is outside, the freshmen can be recognized by their white helmets and green tops. Athletic period ends at 12:45, and everyone returns to the school building for afternoon classes.

The varsity wears shells after school while both the JV and freshman teams are in full pads. The program has great numbers, but the school has a small coaching staff. Very few, if any, 2A programs have the personnel to platoon. The coaches and players all have both defensive and offensive responsibilities.

After a quick stretch, everyone breaks into seven defensive position groups, five by varsity position and separate JV and freshman groups. The groupings change at 4:05, and the varsity defense combines and works against two offenses running D-City plays, a varsity scout unit and the first JV offense.

Across the field, the second JV offense runs live plays against the freshman defense. The contact in practice is inversely correlated to experience. Varsity contact is rare, but the JV backups and freshmen hit quite a bit, learning how to use their pads.

After defense, the three teams switch to offense, first individuals then team, and two varsity huddles run plays back to back. Long stands between the two huddles so he can oversee both units.

The Wildcats offensive scheme is part of the old-school vibe of this program. No spread offense here. Idalou relies heavily on the power running that's carried them to thirteen consecutive playoff appearances and a state championship in 2010. The I with two tight ends is their base formation. The philosophy is time-tested: create push up front and pound the ball with the running game to set up the occasional pass.

Twenty years ago, almost all coaches subscribed to a version of the "run to set up the pass" philosophy; today it's become somewhat rare in Texas. Not that old ways don't work anymore. With the right personnel and coaching, "smash-mouth" football is as effective as it was in the 1950s, but it requires a smart and strong offensive line able to create movement even against defenses specifically aligned to stop the run. With their commitment to the weight room and a big group of kids, Idalou makes it work.

On Tuesday, I arrive at 10:40, and Long is meeting with two student-teachers helping out this semester. Long explains to them the importance of connections in finding full-time jobs. With the dual-contract teacher/coach system in Texas, the HC/AD usually hires all dual positions. Between twenty and fifty applicants may fight for openings. The system guarantees high-quality coaching. With so many people looking for work, connections become important; a call from Long will go further than just sending in an application.

One misperception of the Texas system is that head coaches spend all their time coaching, but AD is an administrative position, with many responsibilities having nothing to do with football. Long comes in most mornings at 7:30 for his AD duties. After practice he usually gets home around 7:30.

This is only Long's second season as the Wildcat head coach. For twenty-two years from 1989 through the championship season of 2010, Johnny Taylor was at the helm. When Taylor retired, Long, his defensive coordinator of twenty-one years, was hired. Long is from Muleshoe, near the New Mexico border. After attending college at Texas Tech, he got his first coaching job in Hereford in 1979, stayed there until 1986, and then spent four years at Odessa High.

He tells me about his decision to return to a smaller town. His social studies class at Odessa watched a video about drug violence. He recognized footage down the street from his daughter's school and his eyes opened to the dangers of raising kids in a city like Odessa. Like many who've returned to small towns, he found the big city a poor place to raise a family.

There are big-city coaches and small-town ones. In a nomadic profession, more often than not, coaches return to places like their hometown. It's no coincidence the small-town coaches in this book—Scott Surratt at Carthage, Wayne Hutchinson at Stamford, Mike Reed at Throckmorton, and Don Long at Idalou—all grew up near where they landed. So did many of their assistants. Education is among the few professions employing and recruiting large numbers to the towns. It isn't surprising so many small-town natives seek jobs in these places. For those who go off to college (a huge percentage), there are few other jobs that bring them home.

Taylor was head coach from 1989 through the 2010 season. He decided 2010 would be his last season. After a 1-3 start, it looked like he might have picked a bad year to go, but the Wildcats ran off eleven straight victories to win their first state championship in his final game. Taylor is still a fixture around the fieldhouse; he hosts a bible study for the coaches every Wednesday evening and is on the school board.

Today, the offensive focus is the passing game. Quarterbacks and defensive backs coach Russ Reagan is the father of quarterback Seth Reagan. Coach Reagan is fun to talk with; he's forever telling stories about places he's been, restaurants to visit, the state of the nation, Texas, education, and anything else that comes up. He's been on the Idalou staff for twenty-six years. His older son, Shae, was the quarterback in 2003, before going on to TCU. Shae is widely regarded as the best player in Idalou history.

Idalou runs a 4-3 defense, with the front seven reading line keys. Long brought this defense with him from Odessa, and it serves him well. The practice schedule is much like yesterday: offensive indy, offensive team, defensive indy, and defensive team, with a kicking circuit where linemen shag field goals in the parking lot. The only real difference happens during offensive team; it's passing instead of running.

In West Texas, I've hardly heard a cuss word stronger than the "Gosh Almighties" and "Goo-oolllies" that are standard expletives hereabouts. It's rare to hear players using bad language, even when coaches aren't around, something that isn't true elsewhere in Texas. While traditional bad words never come out of his mouth, Long says some colorful and creative things. Today, when a receiver runs the wrong route, the incensed Long yells, "Kiss a fat dog!!!"

When Taylor accepted the job in 1988, he inherited Coach Reagan. Long and Turner, the offensive and defensive line coach, came over two years later in 1990. Five of the eight coaches have been in

Idalou over ten years, and Coach Lofton, while younger than most on the staff, has deep Wildcat roots, playing for and graduating from Idalou in 1997. He returned to coach in 2009.

When Taylor retired in 2010, the program stayed on path. By promoting from within and hiring then-defensive coordinator Long, the program avoided the upheaval a new coach often causes by bringing in new schemes and people. Such stability is rare in this state, where assistant coaches often move every few years, climbing up the ladder.

This stability is a big reason for Idalou's success. This was the winningest class 2A program in Texas during the 2000s. A coaching staff is a team. This one is more efficient than most after so many years together. Each coach knows his role and how what he teaches fits into the big picture.

As much as I like the Texas model of athletics and coaching professionalism, the transitory nature of the job is something I struggle with. The coaches gain tremendous experience, learning different things at each stop, and have added motivation to put their best foot forward or risk losing their jobs. Coaches with five years' experience here are further along than five-year coaches elsewhere. The Texas system guarantees assistants won't shirk on coaching responsibilities, as those duties are as important to their continued employment as their teaching. The need to win is a purifying factor. Hires are made with that bottom line in mind. It's a two-way relationship; the assistants truly are employed by the head coach, and everyone is in the same boat. If the head coach doesn't win and is fired, the staff is in danger of losing their jobs, as well.

The downside is that without stability in assistant positions, coaches rarely develop relationships with their players. Professionalism can create a mercenary atmosphere, where certain jobs are openly known as stepping stones for better positions. There's very little loyalty from coaches when building a resume. The head coach is often in a tough spot. The need to win makes school boards impatient for results, and sometimes coaches are fired too quickly. It's nice to see a school like Idalou, where so many coaches have been together for years.

I love the football I've seen in Texas. The preparation, coaching, and execution are everything I'd hoped to find. However, I've purposely chosen these programs because they're exemplary. Is it a cheat to stack the deck this way and use the results to validate my original opinion? I'm not sure. I worry that eleven different programs would paint a different, less attractive picture. Can the quality I've seen in these programs justify the system as a whole? I *think* so, but the question bothers me.

Wednesday, during freshman-junior high athletic period, one coach talks about the upcoming presidential election, telling a younger coach who to vote for. The young coach clearly doesn't want to talk politics. This points out how rarely I heard political talk in Texas.

I was often asked about being in Texas during the presidential election. After Barack Obama won, there was well-publicized talk about Texas' secession, and people outside the state wondered about the atmosphere. Honestly, I rarely heard political talk at all. Politics are divisive, and it can be dangerous to inject it into discussions when a team is trying to focus. Arguing about politics can only get in the way.

A second thing worth noting is that like everything else in Texas, the politics are not simple. The politics are as diverse as the population; some parts of the state are "red" while others are very "blue." The week of the election I was in Cedar Hill, a majority black exurb of Dallas. Driving through neighborhoods, it was hard to find a Mitt Romney sign. The same was true during my previous week in the Rio Grande Valley (the Valley voted heavily for Obama).

After athletics, Long sits in the locker room as the players change for their afternoon classes. Either he or Turner do this before and after every practice. There is a liability issue addressed by having a coach supervising, but more importantly, Long sees it as an opportunity to get to know his players.

"I might have had to yell at a player on the field," he tells me. "I use this time to talk to him in a friendly way before he goes home."

During the afternoon I meet with Janet Thornton, Idalou's principal. She and her counselors go to the middle school during the spring and try to find a niche for each incoming eighth-grader. The policy of involvement has been successful—she estimates that 80 to 90 percent of Idalou students participate in something. The one hundred members of the football program and the eighty in the band make up more than half the student body by themselves. Besides football, Idalou has excelled at other activities. The boys' basketball team won a state championship in 2010, making this the only 2A school to win state in football and basketball during the same year. Girls' sports, the band, UIL academics, and the FFA are all successful, as well.

Football PR starts even before middle school. Elementary kids are made a part of things. Each Friday during the season junior players go to the elementary school and meet the kids for the "Wildcat Growl." Thornton tells me that when her boy played, the growl was his favorite part of the week. Just as important as getting players involved with younger kids is getting future Wildcats excited about the program. Traditions like this eventually pay huge dividends.

Thornton sees nothing but positives coming out of the program.

"Coach Long is interested in turning out fine young men," she says.

She tells me the staff takes it personally when kids aren't successful after leaving the program. Several players echo her opinion. Senior offensive and defensive lineman Chandler Shields tells me, "Coach Long does focus on life skills. We've learned a lot of great tools that will help us a lot in the next step of our lives." Another senior, running back and linebacker Tylo Kirkpatrick, agrees. "It's not just about being a leader on the football field, it's for when we get out of here, as well."

Wednesday starts with weights again. It's another quick but intense workout. The focus is on the upper body, so as not to tire their legs this late in the week. Outside, the varsity focuses on the defensive side of the ball. Two offensive huddles run against the starting defense. Coach Reagan plays scout quarterback for the JV group. By the end of practice, most of the prep work is done. Now, it's just about fine tuning.

On Thursday during athletic period, the varsity is on the field doing the "play the game" drill that most schools do. The JV and freshman teams are headed to Denver City today, while the seventh- and eighth-grade teams play in Idalou.

Seventh- and eighth-grade football are very different. For many seventh-graders, this is their first season in pads, and it shows. The blocking is mostly belly-bumping, and tackling usually consists of jumping on the ballcarrier's back or swinging him around by the jersey. The seventh-grade Wildcats lose, 28-0. The game goes quickly with only 6-minute quarters.

The eighth-graders win big and look much more polished. The tentative play is gone; the kids move with greater purpose and have some technique. One year makes a difference. Over in Denver City, the freshman team ties and the JV loses a close game.

This evening the moms decorate the varsity locker room. Green and gold streamers and banners drape the ceiling. Bags of candy and cupcakes are placed in lockers for the players to snack on throughout the day. Halloween is still two weeks away, but you would be forgiven to think it had come early.

Middle school and freshman athletic periods lift with Lofton Friday morning, a postgame workout. During varsity athletic period, juniors put on game jerseys and head to the elementary school to fire up the young kids with the Wildcat Growl. Seniors wear grey game-day polo shirts with green helmets and numbers on their chests. They join Long in the locker room for their weekly leadership meeting.

This is the first season of leadership lessons. Long felt that this group needed something extra. He found a packet used by a school in the Metroplex. It's full of lessons on topics ranging from work ethic to trust to competitiveness to passion.

Long often googles a topic and looks for YouTube clips of coaches and other notable people. Today's topic is pride.

"The players get sick of me talking to them all the time and might follow better when it comes from someone else," he tells me.

For the lesson on pride, Long starts a conversation about the dangers of taking too much pride in accomplishments. The talk speaks to the tendency of becoming complacent if one allows pride to keep him from reaching greater goals.

There's a short pep rally at the end of the day, after which the coaches and players head out to take their naps before getting back to the fieldhouse around 6:00. I check out of my motel in Lubbock and spend a few hours relaxing in the coaches' office. I have a long drive after the game, heading down to Austin, and use the downtime to get a little rest.

I don't know if it's a byproduct of such an experienced staff, but the atmosphere is remarkably relaxed before the game. Although Long seems just as cool as everyone else, he is superstitious. After his pregame speech, Taylor always comes into the office and accompanies Long as he locks up; they walk out together as they've done for years, always the last two to leave the fieldhouse. I'm told no bus for road trips may have more than twenty-nine players on it, and whatever color pants they're wearing are scrapped for the rest of the season after a loss. Fortunately, the Wildcats haven't lost more than four games in a season since 1999, as I've never seen a team with more than that many sets of game pants.

Reddell Field in Idalou is modest, with only 1,200 seats and a small press box. The game is the big thing in town, as in every small town in West Texas, but with only 2,000 residents in Idalou, the small stadium is all they need.

Tonight the home side is three-quarters full. The red-and-silver Denver City Mustangs have brought a good crowd, as well. Many Wildcat supporters set up lawn chairs behind the end zone and along the sidelines on either end of the bleachers. There is really no crowd control at all; young kids wander among the cheerleaders, heading in and out of the stands. Thornton worries little kids will be kicked by cheerleaders, but so far all have been safe.

The Wildcats start slowly, falling behind 7-0 in the first quarter on a 29-yard touchdown pass from Clancy David. The rest of the half belongs to Idalou. They tie the game with 4 minutes to go in the first on a 13-yard run by quarterback Seth Reagan. An interception leads to another Wildcat score a few minutes later, giving Idalou a 14-7 lead. During the second quarter another run by Reagan and a screen pass make the score 28-7 at the half.

After the break, the Mustangs pass for a touchdown to close the score to 28-14, but Idalou effectively puts the game away with on a 58-yard run by Travys Bravo, giving the Wildcats a 35-14 lead. Backups finish the game. The final score is 35-20 in a game that really isn't that close. Idalou is just too strong up front for the Mustangs and dominates the line of scrimmage. The Wildcats are in good position to make their thirteenth straight run to the playoffs.

After each game in Texas it's a tradition for the teams to face their stands and acknowledge the playing of their school's alma mater. As the band plays, the players, supporters, and coaches all make little hand signals, usually holding one or two fingers up and waving them to the music.

If the word "patriotism" can be applied to a person's connection with high school, it describes the ceremony I see each week. In small towns like Idalou, the alma mater is especially important—it represents both the school and the community. The music is solemn and reverent. Players and coaches face the stands making hand signals, along with spectators. Oftentimes, the opposing team stands respectfully as the song plays. Texans might be surprised to know this isn't a common practice outside their state.

Following the song, Idalou holds an additional ceremony. After wins, the players run a flag emblazoned with a green "I" up a special flagpole in front of the fieldhouse. As the school fight song (not the alma mater) is played, the "victory flag" is raised and players shake the pole in time to the music. No one knows when this tradition began. It's been going on as long as anyone has been here.

The coaches celebrate with their families after the game. The wives have brought dinner and everyone eats at folding chairs in the weight room after the players are hustled out. I stay and thank everyone before hitting the road. I've enjoyed my time in West Texas. I leave hoping I'll get a chance to see these guys again during the playoffs.

The Idalou Wildcats sweep the rest of their schedule, winning the District 2-2A championship with a 5-0 record. Unfortunately, I never make it back again to see Idalou. The Wildcats are surprised in their first playoff game, falling to the Bangs Dragons, 23-6.

An even bigger surprise comes in January when, after twenty-three years at Idalou High School, Long resigns as head coach to take the defensive coordinator position at the high school in Andrews. It was a tough decision.

"Sometimes God just opens doors for you and you don't know why they're open," Long said. "But we just felt like this was the place we're supposed to be. That's kind of it."

He gives his staff the credit for the program's success over the years.

"The staff here is so good and so good to work with and all," he said. "The staff, the administration, the kids made this a tough place to leave. But we're looking forward to the move . . . hopefully we'll be able to do good things."

Idalou stays in-house and hires Lofton to replace Long, choosing him over seventy-four other applicants. Superintendent Jim Waller acknowledges Lofton's experience at Idalou as an alum and assistant coach is a factor in his hiring.

"When looking at all the applications, what it boils down to is that," Waller said. "You'd be taking a chance on someone just going on references. But he was here and we got to see his work ethic and his values and the way he handles kids and motivates kids. That put him over the top."

Moreover, Lofton keeps the continuity of staff, an important factor at a school that's been so successful with the same core group of coaches. The first indication that this is a good hire is that, except for Long and one other coach, the staff plans to return in 2013. As the saying goes, "If it ain't broke, don't fix it." Who better than an Idalou native and alum to continue the tradition? Under the leadership of Coach Lofton, the success of Idalou football will continue.

9

THE OTHER SIDE OF THE COIN

Week Nine: Stony Point Tigers

"I am only one . . . But still I am one . . . I cannot do everything . . . But still I can do something . . . And what I can do, I ought to do (by the grace of God) I will do."

—Motto on the door of the Stony Point coaches' office.

Craig Chessher is "an old Texas ball coach," I'm told. It's said as a compliment, but also to describe a throwback from an earlier era.

Some practices are better left in the past. Old-school coaches often didn't allow water breaks, believing dehydration built toughness. Creative but illegal recruiting methods such as paying high school players and having boosters buy families' homes to attract blue-chip players were common during much of the twentieth century. Coaches ignoring kids' injuries and other old-school abuses are mostly long—and well—gone.

"Old Texas ball coach" puts one in notable company, though. From Gordon Wood and Chuck Moser to Bum Phillips, the roster of legendary high school coaches from Texas is impressive.

Texas high school football has been played and documented for more than one hundred years. The traditions that made the sport great aren't modern inventions. Many are rooted deep in the past.

Just as there are many ways to move the ball, there are many different approaches to coaching. Some head coaches are hands on, putting themselves into every aspect of the game, planning, coaching a position, and running drills during practice. Others focus on one side of the ball. Some are disciplinarians, and others are CEOs. During my time here, I've seen many approaches. With Chessher, I would see a method and style with a long tradition in Texas.

Round Rock is in the fastest-growing part of the state. The town has blown up over the past twenty years as part of Austin's metro boom. The I-35 strip between DFW and San Antonio is increasingly the center of Texas' population. This comes as no surprise to anyone on the freeways around suburban Austin.

There are good reasons for the traffic and growth, though. The area surrounding Austin is a desirable place to live. Austin itself is an exciting town, with the university, good job opportunities, and great nightlife. It's also the gateway to the Hill Country, the most beautiful part of Texas, with nice little towns, rolling hills, and inviting rivers.

In north Round Rock, amid suburban subdivisions, Stony Point High School isn't especially remarkable. The campus is nice but nondescript. The athletic facilities are functional but not extravagant. Round Rock ISD has five high schools. At one time it was a one-school district, but it is growing rapidly. It's generally accepted that the fewer schools an ISD has to support, the stronger that support is.

The Stony Point Tigers rolled between 2007 and 2010, making the playoffs four straight years and advancing to the final four in Class 5A three consecutive times. However, with so much growth in Round Rock, demographics, zoning, and enrollments are volatile. It's a common pattern in booming parts of Texas. Schools open as 3A programs and are quickly bumped to 5A as new housing explodes. Zoning lines move and the cycle repeats.

Whether the adjustments help or hurt a particular school is unpredictable. When Stony Point opened in 2000, it threw a monkey wrench into a three-high school ISD. Nine years later, Cedar Ridge High School opened and Stony Point had the wrench thrown back at it. Cedar Ridge is just a few miles away, and boundaries for Stony Point were redrawn.

Stony Point's enrollment dropped from 3,550 to 2,277 in one year, and the school lost many of its more affluent families to the newer school. The enrollment drop hit football hard. After advancing to the state semifinals in 2010, the Tigers were 4-6 in 2011. This season has been frustrating. The Tigers are 3-4, but lost games by 1, 1, 2, and 10 points. They could easily be 6-1 instead of fighting for a playoff spot. They've spent this season on the cusp of success; one play here or there is all that stands between the Tigers and a winning record.

With a 366-mile drive from Idalou to Round Rock, I decided not to torture myself by rushing to Central Texas for Saturday morning meetings. After sleeping in Brownwood, I arrive at Stony Point early in the afternoon after most have left. The Tigers suffered their worst loss of the season in their last game, falling to Cedar Ridge, 40-30.

The Stony Point staff usually puts together scouting reports on Sundays from 8:00 to 5:00, but they're coming off a bye week. The extra time lets them spread out their work. It also gives me time to relax. Saturday evening I go to the University of Texas game against Baylor University, buying a ticket from a scalper to sit in the top tier of Darrell K Royal-Texas Memorial Stadium, seemingly a mile above the playing field. After a Sunday of watching the NFL in my motel room, I get to Stony Point before the sun comes up Monday for the first meeting of the week.

The Tigers meet three times daily during game weeks (twice a day during the off-season). The first time is before school, for film and scouting reports. At 7:20, players file into a classroom for their first information about this week's opponent, the Round Rock Westwood Warriors.

Special teams coordinator Todd Schonhar has the floor and excitedly talks through each Westwood special teams unit while standing in front of a whiteboard showing diagrams of each one. Schonhar looks as though he's spent the weekend champing at the bit for this presentation. He's enthusiastic and demonstrative, giving the impression that kickoff coverage or punt returns will be the difference between winning and losing. After his talk, the classroom's dividing curtain is shut, separating offense and defense. In half the room, offensive coordinator Mark Mullins shows film and talks coverage with the skill players. Offensive line coach Jonathan Luke takes his group into a separate room to look at Warrior fronts. On the other side, defensive coordinator Scott Stewart shows film of Westwood's spread offense.

Alone among the teams I've visited, Stony Point doesn't use Hudl video editing, but rather CoachComm. I wasn't aware this system still existed, assuming it had been bought out along with most of Hudl's other competitors.

Chessher tells me he stayed with CoachComm due to stubbornness and brand loyalty. The coaches may not like it, but he'll keep it as long as it works. The meeting breaks at 8:25. The school week hasn't yet begun, but Tiger players already have the basics of the game plan.

After lunch, the kids return for athletic period. They use a block schedule at Stony Point, meaning each class is well over an hour long, providing time to do a lot during athletic period. Chessher talks to the team, setting the tone for the week. He tells them he's proud of the way they fight, despite the setbacks and tough losses. He reminds them that although they're 1-2 in district, they have an excellent chance to make the playoffs. Theirs is a seven-team district, and with the top four making the postseason, anything can still happen. With that, Chessher lets the coordinators talk briefly before they dress and take the field.

Outside I see further signs of the old-school nature of this program. The trend nationally has been to limit contact during practice. Not at Stony Point. Chessher still believes in daily contact during practice. His team dresses in full pads every day, and *uses* those pads every day. Contact isn't saved for game night. Not only do they hit daily, but the Tigers have at least ten minutes of "good on good" contact every day, pitting the starting offense against the starting defense. The contact is designed to make the Tigers tougher than teams who aren't as physical.

Chessher's role is the second notable thing about a Stony Point practice. Most large-school head coaches aren't responsible for any position, but he's the first I've seen who coaches from a golf cart.

Chessher tells me he'd once been much more hands on but developed this style over time. Several years ago, he suffered from untreated high blood pressure that caused bleeding inside his skull. The situation could have killed him had it gone on much longer. Ten hours of surgery left him with a steel plate in his head, but otherwise healthy. The stress Chessher put himself under was a contributing factor, and he had to make some changes.

The first decision was to give up the defensive coordinator job.

"When I gave up the DC job it drove me nuts," Chessher tells me. "I'd stand behind the coaches making corrections; the kids knew they had to listen to me and the coaches didn't want to step on my toes. I needed to back off and let the guys I hired do their jobs, so I decided to stand on the thirty-yard line and watch. That still didn't work, so I backed off to the fifty."

From there the cart was a logical progression. Before this year the team was spread over four practice fields. To oversee everything was a good hike. "The golf cart just made sense."

It would be a mistake, though, to think Chessher is not in charge. He misses little, and while the assistants have a lot of freedom, there's no question they're held accountable.

After practice, Chessher will often pull a coach over to discuss things he didn't like. He can be brutally direct.

"Why are you letting Billy get washed out like he did on the GT play, didn't you see that?!"

"Yes, sir," a defensive coach answers.

Chessher follows up, "If he does that during the game, we're screwed," making sure the young coach knows it's his job to keep this from happening.

The relationship between a head coach and his assistants is an aspect of the Texas game some coaching friends in Reno have trouble understanding. With volunteer coaches there isn't anything like this hierarchy. A Reno head coach must bargain with assistants and be careful not to hurt feelings or step on toes. Assistant coaches *choose* to help out most places. Head coaches who are too demanding or abrasive have trouble filling staffs, since there's little financial and no contractual incentive. Assistants have the power, and head coaches are at a disadvantage. If they let go of a weak assistant, there may not be anybody to replace him.

In Texas, the head coach is the boss. Coaching is not a hobby, but a full-time job. As with any job, the boss/employee relationship takes many forms. Assistants here are aware they're in the same boat as the head man. If the assistants buck the head coach and the team loses, the coach may be fired. If the HC goes, all jobs are in jeopardy, since incoming head coaches are often given power to replace assistants with their own people. The reverse is true, as well. If things go well, assistants can count on promotions or better positions at other schools. Quality assistants have opportunities to advance up the ladder, eventually leading to head jobs.

After athletic period, several coaches sit in the office talking about the new chain restaurant, Raising Cane's, which just opened nearby. Chessher had been there over the weekend and tells the other coaches it was good but too slow. This staff talks about various restaurants around town. Freddy's is recommended by one coach (nothing special), as are the Salt Lick Bar-B-Que (good) and Round Rock Donuts (very good). I go there every morning on my way to school.

During afternoon practice, senior starting running back Xavier Mays makes a cut on the artificial turf and blows out his ACL. The injury isn't caused by the extra contact that distinguishes a Stony Point practice. He simply cuts and his knee goes out from under him.

A few weeks ago, I saw an Abilene High team win even though they should probably have lost. Self-confidence leads to good fortune and success. This week I'm seeing the other side of that coin. The competition is so tough at the 5A level, the teams so well prepared with so many tools, that the line between the district champ and the cellar is often thin. During the last two seasons, the Tigers have been snakebit. It seems as though every break goes against them, and with each loss it gets harder to summon the belief that those breaks will balance out.

Convincing a team on a bad run that things will turn around is incredibly difficult, especially when every piece of evidence points the other way. It's unspoken, but the freak, season-ending injury to Mays fits the pattern in recent years. That it comes the same week that two other important players return from injuries just adds to the cursed feeling surrounding this team.

Around twenty JV players miss practice today. Chessher summons two assistants and angrily tells them these players must be dealt with, and that if they miss again, "I want them gone."

Instead of delegating parts of unpleasant jobs to groups of coaches, Chessher gives each assistant one task to take ownership of. He names one coach academic coordinator; another makes sure middle school programs are aligned to the high school. Another is in charge of fund-raising, and somebody is in charge of special teams. This way, Chessher will know who to go to if there's a problem and who should get the credit for a job done well.

The lack of recent success is unsettling for this staff. Stewart is the son and grandson of coaches who attempted to warn him away from the profession. It's a crazy business that puts your livelihood in the hands of eighteen-year-old boys. Stewart says he never regrets his decision to coach; he can't imagine sitting behind a desk.

As for job security at Stony Point, Chessher thinks his previous success has bought him time to get things turned around. But there are no guarantees. He's most concerned about his ability to attract good assistant coaches. As long as he can continue to bring them in, the Tigers have a chance to get back on track.

This past season Chessher replaced seven assistants, a little higher number than usual, but not unheard of. Working for an old-school coach like Chessher, who gives assistants a lot of autonomy, can be a good way for a young, ambitious coach to build his resume. The experience has paid off for many who got promotions after leaving Stony Point. The school treats its coaches well, giving them good schedules. Most assistants teach only two classes, leaving the entire afternoon to coach. Coordinators teach only one class. Chessher would like to have a more stable staff but knows hiring ambitious people makes losing them part of the deal.

"I don't hire coaches, I rent them," he tells me several times. One of last year's assistants who left for a coordinator position in Austin tells me that Chessher is "the best coach I've ever worked under. He expects a lot but lets everyone do their job."

It's a lonely position. Chessher has a sense of humor, and he likes to talk and joke with his staff in the office. Still, he keeps social interaction strictly on campus. He may need to fire coaches if they aren't doing their jobs. That might be too difficult it he allows himself to get close to the people working for him.

Tuesday morning before athletics, Chessher takes me by the Kelly Reeves Athletic Complex, or "the Palace," as it's more commonly known. The five Round Rock ISD high schools share the Palace as a home field. The 11,000-seat stadium is also headquarters to the ISD's athletic brass, with offices on the first floor of the press box. Chessher has applied for the open district athletic director position. He *does* want to coach, but wouldn't mind the stability of a bump upstairs. Chessher has time to get Stony Point winning again, but not unlimited time; he won't keep his job unless things turn around.

After a tour of the stadium we stop at one of Chessher's regular places, the Rio Grande Tex-Mex Restaurant, before heading back to school. Over lunch, he talks about his career. He grew up in Houston, and after graduating from Sam Houston State University, spent several years coaching in the area before returning to Sam Houston as a graduate assistant. He coached college football in Arkansas and North Carolina the next four years before deciding to return to high school.

Money was a factor in the move. After four years of small-college football, Chessher was making $28,500 a year. A friend who was making $42,500 as a high school assistant in Texas encouraged him to come home.

More important, though, was the difference between high school and college. "After going out on recruiting trips, I came back to my room and felt like I needed to take a shower," Chessher explains. He's a blunt talker who says what's on his mind even when it may not be the smartest thing to do. College coaching is about recruiting, and recruiting is about telling high school kids whatever will get them to sign. This didn't sit well with him.

This points out an important and often lost distinction. Whenever stories of corruption arise, "big-time" high school football is frequently lumped in with college and pro. Big money, big stadiums, high expectations, and coaches who must win to keep their jobs necessarily lead to abuses, right? Wrong. Most high school coaches in Texas are here precisely because they can coach at a high level *and* build character. Chessher and many coaches I met in Texas have had opportunities in the college game, but found their calling teaching and coaching in high school.

Chessher spent the next nine years as a defensive coordinator at various schools. He was at Galena Park North Shore for four seasons, from 2000–2003, a run that included a state championship with the Mustangs in 2003, before taking a head job. As a successful defensive coordinator at a good program, his problem wasn't finding a head job, but finding the right one. A coach taking a bad job where he can't win will probably be fired and never get another shot, so picking wisely is important.

Chessher turned down three jobs before accepting the Stony Point position. It wasn't an easy decision. Stony Point had been open a few years and never won, but between the pay and the chance to live in the Austin area, he took the offer in February of 2004.

Back at school the kids arrive for their athletic period meeting. Each player hands in the daily progress report he's required to bring from his teachers. The coaches check grades daily so any missed assignments or poor quiz scores can quickly be dealt with. With fifteen coaches assigned to the period, one can always tutor student-athletes who fall behind. Texas has a very stringent "no pass, no play" rule, so athletic period with professional coaches has a major impact on academics. Players need Cs or above in all classes, but by using athletic period to help monitor grades, most programs keep players eligible. All coaches are available all day, and the kids know they will be held accountable. This positively affects how Texas athletes perform in the classroom. Elsewhere, less on-staff help makes academic accountability much tougher to maintain.

In the defensive meeting, Stewart shows a YouTube video, motivational stuff from the University of Oregon. Afterward, he tells his players they have a great chance to win this week if they do their jobs. As he sends them out he tells me, "It can't hurt."

Outside, I watch Coach Luke drilling offensive linemen. The players hang small towels off the backs of their jerseys for defenders to try to snatch away. It's a fun game that trains linemen to keep separation when in pass protection. Chessher watches practice from his cart with the head trainer, Brooke Kneuper. "Coach K" has many roles beyond his training duties. He's a jack-of-all-trades, fixing equipment, working with kids, and keeping Chessher company during practices. Chessher raves about Coach K, telling me he works tremendous hours overseeing Stony Point's athletic programs.

Before after-school practices each day, the varsity meets in the weight room for a joke from one of the coaches. Today Coach Stewart tells one that probably wouldn't go over well in West or East Texas—funny, but kind of risqué. Central Texas and the big cities of Houston, DFW, and San Antonio have a different feel than the West and East. Much is familiar: everyone goes to church on Sundays, and Texas Pride is everywhere. At the same time, speaking patterns are less distinctively Texan, and casual profane language is tolerated. The I-35 corridor generally consists of big-city suburban centers. Anywhere more than twenty miles east, west, or south of this spine (excepting Houston and the Rio Grande Valley) is more rural and more culturally traditional.

After practice Chessher calls over defensive ends coach Vincent Hawkins to talk about one of his starters whose body language looks lazy. The kid also has technique problems, and Chessher is worried about his attitude. Hawkins explains that he doesn't have anyone else to play the position. Chessher finishes the discussion by telling Hawkins, "Do what you want with him, but if he plays and screws up, who do you think I'll be getting shitty with?"

The Harris Poll puts the Tigers as 14-point underdogs, but the coaches believe that this is a winnable game if their kids play four good quarters and limit mistakes. This isn't a team that can easily overcome mistakes, Chessher tells me. "We can win if we play very well. If we don't, we'll get our asses kicked."

When Chessher got to Stony Point, he took over a school that, in its short history, had never won. Part of the problem was that zoning boundaries between Stony Point and Round Rock High School weren't being enforced, allowing good athletes to attend the more successful school regardless of where they lived. With the help of community members, Chessher had that policy changed, and Stony Point started to get better athletes.

Success came quickly. Three straight years from 2008–2010, the Tigers advanced to the semifinal game. Chessher was given a lot of credit by the football media for the turnaround. He was named 5A Coach of the Year in 2008 by *Dave Campbell's Texas Football* magazine, and four times was Central Texas Coach of the Year.

Chessher doesn't talk about his accolades, though.

"There are no secrets to success," he tells me. "It's all about having good athletes, hiring good people, and working hard."

Too often, Chessher believes, coaches think winning is about their genius, when it's mostly about the chair they find themselves sitting in. Anyone could win at some places, while Vince Lombardi wouldn't get results at others, something Chessher knows well with the bottom dropping out at Stony Point after Cedar Ridge opened.

During his run, Chessher spoke at numerous coaching clinics. He tells me he always wanted to give a talk about "losing with dignity" but never had the guts to go through with it, instead opting for more traditional clinic topics like "running the Tiger 4-3." After all, who would pay money to attend a talk on losing? The reason coaches go to clinics in the first place is to lose *less*.

That does bring up a great point, though. For every winner there is a loser. Losing is exactly as big a part of any team sport as winning. Nobody likes to lose, but ignoring the possibility or thinking you can coach your way out of it is foolish. Winning isn't always possible, no matter how hard you work, how much you want it, how good your athletes are, or how well you coach. Winning comes from a combination of factors, many of which are out of anyone's control. Desire, quality coaching, work, and talent can only put a team in a better position to win. The rest is up to fate; football, like life itself, is not always fair.

As little as it's talked about, there *are* many lessons learned in failure. The measure of a coach, a student-athlete, and a man is how he deals with defeat, not success. Winning is the easiest thing in the world to do gracefully. Keeping composure and having the discipline and drive to come back after tough losses are life skills only learned through defeat. On this trip I saw many more happy locker rooms than unhappy ones, but I learned far more about a coaching staff and a program from watching them deal with defeat.

Wednesday, after my stop for a doughnut, I get to school for morning meetings. Today, the defense is in the weight room for their second of three lifting workouts this week, while the offense watches practice film by position groups. After twenty minutes, the defense goes to watch film, while the offense takes over the weight room. Again, the Tigers have accomplished a lot before the school day starts.

Chessher is interviewing a teacher today. One of his freshman coaches was hired this week as an assistant principal at Westwood High School. The young teacher Chessher is considering has been volunteering with the freshman team, hoping to get his foot in the door. As an "official" coach he'll have to find a second sport to work in the spring. Except for the head coach, almost all assistants in Texas are contracted to work a second sport, as well. Chessher is happy with the interview and says he's 90 percent sure he'll make the hire.

Athletic period and the after-school session follow the same patterns as the two previous days: meetings inside, followed by padded and physical practices outside. Stewart and Mullins watch their position coaches and units on either side of the practice field while Chessher sits with Coach K and watches everything from his cart.

After practice, there's more talk about restaurants, and Raising Cane's is brought up again. Coach Schonhar recommends a good bar and grill downtown where I can watch the first game of the World Series; surprisingly, my team, the Giants, has returned to the series and opens tonight against Detroit.

Thursday morning before school, the Tigers are finally in shells instead of full pads, but they are still on the field working special teams. Unlike the rest of the week, where the practice plans are organized by the offensive and defensive coordinators, this morning's session is run by Schonhar, the special teams coordinator.

I don't see Chessher today. He's at The Palace for a district AD meeting, and assistants run the show. After school, the offense wears T-shirts while the defense has on shoulder pads and works on form tackling before stripping off the pads for formation recognition. This is the final walk-through before tomorrow night's game—the last chance to make sure every piece of the plan is in place.

After school, coaches hang around waiting for the first JV game at 5:00. Some look at Pflugerville film in early preparation for next week. I spend some time talking to Schonhar. Like most coaches here, he's a high-energy guy full of enthusiasm. He's the designated "fire up the team" guy many programs rely on to get everyone going before pregame warm-ups. They may not be winning right now, but this staff loves their jobs. Schonhar has spent most of his career coaching college ball and may be there again eventually. Like many coaches with his experience, he tells me, "If I'm going to coach high school ball, it's going to be in Texas."

I head over to the JV field for the JV B game before leaving to watch game two of the World Series. The Giants end up winning the first two games of the series and go up, 2-0.

Athletic period on Friday is all talk. Convincing a 3-4 team that's lost its last two games that winning is possible is the biggest hurdle facing the Tigers. First Chessher talks, then a preacher from the Fellowship of Christian Athletes (FCA) speaks about doing the right thing, even when it isn't popular.

Chessher next talks about the courage needed to continue fighting despite the rough year. He tells the kids, "I feel good about tonight. We're going to play hard like we always do." Without the wins they'd prefer, the signature of the program is its willingness to fight regardless of what's in front of them.

After Chessher finishes, the coordinators take over for film review or whatever else they feel necessary. After their morning classes, most coaches have a long, free afternoon to stare at the clock and wait for the buses to the Palace. The weather is very cold and windy; it will be ski jacket weather tonight for the first and only time during my months in Texas.

I head to the academic building and meet with the school registrar, Rose Trevethan. She's had three sons in the Tiger program and was the president of the booster club.

People unfamiliar with Stony Point assume it's an upper-middle-class suburban school with great facilities and no money issues. This isn't the truth. By Texas 5A standards the facilities are subpar. There are few frills; the turf practice/middle school field was installed a few months earlier, the offices and locker rooms are basic, and the enrollment is majority-minority, with almost 50 percent of the students classified as "at risk."

Trevethan tells me her club raises about $30,000 a year. With more than 230 kids playing football, these funds are necessary. She says the demands made by the program are "pretty brutal," but that this commitment was outstanding in terms of building character in her boys.

"The kids who play are more committed than a lot of people I know who have jobs," she tells me. The discipline and work ethic learned by playing football has helped her sons become better men.

After I finish with Trevethan, I sit down with Albert Hernandez, the high school principal. A former coach from El Paso himself, he thinks the Texas system of athletics is the best in the country and loves having coaches on his teaching staff. He thinks athletics during the school day is what sets Texas apart from other states.

"It's an advantage that these clubs and organizations can monitor the success of their athletes in regard to no pass-no play. There's an advantage to athletics during the school day."

Of places that have athletics only after school, he believes, "They haven't done enough research on what exactly we do in Texas."

He doesn't understand how other states leave such an important role to off-campus volunteers, claiming professionals are usually superior to "contracted people" in working with students. Born and raised in Texas, he gives a lot of credit to high school football in his personal life. "If it hadn't been for Texas high school football, there is no way I'd be sitting where I am today."

Back in the coaches' office, the staff talks about Round Rock restaurants again. Chessher finds somebody else to tell about Raising Cane's as the hours tick by.

The coaches at Stony Point come from many backgrounds. Coach Hawkins has a law degree from Rice, but after working in that field and then in banking, he decided to return to what he really wanted to do. Defensive tackles coach Will Janson is a musician who fronted a Texas country band before coaching and family demands became too pressing. Janson had a busy spring, briefly holding four jobs in three months. The whirlwind tour started when he left his job at Westwood for a defensive coordinator job at Taylor. On the first day of that job last April, the head coach took a new job in Houston. The new Taylor coach brought in his own guys, so Janson resigned and took another job, this one in the Metroplex at Lovejoy. But during his second week there, his wife's father had health problems in Round Rock. Janson's job at Westwood had already been filled, and eventually he landed at Stony Point. While his story is dramatic, almost everyone here has bounced through many different jobs.

This is fairly typical in Texas. Coaching is a very different job here. To attract quality applicants, Texas school districts sometimes offer salaries into the low six figures. In many cases new hires bring assistants from previous jobs. High school coaching in Texas is much like college coaching elsewhere. Coaches are fired for not getting results; when the head coach is let go, the assistants are also at risk. It's a harsh bottom line. If you give a coach all he needs to be successful and he can't win, the school will find someone who can. The incoming coach is often given the authority to clean house. The carousel is made more crowded by successful coaches leaving jobs to move up the ladder, assistants becoming coordinators, coordinators looking for that first HC job, and head coaches looking for *better* head jobs. In 2012, one-third of 5A and 4A coaches in Texas were new hires.

The competition makes coaching here a true meritocracy. From junior high, to freshman assistant, to varsity/JV assistant, to coordinator, to head coach, and from 1A up to 5A, there's a clear progression for a coach to follow. It's a sure bet any varsity assistant has paid his dues, either rising through the ranks in one school or, more often, coming up through other ISDs.

As with any system, there are politics; who you know is important in getting a leg up. But once he's in, at least in good programs, a coach is measured by success. To keep moving up, a coach must stay on top of his game.

As it often does with coaching staffs with varied histories, the conversation turns to coaches they've worked with or for. Chessher tells a story of his first job at Baytown Lee coaching junior high.

"I was just starting out, twenty-two years old in my first job. On the first day of spring ball, the head coach gathered all the junior high coaches around to give us some advice. 'I have two things to say to y'all. One: try to learn something while you're here because none of you knows shit or you wouldn't be slapdick junior high coaches in the first place. Two: STAY THE FUCK OUT OF MY WAY!' Then he stomped off."

Chessher laughs and admits to his coaches, "I was twenty-two and I *didn't* know shit, but it wasn't nice to hear it that way."

Later at that same practice, Chessher recalled, he was standing by as the head coach dressed down his quarterbacks coach.

"THAT'S NOT THE WAY I FUCKIN' WANT IT DONE!" the head coach bellowed as the quarterbacks coach taught option technique, "IF I WANTED IT DONE THAT WAY, I'D FIRE YOUR ASS AND HAVE THIS SLAPDICK JUNIOR HIGH COACH DO IT!!" By the end of the day, Chessher was on the phone looking for another job.

This is the ninth staff I wait for a game with, and for the first time, I sense a vibe in the room I know too well from my own career: an uneasy feeling that something will go wrong tonight.

On paper there's no reason the Tigers can't play with Westwood and come out on top. Stony Point's 3-4 record is deceiving. They've lost three games by less than a field goal. One more break in each of those contests and the Tigers would be sitting in the district driver's seat with a record of 6-1.

What might have been doesn't matter; the reality is that something *does* keep going wrong. The weight of how this season has gone makes it feel as though the Tigers not only will be battling Westwood, but also their own recent history. Nothing is said—the coaches are optimistic about their X's and O's and in the matchup with the Warriors—but they don't seem confident.

Over at the stadium, the Tigers warm up in their yellow practice jerseys, not wanting the Westwood staff figure out who is playing where. Tonight, Stony Point wears visiting jerseys, greyish-white with blue numbers, with "STP" on the sleeves, matching the logo on their helmets. The Palace is a home for both schools, and it's Westwood's home game this year. In the coaches' locker room Chessher looks nervous as he sits on a stool before kickoff and says, as much to himself as to anyone in the room, "This is my chosen profession; I need to keep reminding myself of that."

As loose as everyone's been all afternoon, there's a lot on the line. A win or two can stop the negative momentum that's been building after each loss. Chessher knows his ability to continue "renting" good assistants will be reduced if the Tigers keep losing. Continuing to find good coaches, more than anything, will be the main factor in bringing this program back and saving his job.

The crowd is sparse in the big stadium. I'm sure the cold weather has kept many away. The support of most suburban schools is different than in one-school towns. High school football is big throughout the state, but suburban fans are more fickle than those in small towns. Stony Point drew well when they were winning, but fans in Round Rock have little patience, and many have jumped on the bandwagons of other local programs.

The game starts well for Stony Point. The defense plays lights out, hardly giving up a first down, and the Tigers grab an early lead on a 34-yard field goal with 4:13 left in the first quarter. Westwood's quarterback has a big reputation, but tonight, the Tiger front four are all over him. The run defense is outstanding, as well, giving Westwood's backs nothing to work with.

The trouble is on the offensive side. Running back Joseph Marrero gets banged up early. He returns, but the Tigers play the rest of the game without any offensive speed. They gain 3 or 4 yards on most running plays behind good push from their offensive line but don't have an explosive athlete to turn those gains into more.

With their passing game ineffective, the running game needs to be perfect. Three or four yards is fine as long as the chains move every three plays, but Stony Point's execution isn't flawless. On each Tiger drive, eventually a penalty or a missed block puts them in a third-and-long situation they can't run out of. Turnovers are the other factor in the first half. The Tigers put the ball on the ground four times and are intercepted twice.

With 2:33 remaining in the half, the Stony Point offense makes its biggest mistake of the night. The Tigers attempt a bubble screen on their own 5-yard line; Westwood intercepts, and the Warriors capitalize two plays later, scoring a touchdown and taking a 7-3 lead. On their ensuing possession, the Tigers move the ball into field-goal range, but an interception in the end zone with just 27 seconds left in the half ends that threat.

During halftime I overhear one defensive player say to another, "We're doing hella good." It's true—the defense is playing great— but I'm struck by how different this game is for players and coaches. The players will be fine in two hours whether the Tigers win or not.

Little hangs in the balance for them. They are kids playing a game, as they should be.

But this is the coaches' livelihood. Winning and losing may be the difference between staying in Round Rock, getting promoted to head jobs, or having to move elsewhere after being fired. I remember what Stewart said about a coach's professional success being decided by eighteen-year-old kids and realize what a crazy business this is.

Stony Point has a chance to take the lead halfway through the third quarter when Westwood's return man muffs a punt deep in his own territory. But a penalty on the Tigers returns the ball to Westwood and tacks on 15 yards, as well. A personal foul is called on the following play, and though the Warriors have to punt, now it's Stony Point that's backed up.

The game is not over. During the final minutes the Tigers have good field position, but again, they can't capitalize and time runs out.

Stony Point moved the ball 231 yards, to under 100 for Westwood. Westwood was held to 15 yards rushing, but the outstanding defensive effort wasn't enough. Once again, mistakes and breaks cost the Tigers. Stony Point outplayed Westwood in almost every statistical category but could never get the one big play they needed to put them over the top.

It's another frustrating loss in a season of disappointing endings, but Coach Chessher gathers the team and says the right things.

"I know you're tired and I'm telling you this is just one of those years right now . . . it's tough. And every fiber in your body right now may say, 'I don't know if I want to do this anymore.' You have two more games left and we'll finish strong. There is no quit in Stony Point. I saw a lot of good things tonight, but we've got to keep working to get better. I'm very proud of this group."

The Stony Point Tigers fall to Pflugerville the following week, but despite a 3-6 record, they still have a slim chance of making the playoffs. If they win their final game against Round Rock and lowly McNeil beats Cedar Ridge by more than 10 points, Stony Point will get the fourth playoff seed in district 16-5A. McNeil does its part, shocking the Raiders, 42-21, for just its second win this season. Stony Point is on the verge of fulfilling its part, as well, leading 29-24 until the final two minutes of the game. The Tigers can't hang on, though, giving up a touchdown with 1:22 remaining. They fall to the Dragons by 1 point.

Early in December, I return to Round Rock while doing interviews in the Austin area. I drop by Stony Point and catch up with everyone. Despite the frustration of the game I attended, this was a really fun group to be around and I enjoy being back.

Once again, Chessher takes me to the Rio Grande, and he tells me about the trip to Disney World he'll take with his wife and daughter during Christmas break. We also talk Stony Point's future. He's optimistic about this coming group. The 2012 team was very young, and he loves the way next year's team is working. Enrollment projections have the high school heading back above 3,000 students. He's officially applied for the AD job but says he doesn't really care if he gets it. As it turned out, Chessher would be a finalist, but wouldn't get the job.

After lunch, I watch an off-season athletic period, the first "off-season" I see during this trip. By this point I've seen about everything and know Texas football about as well as an outsider can, but this new aspect amazes me. It's incredible how much a football program can get done when every coach works with his players every day.

From December until spring practices start, the Tigers meet twice a day, in the morning before school for upper-body lifting and then again during athletic period for lower-body, conditioning, and speed work.

The modern game is predicated on speed, and spending the spring devoting time to getting faster only helps. During the spring season, track coaches (usually football assistants) often take the lead, teaching speed and promoting their programs. Consequently, Texas football players are playing at their top speed more often than those players in other states. Elsewhere, coaches may want their kids in track, but most have no way to make it mandatory. Texas coaches simply tell their team they *will* do track during athletic period. If they're going to do the workouts anyway, they might as well run in the meets, and most do.

During athletics, players are equally divided between the field and the weight room. Those on the field work a speed-training circuit with five coaches covering different aspects of explosive running. The coach at the start has an iPad and records each player's technique for immediate analysis. The detail and thoroughness in this one workout answers any questions remaining about how so many kids in this state are so proficient. What passes for the off-season where I'm from, with one coach in the weight room with fifty-some kids, just doesn't compare to what I see at Stony Point. If the Tigers haven't won enough over the last two years, it's not for lack of effort or expertise from the coaching staff or kids.

The off-season motto at Stony Point is "Right Way Every Day." Whether this commitment to doing things right will pay off on the field next year or ever, who knows? Work ethic isn't just about victories. It's about doing things the right way simply because giving your all is the right way to do *anything* and the only way to hold your head up when things go against you.

While winning is important, the real reason public schools support and sponsor football is to help build boys into men. The growth comes through a *process* of sacrifice, teamwork, and discipline needed to fight for victories, not in the victories themselves. By this measure, Stony Point High School is a successful program.

10

THIS IS OUR TOWN
Week Ten: Harlingen Cardinals

When Texas was admitted into the union in 1845, the United States Congress offered the new state a unique option. If the legislature ever chose to, the state was given permission to separate into five separate states, thereby increasing its representation in Congress. Texas Pride being what it is, the likelihood of this happening is remote, but the option exists.

In many ways, Texas might as well already be multiple states. Texas State University geography professor Don Huebner pointed out that Texas is one of a few states that describes its regions in terms usually reserved for separate states. There is no *North* California, *West* Tennessee, or *South* Nevada; instead the suffix *–ern* is usually included. In this state, however, North Texas, West Texas, East Texas, and South Texas are the correct usages. The terminology recognizes these regions as very distinct places.

In essence, Texas is a borderland where four separate cultures meet. The American Southwest enters from the west, the Midwest from the north, the South from the east, and Mexican culture from the south.

To confuse things even more, the Gulf Coast crescent from Beaumont through Houston and around to Galveston is part of the Tidewater South, stretching east to New Orleans and Gulf Coast Mississippi and Alabama, while the rest of East Texas is effectively part of the "Old South."

The Metroplex is its own little world. Dallas is almost like a northeastern city stuck in the middle of Texas, while Fort Worth, less than fifty miles away, belongs to West Texas. Central Texas is an entirely different mess, with the crashing together of cultures from the four compass points on top of the academic-liberal enclave of Austin and the German and Czech influences of the Hill Country.

Texans from other parts of the state hardly recognize South Texas as part of the United States, much less Texas. Every Texan loves San Antonio, but the triangle of land to the south of the city of Alamo is described as North Mexico as often as South Texas. At the bottom of this triangle is the Rio Grande Valley, often referred to within the state simply as "the Valley." One cannot go further south and still be in the United States. West and south of the Valley is the Rio Grande River and Mexico; east is South Padre Island and the Gulf of Mexico. To the north, 250 miles of sparsely populated farmland and desert separates the Valley from San Antonio.

The Rio Grande Valley is isolated from the rest of Texas in many ways. Part of this isolation has to do with race and nationality. The Valley is nearly 90 percent Hispanic; Anglos are a distinct minority, a fact the rest of the state is well aware of and cause of the commonly held view that the south isn't quite Texas at all. The cities of Brownsville and McAllen on the American side and Matamoros and Reynosa on the Mexican side form, in effect, an international commerce zone.

The "North Mexico" slur has a sliver of truth to it. The border crossings at the river have been likened to "toll booths across an irrigation ditch," as traffic across the river is routine and quick for Americans heading south to buy medication and Mexicans going north to shop, work, and visit family. Mexican nationals can cross into the Valley with only a flash of a card to do business north of the river. To the people who live in the Valley, Mexico and its affairs have as much impact on day-to-day life as what's going on in the rest of the Lone Star State.

The isolation is physical, as well. Long after the rest of Texas was connected by highways, the only way to get into or out of the Valley was the railroad (incidentally, these same two distinctions and the attitudes caused by them also apply to El Paso). The look of the area is not what most would consider Texan, either. Palm trees planted by make-work programs during the Depression, colorful sunsets, and the suburban sprawl of the Valley give it a tropical, almost Florida-like feel. The winters are mild, with temperatures rarely requiring long pants or even light jackets. The warm weather has drawn many "Winter Texans," retirees from Canada and northern states who've moved to the Valley.

The Valley is an outlier from a football perspective, as well. The coaching community in South Texas is largely self-contained. Rio

Grande Valley coaches rarely leave for jobs elsewhere, and coaches from other parts of the state don't often make South Texas part of their circuit when climbing the ladder. On the rare occasions when coaches from "up Texas" make it to the Valley, there's a perception they come with an attitude that they know better than the locals how things should be done.

When a Valley coach tells me about working with a coach from "up north" (Central Texas, in this case), he says, "He thought he was going to come down here and show us all how things ought to be done." This outsider lasted just two years. "He thought he was in Mexico . . . not South Texas," the Valley coach says resentfully.

None of this is to say South Texas or the Valley doesn't fit into Texas Football Culture. They absolutely do. The fanaticism here rivals and often surpasses that of any other region in the state. Loyalties are strong through generations and the competition is fierce.

I'm here to visit the Harlingen High School Cardinals, arguably the most storied program in South Texas and inarguably the one that's made the biggest splash in recent years. Even by Valley standards, the Cards enjoy tremendous support. Families have held season tickets for thirty or forty years, sitting in the same seats at Boggus Stadium season after season. In 2011, the Cards played a neutral-site game against Abilene High in San Antonio. As great as Abilene fans are, they were outnumbered by the 5,000 Harlingen supporters who made the 250-mile drive.

All the Valley is missing is championships. Every South Texan knows that no Valley school has won state since Donna took the 2A crown in 1961. The kids here are tough and hard working, and they love football. But it's rare when a majority Hispanic demographic has enough speed at the skill positions or size on the line to compete with teams from other parts of Texas.

"We don't have as much athletic talent down here as other parts of the state," Harlingen trainer Raul Zamarripa admits. "But we get a lot done without a lot of talent. Give us three D-I players and we'd make a run, too." The competitive imbalance with other parts of Texas, however, isn't a factor during the regular season. It isn't until the third playoff round, when the Valley's best head north to play against schools in San Antonio, that the imbalance is usually felt.

The staff is tense and busy, hardly noticing when I arrive late Saturday morning for the scout meetings in preparation for the Cardinals' crosstown rivalry game against Harlingen South. For most of the twenty years that these schools have met since South opened in 1993, the "Bird Bowl" was a rivalry in name only. The Cardinals have won sixteen of the nineteen matchups, including the past four.

This year, however, the city of Harlingen and much of the Valley is buzzing that the mighty Cardinals are ready to fall. Harlingen South has not often been a factor in District 32-5A, but this year the Hawks are 7-1 while the Cardinals have had an uncharacteristically tough early season, losing their first two games before going 5-1 in district play. Everyone in town expects Bird Bowl XX to live up to the hype.

Only two weeks before the playoffs begin, the Bird Bowl is likely for the district title as well as bragging rights. Cardinal haters from around the Valley anticipate the Cardinals being brought down a peg. Of the twenty-seven 5A schools in the Rio Grande Valley, the most loved, hated, reported on, respected, and influential is the Harlingen Cardinals.

"This town is ready for the Cardinals to lose the Bird Bowl," according to head coach Manny Gomez. The feeling in the Cardinal coaches' office is that people don't want to see the Hawks win so much as they'd like to see the Cardinals lose.

Gomez doubles as the defensive coordinator, and he alternates between the conference table and the whiteboard at the far end of the office, scribbling defensive looks on the big board, on a pad of paper, and on a clipboard-size whiteboard. The players watch film in separate locker rooms, half in the JV room with offensive coordinator Robert Fraga, while the rest are in the varsity room with some of the defensive staff. Other coaches put together game plans and scouting reports. Hudl film of South runs on laptops and iPads in the individual coaches' cubicles lining either wall of the rectangular office.

The overall theme is that South is not as good as advertised. The coaches highlight weaknesses. Body language, how the Hawks break huddle, how the offensive players loaf when the play is away from them—all of these are pointed out by the defensive coaches. The narrative is that South hasn't faced adversity and is made up of prima donnas with "me first" attitudes who will turn on each other if things get tough.

Gomez comes in at 11:40 and tells his defense that the key to stopping the Hawks is containing sophomore running back Jaedon Taylor, number twenty-four. Taylor is big and fast and has accounted for most of South's offense this season. The competition the Hawks have faced so far hasn't been able to slow him down, but Gomez is confident the Cardinals will.

After the kids leave, the coaches continue working while eating from Styrofoam box lunches of catfish, fries, and tortillas. I'm not sure if it's the opponent or just the nature of this staff, but this is the most businesslike group I've seen on a Saturday this season. There's none of the small talk, coaching gossip, or joking that's often mixed with the Saturday work.

Part of the intensity is this week's matchup. Some rivalries are traditional; most have to do with proximity. There's always talk about "bragging rights" and "bad blood," but usually the talk is just that, talk. Rarely is there much to back up the clichés. Rarely is there anything close to genuine dislike, much less hatred. Of the four rivalry games I attend this regular season, Harlingen High versus Harlingen South would be the only one with true animosity.

One week isn't enough for me to understand the love and hate of Harlingen High School in the Valley, but it's long enough to know that any rivalry involving the Cardinals involves deep feelings. Now in their one hundredth year of football, the Cardinals have been a major Valley power for generations, regularly winning district championships and embarrassing opponents. Harlingen has had only four losing seasons since 1970; they've made the playoffs twelve straight seasons and have won ten or more games each of the past four years. This much success can lead to jealousy, arrogance, and resentment, words I heard repeatedly from locals inside and outside of the program.

Most Harlingen coaches are alumni of the school. Successful programs often take the structure of a family and use it as a rallying point. Most often this family is a seasonal thing, changing each year as coaches move, kids graduate, and new members join. At Harlingen, the family connections are real and deep.

Harlingen's "family" is an exclusive club—one either is a Cardinal or isn't. Local sportswriter Eladio Jaimez says the Cardinal football program is the New York Yankees of the Valley. Like the Yankees, the Cardinals have a large and passionate following, and like the Yankees, the Cardinals are hated by everyone else. There is no middle ground. If you live in the Valley, you either are a Cardinal or you can't stand them.

While Gomez has maintained the tradition of his school, what sets him apart from others in the Valley is his ambition. Unlike other Valley programs that are content to win their ten or so games before running into a buzz saw when they face San Antonio schools in the playoffs, Gomez is unwilling to accept that Valley schools can't compete statewide.

Monty Medley, Harlingen's booster club president, says, "Coach Gomez isn't satisfied with just winning in the Valley, but wants to go against the best in the state and prove we can play with anybody."

Jaimez says, "Coach Gomez paints a picture in the players' minds that they can be playing in Cowboys Stadium in December." At practice, I hear Gomez talking about the ultimate goal of making deep playoff runs, consistently putting that possibility out there for the players.

The mindset Gomez instilled in the Cardinals began to pay off in 2011, when Harlingen made it further in the 5A playoffs than any Valley squad in recent history. They've always been a name program in the Valley but got on the statewide radar only when they made it past "Valley Weak" and advanced to the fourth round of the 5A playoffs. "Valley Weak" is a derisive term coined by San Antonio-area teams for the third round of the playoffs, when their schools usually breeze by overmatched opponents. In 2011, however, Harlingen High would table that slur for at least a year.

After the undefeated Cardinals beat Los Fresnos in bi-district and Del Rio in area, they faced San Antonio Warren in "Valley Weak." This time, however, Harlingen had a special group and did something no Valley squad had done in many years, thumping Warren, 53-28, and advancing to the state quarterfinals.

The win electrified the entire Valley. The Cards have always had great support, but now the support went beyond the usual "family." Could the championship drought finally end? Could the Cardinals bring the first title to the Valley since 1961? Ten thousand Valley residents traveled one hundred miles up to Kingsville for the quarterfinal matchup with San Antonio Madison to see for themselves.

There are two schools of thought on why so many made the trip. Outsiders saw the Valley unite behind the Cardinals, forgetting past bad blood in the hope the Cards would end the championship drought, proud that the "Valley Weak" knock had finally been overcome. Locals say many Valley "supporters" made the trip hoping to see something else the Valley hadn't seen in a while: a Cardinal loss.

Whatever the truth, the ride would end in the quarterfinals. The 2011 Cardinals fell to Madison, 42-27.

The coaches put in a long afternoon on Saturday. Gomez tells me they're trying to get everything done so they'll have Sunday free for families. It wouldn't work out that way, though. On Sunday the defensive coaches return to the office, watching film and working for five additional hours. It's a short weekend before they come back to school early Monday for freshman early-morning athletic period.

Less than ten miles from the border, Harlingen is very different from Brownsville and McAllen. It's basically a middle-class suburban town. The residents have little connection to Mexico other than ethnicity. They come from families who've lived in Texas for generations, speak English, and embrace American customs.

Crossing the farmland heading southeast to Brownsville, the Valley rapidly changes. Where Harlingen is a sprawl, Brownsville is more compact, older, and poorer. Signs are more often written in Spanish, and the place has a greater Mexican influence than Harlingen. More residents are first-generation Americans and have strong ties south of the border. With the larger city of Matamoros located just across the river and four bridges connecting the two, Brownsville feels more Mexican than Texan. When driving through the shopping district just north of the river, one would have a tough time knowing whether he was in the United States or Mexico.

Later that evening, back in my motel room, I watch the Giants wrap up their second World Series title in three years. I wish there were someone to celebrate with, but here in South Texas, more people are already talking about the Bird Bowl than the Series.

On Monday, I arrive at Harlingen in time for athletic period and varsity lifting. The fieldhouse was built by a bond issue in 1999. The weight room is beautiful, with high ceilings, painted in red and black; the equipment is clean, well-maintained, and functional. Motivational quotes ("It's amazing what can be accomplished when no one cares who receives the credit," "If you fear failure, you will be successful," and "The more you sweat in peace, the less you bleed in war") are everywhere inside the weight room and fieldhouse. Above the weight floor is a mural of a giant avian eye and the words, "Cardinal Tradition watches over you."

The lifting routine is organized in almost military fashion. Today's workout consists of hang cleans, front squats, and incline press. Not a single move is made without a coach's prompt. Groups of three lift, spot, or perform secondary exercises. Every rep is done on a whistle, and after each whistle toot, the players count off a cadence, "One, sir! Two, sir! Three, sir! . . ."

After lifting, the offense and defense break out with their respective coaches to review the game plan. On the offensive side, Coach Fraga goes over new plays the Cardinals will add. Harlingen runs a multiple pro-style offense with some spread looks, but also some two-back smash-mouth attack, taking advantage of their weight training. Fraga installs an influence trap play this week, with both guards pulling the same direction, hopefully moving the defensive tackle and front-side linebacker out of position.

Over with the defense, Gomez and his staff have found some Hawk tendencies. Number four and number one are South's top receivers, and film shows that when they line up in the inside or slot position, the Hawks usually pass. The Cardinals play an attacking, gap-control defense, reading keys on the fly but always coming hard to fit into their assignments. When they see the Hawks line up with number one and number four in the slot, they'll bring extra pressure and get after the quarterback.

As the coaches straggle back to the fieldhouse after afternoon classes, Gomez sits on a stool watching a cut-up of South plays from the trips open formation. A sign on the office door reminds everyone who enters, "A man must be big enough to admit mistakes, smart enough to profit from them and strong enough to correct them." Reggae music plays from little speakers on the video cart as Gomez watches each play repeatedly, looking for any little pattern or edge.

The Cardinals go outside for practice at 4:15 and spread over two fields. The defense is on the practice field close to the access road behind the school, while the offense works on the adjacent JV game field. The dress today is full pads, with the varsity wearing white jerseys and the JV players in red. Like most large-school programs, there's very little contact between the two units once practice begins.

On one side of the tall filming tower between the fields is a sign listing the years the Cardinals have won Bird Bowls (a total of fifteen), the Battle of the Arroyo (sixty-two), district championships (thirty-three), and playoff appearances (thirty-five). On the opposite side is a statement, "The pride and winning tradition of the Harlingen Cardinals will not be entrusted to the weak nor the timid." The pace of Monday's practice is a little slow. There is a lot of walking and talking as coaches install this week's adjustments, first with their position groups and then with their units.

It's now late October, and the sun sets earlier each day. It's dark when practice ends at 7:00. In the twilight, a flock of wild parrots lands on power lines running parallel to the practice field. The Rio Grande Valley is a destination for bird-watchers attracted by the huge variety of birds migrating from South America. Tour buses full of bird-watchers often pull into the parking lot to see the parrots perching on the power lines at sunset.

It had been a tough early season for Gomez and the Cardinals. After a memorable 2011, only two starters returned on each side of the ball, so a drop-off from their 12-1 season shouldn't come as a surprise. Gomez's ambition also made life difficult for his team from the start. Instead of playing it safe and opening with a Valley team from another district as most do, the Cardinals traveled to San Antonio and got shut out.

One would think the success of the past three seasons would have bought Gomez a little time and patience after the poor start. Instead, he heard so much negative stuff that he stopped going on Facebook and changed his phone number.

"People are spoiled here," says one of the trainers. "Coach Gomez is under a lot of pressure."

The tradition of Harlingen football can be harsh. Gomez knows this as well as anyone. He graduated from Harlingen in 1990 and went to college at Texas A&M University-Kingsville before returning to Harlingen High. He began coaching here just a few months after his college graduation, under previous head coach Randy Cretors.

After twelve years as an assistant—the last three as defensive coordinator—Gomez got the head job in 2007. His success was steady and immediate. Since getting the head position, he has a record of 59-13. According to Jaimez, "Gomez coaches with a chip on his shoulder. He wants to prove a Valley coach can compete with coaches from upstate and that Valley teams can play with anyone." This chip may be another factor in this season's Bird Bowl, as South is coached by an import from "up-Texas."

Unlike most 5A coaches, Gomez remains the team's defensive co-ordinator as well as head coach.

"I couldn't be one of those guys who watch everyone else coach," he tells me. Watching him during practice, it's hard to imagine him overseeing practice instead of working directly with players. It just doesn't fit his personality. I suspect that if given the choice between being head coach or a coordinator, Gomez would stay as the coordinator. He comes across as a tough, no-nonsense, somewhat intimidating man. At forty years of age, he looks as though he could still line up at linebacker, as he did at Harlingen and A&M-Kingsville.

Gomez's career path to coaching at his alma mater—in fact, never coaching anywhere *but* his alma mater—may be unusual, but at Harlingen it's the norm. Fourteen of the sixteen coaches on the Cardinal staff are graduates of Harlingen High. The staff is truly tied to the school in a way that most aren't. They know what it means to be "Cardinals" and they've had that identity much longer than the kids they coach. Most don't want to be anywhere else.

They often stay, remaining loyal to their colors despite low pay, sometimes forgoing offers from other schools in order to contribute to the tradition of their school. The traditions are ingrained into this coaching staff, and the results are personal in a way that can't be the case with outsiders. The coaching legacy in the Valley is so strong that other staffs are made up of ex-Cardinals, as well, coaches who would prefer to be at their former school but can't find positions. The ethos of Harlingen High has become the dominant philosophy in the Valley; five competing Valley head coaches are alumni of the Cardinal program.

On Tuesday, athletic period is outside with a special teams focus. It's a hot late October day, humid with temperatures in the mid-eighties. The kids wear shells, and many of the coaches are in sleeveless black T-shirts. Coach Fraga uses the time to work some sled drills with the offensive line. The linemen aren't very tall, but are thick and stocky, solid-looking boys who are very strong.

After lunch, back in the fieldhouse, Gomez sits in his spot watching film with a portable whiteboard on his lap as assistants wander in. Today the film is of South's punt team; Gomez looks for the clue that will help the Cardinals block a punt. Does the punter or snapper do anything to key when the ball will be snapped? Does anybody up front take a bad step? The only way to know is to watch over and over.

The snapper and punter *do* telegraph when the ball will be snapped. Gomez puts in a stunt designed to capitalize on this tell. Yesterday was reggae and a little country; today, Gomez listens to some awful, almost pornographic rap music while watching film. I'm just too old to appreciate it, I guess.

Practice moves faster and is more intense today; again, the kids are in full pads. The offense and defense meet on the JV field for twenty plays of "good on good" passing scrimmage, the only time the two units will be together all week. "Good on good" is followed by more scrimmaging between the varsity and JV units.

After practice, Gomez talks to the team about being champions.

"Everybody wants something in this world. Are you willing to pay the price is the question? Are you willing to pay the price to be a champion?"

The kids respond, "Yes, sir," but Gomez isn't convinced.

"I'll tell you what, it's one of those things that's easier said than done. I can say 'Yes, sir!' but really what's down there?" he asks, pounding on his chest. He reminds them that time is running out, "like sand running through an hourglass . . . once it's over, it's over. Opportunities are slowly getting away from you. We got two opportunities left and it starts Friday night."

On Wednesday, I meet with the principal, Imelda Munivez. Like all administrators I met during my trip, she talks about the importance of getting kids involved in extracurricular activities. However, she's worried that if the testing protocol in the state doesn't change, soon her low-achieving students may be forced out of athletics.

Remediation is an educational buzzword that essentially requires a student failing in math, for example, to take *two* math classes instead of one, replacing an elective.

Munivez worries that taking away the activities that make kids want to come to school may lead to the loss of those students altogether. So far, Harlingen has found other ways to remediate, but the day may come when in-school athletics in Texas go the way it's heading in so many other states—pushed out to after school.

Harlingen High was among the largest schools in the state before being split by the opening of South in 1993. Today, it has an enrollment of around 2,600 students. Of those, Munivez estimates 65 percent are involved with some sort of activity. The band has around 250 members. Football is well represented, as well, with about 300 students on the school's five teams.

It's an interesting practice today. I see something I'd never seen in twenty-two years of coaching and a season of doing nothing but watching practices and games. The Harlingen offensive unit spends the entire practice running plays versus air. Every personnel group for both the first and second team runs every formation, motion, and play at thirty-second intervals, moving the ball in 5-yard increments until reaching the end zone, then turning around and repeating the process. A quick calculation tells me that Cardinal offensive players run roughly 240 plays during the two hours this drill runs.

"Reps" is a mantra of many coaches, myself included, but I've never seen the philosophy taken to this extreme. Fraga tells me this is a normal Wednesday practice with the goal of preparing his offensive players mentally to do the little things correctly. How many football games, from peewee to the NFL, have been lost because somebody lined up wrong, missed a snap count, or ran the wrong route? Just getting all eleven offensive players moving together, in time, and with purpose is half the battle. This drill forces players to focus exclusively on the little things without the distraction of a defense.

While watching this drill, I talk with coach Bobby Lucio. Lucio is the senior staff member, having coached at Harlingen for twenty-six years, meaning he's coached many of the current Cardinal staff. He started here at nineteen years old as a junior high coach.

Where Gomez is fiery but somewhat distant, Lucio serves as the team elder, a father figure who provides a spiritual foundation for the program. For the past seventeen years, the Wednesday practice has traditionally been followed by a speech/story/sermon given by Lucio.

This talk is eagerly anticipated as the team gathers around after practice. The sun is setting as Lucio gives a strange but memorable rambling rant about an obscure movie the kids have never seen, *The Last Dragon,* where the hero finds he has a dragon within himself. He then talks about old *Mad Magazine* cartoons that show shadows being different and more ferocious than the objects that throw them—for instance, a Chihuahua with the shadow of a lion.

The moral: find that beast within yourself and unleash it Friday night.

"We don't know who we are, we're still trying to learn . . . I hope Friday . . . I HOPE FRIDAY we learn who we are . . . because there's nothing I can do . . . there's nothing Manny Gomez can do, there's nothing ANYONE CAN DO . . . This one's you and this one's YOU ONLY. This is YOUR Bird Bowl. I hope when the lights are on and focused, and I look out there what I hope to see is a BIG DRAGON, WITH WINGS AND HORNS AND FIRE OUT OF HIS MOUTH!!!" With this, Lucio rips off his shirt and runs off amid the cheers of Cardinal players.

Today is Halloween and Coach Gomez, his wife, Melissa, and their two daughters—Alysa, a freshman cheerleader at Harlingen High, and Alexis, a third-grader—meet at the Garzas' house just around the corner from the school. Brandon Garza is the Cardinals' quarterback, and we all sit in front of the house in lawn chairs as Alysa takes her sister trick-or-treating. It's a nice neighborhood, and because of this—or just due to local tradition—people from all over town drive their kids here for trick-or-treating. Nobody needs to worry about their children running into traffic tonight, as cars cannot drive down the streets at all. It's wall-to-wall people, and the Garzas carefully dole out the candy lest they run out.

I talk to Brandon's father. Brandon is a junior and he's getting a few preliminary looks from college recruiters. One of Gomez's main frustrations has been how college recruiters treat the Valley. Texas is the prime recruiting area for many colleges, but the Rio Grande Valley may as well be in New Mexico or North Dakota as far as scouts are concerned.

The reputation of Valley athletes and the difficulty of getting here keep most college coaches from ever venturing south of San Antonio. Except for A&M-Kingsville and the University of Texas at San Antonio, nobody recruits the Valley. Garza has been doing the right things to get noticed and puts up good numbers, but coming from the Valley puts much more of the burden on high school coaches and players to sell themselves than if they were in other parts of the state.

Even with the tiny portions, the candy doesn't hold out long, and the crowds slowly disperse. It's a beautiful evening, and great to sit outside. I'm happy to have a reason to be away from my motel room. Gomez is a different person with his family in a social setting: very relaxed and enjoying a rare evening without the pressures of his job.

Thursday is a slow day. The JV and freshmen A teams will play at Boggus Stadium tonight, while the Bs will be at the small stadium on campus. Athletic period starts the way Wednesday ended, with another talk by Lucio. It's a calmer one this morning, with a prayer rather than a story. After Lucio gives his sermon, the Cards take the JV field for special teams situations.

I have lunch with Jaimez at Pepe's, a popular Mexican restaurant across from the stadium. He's been the high school sportswriter for his paper for many years and tells me about the background of the Harlingen program. When the second high school was built nineteen years ago, many believed the glory days for the Cards would end. They were wrong. The Cardinals have made the playoffs seventeen of the nineteen years since the split. Jaimez attributed this consistency largely to the coaching staff.

"Other schools have their traditions in trophy cases, painted on the side of their school buildings and on their water towers. At Harlingen the tradition is actually coaching you."

Historically, the Cardinals' biggest rival has been neighboring San Benito High School, whom they play every year in the Battle of the Arroyo. The Bird Bowl has usually taken a back seat to that game, mostly due to the weakness of South but also because South is a new school while the rivalry with San Benito is long and storied. This year, many believe the Hawks have finally caught the Cards. The message boards have been full of predictions that the Cardinals will fall.

After school, Lucio buffs the balls for this weekend's games, making sure enough of the sixty Cardinal game balls are properly "tackified." This being the first day of the month, several younger coaches try recruiting older staff members for a "no shave November," each putting twenty dollars into a pot for the last to shave. Older, hairier coaches like Fraga and Lucio take a pass.

Tonight is a little taste of the atmosphere I'll see tomorrow. In Texas, without full-time lower-level coaches, winning and losing at the lower level isn't usually a priority. Tonight, the JV and freshman Bird Bowls are an exception. The bad blood between the two schools is evident. Both in the stands and on the sideline, there's a definite feel that these games matter. Varsity coaches get fired up, and the thousands in the stands ring bells, wave flags, and jump out of their seats, behavior rarely seen for sub-varsity games. Nobody wants to lose to the crosstown rival, even if the games don't count in any standings. It's a good night for the Cardinals. They beat the Hawks in both games.

Hanging out in the coaches' office Friday morning, I meet Randy Bermea, a rare Harlingen alumnus with an athletic scholarship. Bermea was a running back on last year's team and now runs track at the University of California. He had the opportunity to play football with UT-San Antonio and Rice but chose Cal instead. He credits the Cardinal program with teaching him to be accountable and giving him the work ethic he's using in California. He tells me the off-season track workouts at Cal are nothing like what he'd endured as a Cardinal.

Around campus today, Harlingen High students wear T-shirts saying, "This is OUR town." Nothing subtle here. This game won't be about home ownership ("This is our house"). It's bigger than that. South has been feeling their oats, getting big heads from the successful season. Tonight is about reminding everyone that Harlingen still belongs to the Cardinals.

During athletic period, the Cardinals are in the weight room again. The players aren't lifting heavy; this is the first place I've been that lifts on game day at all. Afterward, offense and defense meet with coaches for last-minute reminders. There's no talk about what's on the line; nobody needs to be told.

Waiting in the fieldhouse, the coaches are on edge. Gomez comes in just fifteen minutes before it's time to leave. The captains pump up their teammates in the locker room while the coaches finish their pregame rituals in the office. The two buses make the half-mile trip to Boggus Stadium at 5:30. The players are dressed in black game pants and white Under Armour tops with their numbers on the back, carrying jerseys and shoulder pads. Coaches wear their game gear, as well, red polo shirts and black slacks with the Cardinal insignia on the pocket. Gomez stands out from his staff in a white shirt.

South's buses arrive right behind the Cardinals. Everyone files off, but opposing players and coaches completely ignore each other. Harlingen is a small town; some of these coaches know each other, and you'd expect them to shake hands and make a little small talk. Not tonight. A Harlingen assistant tells me, "There is no love lost between us."

Kickoff is still two hours off, and the Cards sprawl on the floor and bleachers in the gym next to the stadium. Position coaches with portable whiteboards meet with groups of players going over the adjustments. Trainers and student-trainers tape ankles on the tables they've brought for this purpose.

The stadium is buzzing tonight, and the crowd arrives early. By 7:00, with a half hour to go until kickoff, most of the 9,000 seats are full. Harlingen South is dressed in white tops and white pants; the Hawk uniforms resemble the University of Miami Hurricanes, with orange and aqua trim. Even the "S" decal is reminiscent of Miami's two-toned "U." As the Cardinals stretch, Coach Gomez walks though, shaking every player's hand and giving final words of encouragement. The sun is setting as the two squads line up back to back right up to the 50-yard line, neither team willing to give up an inch of real estate.

Before heading out, Gomez addresses the team, reminding them of the intensity it will take to stop the Hawks.

"Put that cage on their freakin' ass over and over and over until you break their will to compete and we ain't going to slow down. Live up to the hype of this football game."

When the teams rush onto the new artificial turf after the national anthem, they're joined by middle school players wearing their football jerseys. It's a Bird Bowl tradition for these future Hawks and Cardinals to take the field with the varsity kids, giving them an early taste of running into a packed Boggus Stadium for a big game. Tonight the excitement is electric. This isn't just a standing room crowd, but an intense one. For the next three hours, the fans will be on their feet as much as in their seats. South fans are chanting, "Red is dead." Banners wave on both the red-clad home side and the aqua and orange visiting stands.

South gives the visiting crowd a reason to cheer early, kicking a 49-yard field goal to take a 3-0 lead, then extending their advantage when Hawk defender Nick Garcia scoops up a lateral and returns it 25 yards for a score, making the score 10-0.

The Cardinal offense has trouble getting started, but in the final minute of the first quarter, Harlingen High finally gets on the board. The Cardinals cap an 88-yard drive with a 56-yard touchdown run by Dion Conde, making the score 10-7 Hawks. South comes right back on a 70-yard run down the right sideline by Taylor a few plays later. After a blocked extra point, it's 16-7 Hawks.

Taylor is impressive. Though only a sophomore, he looks like a man. The problem is that he's responsible for almost all of South's offense, and when the Cardinal defense begins to contain him, the Hawks don't have much of a plan B.

It's the Cards' defense that turns the momentum. After a three-and-out deep in their own territory, a bad snap on a Hawks punt attempt gives the Cardinals a first-and-goal from South's 3-yard line. Two plays later, Garza sneaks the ball across the goal line, closing the Hawk lead to 16-14.

Again, the Hawks can't do anything with the ball on their next possession, and the Cardinals take their first lead of the night, 17-16, on a Samuel Bazan field goal with just 30 seconds remaining in the half.

It's a 1-point game, and South fans are just as fired up as they were before the opening kickoff. As the Cardinals leave the field, Hawk supporters taunt the red players and coaches. The Cards egg on the derisive fans as they head past the visiting stands on their way to the locker room.

While the coaches make their adjustments, I talk with the team doctor, Herman Keillor. Wearing a Hawaiian shirt and baseball cap, Keillor doesn't look like a doctor. He loves helping the program however he can. Originally from Chicago, he moved to the Valley when he was a kid and never left. This is his thirtieth season as the Cardinals team doctor.

He proudly tells me, "We got a bunch of mean little Mexicans! . . . Great kids who play with a lot of heart. I love these guys."

The players sit on benches in front of two whiteboards in the spartan halftime room at Boggus. There isn't a lot to the room, just benches, whiteboards, showers, and a restroom.

It's a 1-point game, but after trailing by 10 early, the momentum is clearly on the Cardinals' side. South still hasn't shown they could do anything but give the ball to Taylor, and the Cardinal defense has pretty well contained him since allowing the 70-yard run.

Before going back out, Gomez tells his squad, "Keep doing what you're doing. Just pick up the effort a little bit. Let's go finish them."

During the second half, the Cardinal defense continues to play well, shutting down both Taylor and the rest of the Hawk offense. On the opening drive after the intermission, Cardinal defensive back Joel Leon intercepts a Sean Montemayor pass. The Cardinals follow with a 40-yard drive, capped by a 3-yard run by Conde for his second touchdown of the night, making the score 24-16 Harlingen.

With this score, South's crowd deflates. The momentum is now completely on the Cardinal side. The defense flies around, swarming to the ball; it's all the Hawks can do to get back to the line of scrimmage. They manage only three first downs during the second half, and the orange crowd on the visiting side begins to file out.

Tonight isn't the night for Harlingen High to be humbled. Taylor would finish the game with 102 yards, but 70 came on one play. He's bottled up in the second half and the Hawks are held to 153 total yards for the game. As good as Taylor is, South's offense is just too one-dimensional. Harlingen's offense, while not explosive, is steady and consistent. Controlling the line of scrimmage, the Cards rush for over 200 yards, and Garza is 11-of-17 passing for 168 yards and two touchdowns. The final score is 38-23 Harlingen High.

The Cardinal celebration has the air of a huge playoff win. Gomez is presented with a crystal football, the Bird Bowl trophy, and the players gather around for the standard pictures, just like those taken after playoff wins. For one more year, anyway, Harlingen remains the Cardinals' town.

The celebration would continue at Medley's house late into the evening. I wish I could have gone, but for the last time this season, I have a long, late-night drive ahead of me. I hit the road as soon as the Cardinal buses get back to the fieldhouse

Unfortunately, my journey doesn't allow me to return to the Valley. The Harlingen High Cardinals and Harlingen South Hawks both win their final regular-season games the following week and share the District 32-5A title with 7-1 records. In the bi-district round of the playoffs, the Cardinals defeat McAllen Memorial; the Hawks advance, as well, beating Rowe.

Both Harlingen schools have their seasons end the following week. The Hawks lose to Edinburg North, 14-3, and the Cardinals fall to Mission Sharyland, 42-2. Sharyland was an undefeated team, and Gomez was quick to give them credit, but at the same time, weather contributed to the lopsided outcome. The Sharyland game was played on a very wet evening, and Garza had trouble getting a grip on the ball, stalling the Cards' screen game. Falling into a hole, Gomez tells me, things just snowballed and got away from the Cardinals. It would be up to Edinburg North and Sharyland to represent the Valley in Class 5A and take their shot at overcoming the "Valley Weak" stigma.

This year, though, no one would carry the Valley's banner north into the deep rounds. Edinburg North loses to Cibolo Steele in the third round, and Sharyland falls to San Antonio Madison, the same squad that knocked the Cardinals out of the playoffs the previous year.

11

LONGHORN SPEED

Week Eleven: Cedar Hill Longhorns

"Protect the Family"

—Cedar Hill motto.

I don't know what to expect when I pull up to Cedar Hill High School after a 500-mile drive from the Rio Grande Valley to the Metroplex. The Longhorns had been highly ranked by preseason polls but started 1-3 before finding their stride. After a tough 27-20 loss to Mansfield the night before, it isn't clear whether the Horns are guaranteed a playoff spot with a 4-2 district record. Head coach Joey McGuire had seemed enthusiastic about my project when I'd last seen him in August, but the stress of a long season after a tough loss and the possibility that this might be a must-win game make me a little apprehensive as I arrive Saturday afternoon.

I needn't have worried. Most of the coaches have already left, but McGuire is still there. When I tell him I'm sorry about the Mansfield loss, he lights up and starts gushing about how great a game it was. Through various tiebreakers the Longhorns *have* clinched a playoff spot, regardless of what happens this weekend, but I doubt McGuire would have acted differently had the scenario been different. He's not a man to brood or to lose perspective. Having fun is as much a part of Longhorn football as winning games.

"You should have been here this morning," he says, excitedly describing today's scout meeting. "One of the coaches brought in a pot of chili, and then some of the younger guys put on tights and started rasslin'!"

The playoffs are clinched, but Friday is important. The Longhorns will play the Midlothian Panthers. Both teams will be in the Class 5A Division II bracket, with the winner getting the top seed and the loser going to the bottom, something that might be huge in surviving the first few weeks of the playoffs.

As I drive onto the Cedar Hill campus for the first time since August, I realize how jaded I've become. On my first visit, McGuire had given me a tour of the facilities. Longhorn Stadium has 7,500 seats, a replay scoreboard, and a two-story, air-conditioned press box with an elevator. I'd been impressed during the summer; by November, I recognize Cedar Hill's facilities are somewhat modest by North Texas big-school standards. There's no indoor practice field, and while the fieldhouse is nice and functional, it is showing its years.

The hallway is filled with motivational reminders in red and black. One describes the "Longhorn Commandments: Treat women with respect. Do not lie. Do not cheat. Do not steal."

Another wall honors former Longhorn players pictured in their college uniforms. With several former Longhorns playing in the NFL and several more expected to be there soon, there's talk about a second wall of Longhorns in pro gear.

On Sunday, there is no wrestling or other goofiness. It's the basic weekend scout meeting I've seen all year. The coaches meet in a large classroom with a curtain divider down the center decorated in school colors and a red Longhorn logo on the cinder block wall. I arrive at 1:30, and offensive coordinator Mike Glaze and his staff are watching Midlothian film. The film is running on a big screen at the front of the room, but also on iPads and laptops the coaches brought.

Cedar Hill runs a variety of offensive looks, "Every formation known to man," McGuire halfway joked when I came to practice back in August. The early part of the meeting is spent trying to predict how Midlo will line up their 3-2 front against the many formations the Longhorns use. As the afternoon progresses, the whiteboard at the side of the room slowly fills up with the formations, personnel groups, and plays the Horns like against Midlothian.

The staff is easygoing and not too busy for conversation. Learning I'd come from the Valley, I get into a conversation with safeties and kickers coach Calvin Ruzicka, sometimes affectionately known as "the hippie" for his long hair and goatee. Ruzicka coached in the Valley at Brownsville and is the first eleven-man coach I've met who had also coached the six-man game. On top of coaching his position, Coach Ru is also the recruiting coordinator, an important post at a school with so many prospects. He makes sure players meet NCAA requirements and is in charge of getting film for the many college coaches who come through to look at Longhorn players.

On the other side of the divider, the defensive staff goes to work at 3:00. It's the same basic scene, with Hudl running on the coaches' personal devices and also on a screen. The defensive staff is a little frustrated by the Panthers' color scheme. With dark blue jerseys and black numbers, the numbers are so hard to read that it's almost impossible to tell who's on the field.

Despite this headache, the staff has already decided that Midlo has strong tendencies based on personnel groups. The discussion is how to adjust the front to best stop the Panthers.

This week the Horn defense will adjust one way when the quarterback is under center, another way when certain backs are in the game, and a third way when the quarterback is in shotgun. The staff won't ask the players to unravel all the variables, but a coach on the sideline will hold up a card for the players after defensive coordinator Steven Lemley makes the call from the press box and relays it down to the field.

McGuire goes back and forth between the offense and defense, but is much more involved on the defensive side. Lemley stands at the whiteboard, draws up proposed fronts, and encourages comments. McGuire isn't shy about adding his two cents, and Lemley seems happy about the input. McGuire's thirteen-year-old boy comes in and out as the afternoon progresses, running odd jobs for the coaches but mostly just hanging out.

It was a frustrating early season for the Longhorns, as they lost three of their first four games. But 1-3 doesn't tell the whole story. Too often, in both football and in life, numbers are assigned deeper significance than they deserve. A 200-pound man may be fat or thin, depending on his height; a one hundred dollar price tag may be exorbitant or a bargain, depending on the item it buys. In football, 1-3 can mean different things depending on the circumstances.

Cedar Hill may have played the toughest first four games of any school in the country. The Longhorns opened with the eventual Class 4A Division I state champion Denton Guyer, beating the Wildcats, 54-28. For their second game, the Horns lost to the second-ranked team in the nation and the eventual Class 5A Division

I state champion, the Allen Eagles. In week three, Cedar Hill fell to Booker T. Washington High School from Miami, Florida. Washington would finish their season ranked thirteenth in the nation and win the Florida Class 4A state title. District play began in week four, and the Horns lost 48-35 to DeSoto, which would eventually lose its only game of the season in the state semifinals to Allen and finish the season ranked third in the nation.

Even with this schedule, the Longhorns had their chances. Starting running back Jared Rayford, the most explosive player on the team (that's saying something) and the player the Horns had planned on centering their offense around, blew out his ACL against Allen. With him, McGuire believes his team would have come out of the early season with more wins, instead of searching for a new offensive identity.

I'm told nobody involved with the Longhorn program panicked as a result of the tough start. In fact, McGuire viewed the DeSoto loss as a positive. The fact that the Horns had shown so much heart and scored 35 points against DeSoto showed potential. The rough start may have been just what they needed, exposing weaknesses and allowing them to be fixed before the games mattered. From the outside, however, many were quick to write off the Longhorns. Cedar Hill dropped out of the polls and spent most of the season under the radar.

Monday morning during athletic period, the defense is in the weight room with tackles coach Cory Jennings. Regimentation isn't part of the Cedar Hill program, unlike what I just left in Harlingen. The kids work hard but at their own pace. Some wear black, others red, still others are bare-chested as they do hang cleans and side lunges. "TTHL" is painted on the wall, "Turn Those Horns Loose," a common mantra within the program ("Hook 'em Horns" is trademarked by the University of Texas at Austin). TTHL is especially appropriate for a team that thrives when playing with abandon.

The offense is outside, walking through adjustments. This week they will go back to calling plays off wristbands. Glaze and his staff believe Midlo has enough film to have broken the signals the Horns have used most of the season.

"Let's go, LET'S GO!! . . . *LET'S GOOOOO!!!*" McGuire yells as he steps on the artificial turf at Longhorn Stadium Monday afternoon. "We're going to have a GREAT DAY!!!" As the music is turned up, he grabs various players in headlocks and bearhugs, looking like an excited kid on Christmas morning. The enthusiasm of a Longhorn practice is something to see. Music is always blaring, coaches are dancing as they run drills, and players are encouraged to be loose and have fun between reps. Good-natured trash talking is common, and the defense celebrates when making plays versus the scout team.

Practice often begins with McGuire playing DJ from the press box, joking and encouraging his players and coaches over the speakers during warm-ups.

"We need a great practice from you today, Quincy! . . . Jaleil Davis is in the house! . . . I love you, Larry Hill! . . . It's a great day to be a Longhorn! . . ." Longhorn safety Tadarrian Luster says, "The coaches are crazy and fun to be around. I look forward to coming to practice every day."

McGuire came from Crowley to Cedar Hill in 1997 as an assistant under a coach with a more disciplinary style. The Horns had talent but poor numbers and didn't play with much emotion. McGuire decided to do things differently. Football can be a grind, full of routine and tedious repetition; the season is a long slog and practices aren't always fun. Only thirty-one years old when he got the head job in 2003, McGuire was the youngest head coach in the Texas 5A. He immediately implemented his philosophy, part of which included trying to make the day-to-day fun.

This staff would treat kids as individuals, not robots. They'd find ways to make the necessary drudgery more enjoyable. Music would be played during practices and pregame. McGuire would hire and encourage like-minded assistants who could function within this style. Family is a big part of the Longhorn program. Like a healthy family, there's a place for the whole gamut of emotion and fun is high on the list. McGuire sometimes sends half-joking e-mails to staff members when he sees them getting too tight, in the vein of, "Coach so-and so, if you can't come to practice with energy and a positive attitude today, I may have to send you inside."

Besides making things fun, the philosophy creates a level of trust when McGuire reprimands his players. McGuire blowups are frequent and impressive enough that the coaching staff immortalizes each one with a "Mag.": a sheet of paper with a capital "M" is hung on the office wall with the date and a relevant phrase for each.

"Who let in the twirlers" and "I'll call your mamma" are some of the more benign examples of the dozens of Mags lining the wall by the final week of the season.

Seeing a few players and coaches get "Magged," I can attest that it's something to witness. If it were possible for smoke to come out of someone's ears, it would happen here. McGuire looks like he's going to come out of his skin. For all the anger, however, McGuire hugs and loves on his players much more than he chews them out. His fury dissipates as quickly as it rises, and everyone seems to know the outbursts aren't to be taken personally.

"The kids know I care about them and they know where the yelling is coming from," McGuire says.

The looseness during the season is paid for with earlier discipline. Each spring, Longhorn players go through something known as boot camp, a big part of which is more traditional disciplinary practices, such as having players do pushups for not being in "Longhorn stance."

The new coaching style paid off quickly. After McGuire arrived, numbers in the program steadily rose and the Longhorns began winning. In 2005, Cedar Hill made their first playoff appearance since 1994. In 2006, the Longhorns went 16-0, winning the Class 5A championship. Since 2005, the Horns have made the playoffs every year, never failing to survive through the bi-district round.

With success come offers, and McGuire has had chances to move both to other high schools in Texas and to the college game. But raising a son and a daughter, he's wanted a more stable environment. "This is where I feel like I should be," he says.

As loose as practice sessions are, they're also beautifully organized, and the staff does outstanding work at fundamental skills. Three four-minute segments each Monday and Tuesday have the defense running through two separate circuits of basic skills. The players rotate through five stations. Scoop and score, stripping from behind, open-field breakdown, and a variety of tackling drills are all worked on daily. Across midfield the offense is busy with their fundamental drills, as well. Receivers coach Kevin Benjamin spends two segments on stalk blocking (a block where the receiver mirrors the defensive back, staying between the ballcarrier and the DB), a skill too often overlooked in receivers, using drills I'd never seen before. When I compliment Benjamin on the drills, he tells me he learned most of them at clinics at Texas A&M and the University of Kansas. He brings me a DVD of the drills the following day.

During team sessions, McGuire makes a few appearances on the offensive side of the field but is mostly with the defense, often holding a big card with a lion and a ram on either end, telling the unit whether to shift to the left or the right.

Daylight saving time ended over the weekend and it gets dark long before practice ends at 6:30. The defense gets off script around segment twenty-four, but no one cares and they keep working as it gets darker, while the offensive players wait along the sideline.

The loose atmosphere continues into the post-practice talk, as players frequently interrupt by blurting out comments. McGuire uses his whistle to settle the kids. It's something you wouldn't see many other places, where a coach's talk means absolute silence, if not hands clasped behind backs and nothing but, "Yes, sirs," at appropriate times. That traditional show of discipline is not what McGuire is looking for this time of year. Longhorn discipline will show itself in more meaningful ways and situations during the weeks to come.

McGuire is happy with today. He'd been worried his team would be down and tight after the tough loss Friday; instead, they are loose and focused.

As we walk off the field he tells me, his voice hoarse from yelling, "When I was young I used to get into it and yell a lot, but I've calmed down."

A map of the Metroplex resembles two wheels side to side, forming a large oval. At the hub of the larger wheel to the east is Dallas; the smaller hub to the west is Fort Worth. Three highways run parallel between the two cities. Highway 183 is the northernmost direct route between Dallas and Fort Worth; I-30 runs a straight line between the downtowns, and along the south end of the two wheels is I-20.

Historically, the south side had been home to most of Dallas' black residents. During the past twenty years, many affluent black families have left Dallas, in large part due to poor schools. This "black flight" didn't take South Dallas' residents far. Just south of I-20 is a string of bedroom communities full of new subdivisions and, importantly, smaller and more responsive school districts. Lancaster, DeSoto, and Cedar Hill all saw demographic shifts as new housing developments filled with black families wanting a better educational system.

Cedar Hill High School has fewer economically disadvantaged students than the Dallas ISD. Cedar Hill's enrollment is 72 percent black as of 2010. It's an important distinction that this didn't happen because the white students left, as is often true with majority-minority schools. At Cedar Hill, the black population moved *in*, creating something unusual outside the South: a middle-class majority-minority school.

According to several coaches, the influx of black families brought something else to the area south of I-20: arguably the greatest concentration of athleticism in Texas. Just a few miles from Cedar Hill, DeSoto would make it to the state semifinals and Lancaster High would advance to the 4A title game.

Aside from coaching, three variables make a successful football program: 1) A large number of great athletes. 2) Solid kids with stable home lives. Stability gives kids time and support to devote to football and the work ethic, coachability, and discipline to improve. 3) Financial backing to organize this very expensive sport. Many minority schools have number one, but struggle with numbers two and three; Cedar Hill and their South Dallas neighbors have all three.

The speed here is incredible. Watching Cedar Hill's practice is more fun than watching most teams play. The kids are well coached in fundamentals. Watching these skills performed so beautifully by such amazing athletes is a joy for a football coach to watch. I've seen it before, but only at college and NFL practices, never with a high school team.

With an enrollment of just 2,145, Cedar Hill is just fifty-five students above the Class 4A cutoff, making it one of the smaller 5As in the state. An accounting error may have put the school above the 5A threshold, and the school could move to the 4A eventually. With the talent here, the thought of Cedar Hill playing in the 4A is scary.

Driving toward Cedar Hill, you notice gigantic antennas rising thousands of feet above the town. At 880 feet, Cedar Hill has the highest elevation between the Red River and the Gulf of Mexico. There's nothing easily recognized as a "hill," but it's high enough to make this the location for the largest collection of antennas in the country. Many of the fourteen towers are more than 2,000 feet tall and can be seen from anywhere in the Metroplex.

Cedar Hill High School is split into two campuses. The tenth-through twelfth-graders attend the main building close to Highway 67, while the ninth-graders are at the freshman center close to the main tower complex. This setup means the freshmen players have less interaction with the varsity than in many schools. The coaches make up for this by regularly sending some varsity/JV coaches to the freshman center for athletic period.

Tuesday is election day, but one would hardly know it in the fieldhouse at Cedar Hill. Other than coaches slipping off to cast their ballots, there's very little talk about it. On Wednesday, the re-election of Barack Obama as president made very little splash here. It's a rare outside event that intrudes upon a coaches' office during game week. One coach mentions his dismay at the result, but another disagrees and the subject is quickly dropped. As with sex and religion, politics is a topic best avoided among friends and co-workers. Nothing takes the focus away from where it belongs.

Senior offensive lineman Anthony Pullins comes into the office before practice to talk to coach Louis Oubre. Above Oubre's desk is a piece of paper stating, "Football is a series of collisions, with tests of strength, skill and will: Big guys clearing the way for fast guys, with countless contests of individual courage and toughness, until one side collectively wears down physically or surrenders mentally." Pullins, who plays both center and guard, good-naturedly tells me to write that he's the "best offensive lineman in the state," making sure I know his number and the spelling of his name. Pullins would eventually sign with Stephen F. Austin State University.

On Wednesday, practice ends with "candy questions." This week, offensive line coach Aaron Woods is responsible for the offensive questions and Lemley is in charge of questions for the defense. Just as it sounds, candy questions involve coaches quizzing the kids on trivial matters to win pieces of candy—a little part of McGuire's "fun" agenda.

While the Cedar Hill-Midlothian rivalry doesn't come close to Abilene-Cooper or Harlingen-Harlingen-South in intensity, the two schools have history. Midlothian is only a few miles south of Cedar Hill but hasn't had as much success. McGuire and several Cedar Hill coaches have homes in Midlothian, making the game important to them personally. The staff worries that this game matters more to the Panthers than the Horns. Two years ago, Midlo beat Cedar Hill, 27-20, despite finishing the year with a 5-5 record. It is a huge deal for the Panthers to knock off their more successful neighbor, while sometimes Cedar Hill has looked past Midlo. This would be a serious mistake, as Midlothian has been surprisingly good this season, coming into the final weekend tied with the Longhorns with a record of 4-2 in district play.

Thursdays after school, the Longhorns always invite a guest speaker to talk about the upcoming game. For the Midlothian game, the speaker is the head baseball coach, Jeremy Fatheree.

Fatheree talks about being ruthless.

"You don't have friends over there," he tells them. "Inflict every bit of athleticism you have on them."

The "ruthless" theme continues, with a video of Mike Tyson describing his mind-set before a fight. McGuire follows up by reminding his team of two keys to keep in mind: number one, Midlothian is a good football team, and number two, "They hate you." On the four losses heading into the playoffs, McGuire says something prophetic, "All we have to do is to keep believing in what we're doing and get hot. Getting hot starts tomorrow night."

During athletics on game day, the defense watches highlights of little things they'd done well the previous week. This isn't the usual cut-up of sacks and huge collisions, but more mundane and important details that are often overlooked: a highlight circle around a defender taking the proper angle and forcing the ballcarrier back into the rest of the defense, or the secondary, all in proper zones, forcing the quarterback to take a sack. Everyone wants to make the big play, but this film is a reminder that great defense is a team activity rewarding disciplined play.

Unlike most staffs, the coaches at Cedar Hill don't have a game-day dress code. Several coaches wear ties, others wear T-shirts, and some dress in the traditional coaching gear of polo shirts and khakis. In the coaches' locker room, Kyle Morales and Brady Bond have an impromptu wrestling match. It's a scene I'll see repeated in each of the weeks to follow. While looseness is a big part of the Longhorn practice week, it's also part of game day. The coaches' antics in the locker room are just the beginning.

Before getting off the defensive bus, Coach McGuire reminds the players about their interactions with the Panther support staff.

"If it's a lady, you be polite," he tells them, "but if it's a guy, you look him in the eye and *you don't blink!*"

From the time they hit the pavement until kickoff in almost two hours, the Longhorns will follow the same routine as they have in every other game this season.

5:40: the scoreboard reads MHS 38, CHHS 36 from the freshman game last evening as the Longhorns walk the field in their grey pants and Under Armour tops with red Superman "Ss" on their chest. After a few minutes of absorbing the surroundings, position groups meet in clumps with their coaches, sitting on the turf while the coaches, in calm, hushed tones, go over adjustments and what to expect.

6:20: the players are back in the locker room. Cedar Hill isn't a "shut up and get your mind right" place. Huge speakers are part of the Longhorns' travel gear. This is the players' time, and for the next twenty-five minutes the locker room resembles a typical "parents out of town" high school party (minus girls and contraband). Loud rap music blares as kids dance and joke while dressing and preparing for the game however they choose.

6:45: the Longhorn version of warm-ups begins. Players line up at 5-yard intervals along each sideline. Receivers coach Stephen Smith stands between the hash marks, leading the kids in a rhythmic clap. On each toot of the whistle, the players trot to the opposite sideline and do a jumping high-five or hip bump with a teammate coming from the other side. Alternating low- and high-fives, they run from sideline to sideline, greeting their teammates as they go. Smith gets the clap going again, waves his hands in the air, stomps around, and tears his shirt in two, exposing the Superman tights he's wearing underneath. Appropriately fired up with enough swagger to last the night, the players break into position groups.

7:05: the players are back in the locker room, music blasting again, when the coaches go outside, take a knee, hold hands, and are led in prayer by defensive line coach Rod Ingram. After the prayer, half the coaches in the circle turn one way and half the other, shaking hands with everyone in turn. The younger coaches finish by jumping in the air to do flying chest bumps (don't know if this is the right term, but you get the picture).

7:10: back inside, the music is replaced by highlights of last week's game. After the film, the players gather and finally it's time for McGuire to speak.

The rip-roaring pregame speech is one of the biggest clichés in football. In truth, many great coaches aren't good at giving such talks and some mediocre coaches buy into the mythical importance of the talk, putting oratory in front of actual nuts and bolts. Good speeches don't win football games; any extra spring in the step from a dramatic speech is gone long before the opening kickoff.

That said, "the talk" does have a place; it's a reminder of whatever theme a coach wants his players to have in mind and draw from at key moments. For McGuire "the talk" is important because of his relationship with his players and the family atmosphere he works to create. As a man who wears emotions on his sleeve, whose emotions will quickly run from love to anger, he is among the best I've seen at giving "the talk."

Standing on a bench at the back of the locker room, he asks for a favor, "Someone says, 'Coach, I need a pair of size fourteen cleats.' I got you. . . . I never ask for anything. I DO IT, because I love you. What you need to understand is even if on that day I think you're a slap, I love you unconditionally. Whatever happens tonight won't change a thing for me, but guys . . . me personally . . . this is a big game for me.

"I've lived in this town for nineteen years. I go to church about half a mile from here . . . all these people in the stands, they all want to see me fail. They all want to say, 'You should have come to Midlothian when you had the chance. You should be *our* head coach.'"

Pointing at his chest, he affirms, "I'm where I belong. I'm where I'm supposed to be. *I'm with my family.* I usually don't ask a lot for myself, but I want you to play hard for me. When you hurt and you're tired, I want you to play for me."

Choking up now, he continues, "It means something to me. When my boy goes to school in this town, he wears red, black, and white. It means something to him. Let's show these guys why I'm where I'm at and where I belong."

Heartfelt emotion changes to intensity and he finishes, "We have the opportunity not only to play the game that we love, but to play for something. The number one seed in the playoffs. We're going to get hot, and we're going to get hot TONIGHT! YOU LOOK THEM RIGHT IN THE EYE! THEY'RE GOING TO BLINK! YOU DON'T BLINK!

"Everybody touch a Longhorn. Close your eyes and visualize . . . offensive line—it starts with you, how you go is how we go . . . Defense—if you get us three turnovers we *can't lose* . . . Special teams—be *special*!

"And last but not least, I promise you guys . . . when we play at Longhorn speed for four quarters, there's nobody in the state of Texas, there's nobody in this *nation* that can hold up. Play your butts off for your brothers next to you and play your butts off for me and I promise you I will coach my butt off for you. Coach I."

In his deep baritone voice, Coach Ingram leads the team prayer, promising that the Longhorns would give God all the credit and glory for whatever happened tonight before the Horns head to battle.

Just two more traditions before kickoff: as players head out, they pass Coach McGuire's father revving a chain saw. This began in 2006, the state championship season, when the Longhorns played Hebron in the second round. Hebron's stadium is known as "The Woodshed," and during that week Hebron's coach gave the Horns bulletin board material, talking about "taking Cedar Hill behind the woodshed." McGuire's theme for the week was chopping down that shed. The chain saw was fired up, CH won 42-17, and the tradition stuck.

Behind the inflatable red Longhorn helmet tunnel sits a Longhorn skull that each player will hug, touch, or kiss before taking the field.

While nowhere near the biggest with only 8,000 seats, Don Floyd Field in Midlothian is one of the best stadiums in the south Metroplex. With a sunken field, good artificial turf, a nice two-story press box, and a big, clear video scoreboard, the stadium is popular for neutral-site playoff games but has rarely hosted big games involving its home school. Tonight, the entire home side is filled with Panther fans, excited by their outstanding season and a belief they can knock off their closest rival.

As I'd seen in Austin, suburban fans can be finicky, and Longhorn supporters haven't jumped on the bandwagon after the early losses. The red-and-black crowd isn't very large, but stadium manager Kenny Hendricks tells me it's a decent turnout. Even with some empty seats on the visitor side, it doesn't get much better than this. It's tough to beat a big game in a great stadium, in front of a large and fervent crowd, on the last night of the regular season in Texas.

The Longhorn offense starts strong, quickly moving to the 15-yard line. However, on his first pass attempt, quarterback Damion Hobbs throws an interception. A few plays later, Panther running back Justin Seeton plunges into the end zone to put Midlothian up, 6-0.

After a three-and-out, the Longhorns are in danger of falling into a deep hole. The Panthers drive to the Cedar Hill 10 before defensive end Xavier Washington puts a huge hit on the Panther quarterback, dislodging the ball. Tackle Calan Johnson scoops it up and runs 85 yards for the score. A missed PAT and the game is tied at 6.

A poor kickoff, a screen pass, and five runs are all Midlo needs to retake the lead, 13-6. The Horn defense is in trouble. Except for the scoop and score, Cedar Hill could easily be down by three touchdowns.

On their last possession of the half, the Longhorn offense puts together a nice drive. They run 85 yards on sixteen plays, all on the ground. Carries by running back Larry Hill and slot/running back Laquvionte Gonzalez and some great scrambles by Hobbs give me my first taste of the "Longhorn speed" McGuire had talked about. When this offense is clicking, it's almost impossible to stop. With the looks they use and the athletes they have, a defense can't key on any one thing. Taking away any one weapon just opens up another option. Hill is a strong, physical back with great forward lean and always seems to get a few extra yards. Gonzalez is blazingly fast and will cut on a dime to find a lane, turning 5-yard gains into big plays. The Horns tie the game at 13 with just 59 seconds left, on a 1-yard dive by Hill.

The Panthers keep scoring. On their first possession in the second quarter, Midlothian regains the lead, looking unstoppable while driving 79 yards on six plays to go back up, 20-13.

The Longhorn defense stiffens. Two consecutive stops deep in Midlo territory and two poor punts set up a short 21-yard touchdown drive late in the third quarter. A pass from Hobbs to receiver Quincy Adeboyejo ties the score at 20.

Again, the Panthers answer with a long drive. Converting once on fourth down and twice on third, Midlo's running attack grinds down the field and for the fifth time tonight to pull ahead of the Horns, taking a 1-yard dive in with 5:02 left. The crowd is electric. A blocked PAT that holds the score at 26-20 does little to dampen the intensity. One more stop and the Panthers will clinch the number one seed in the 5A DII bracket.

During the ensuing drive, the Longhorns use the formula of Hill, Gonzalez, and Hobbs on the ground, and the clock rarely stops. With every tick, it becomes clearer that the game will be decided here and now.

A fourth-and-2 run by Hobbs for 3 yards keeps Longhorn hopes alive as the clock continues winding. Runs by Hobbs and Hill move the ball inside the 20, but less than a minute remains and the clock is running. The huge Panther crowd is on its feet. One big defensive play is all that stands between the Panthers' victory and the number one playoff seed. On third-and-5 from the 15, Gonzalez takes the handoff in full stride, turns the corner, and tiptoes down the right sideline, showing the agility and skill that make him a blue-chip recruit for Texas A&M.

A season turns on so many little things. No one knows what would have happened in the six weeks to follow had Midlothian's quarterback kept the ball in the first quarter, made that late extra point, or stopped Hobbs on fourth down during the last drive, or had Gonzalez been a step slower. A hundred little things brought this game to this point, any of which would have changed the outcome. We *do* know that Cedar Hill would have been the number two seed and would have had to open the playoffs against an undefeated Midway after two consecutive losses.

As it happens Gonzalez *does* turn that corner, tiptoeing down the sideline just inside the pylon for the score with just 37 seconds to go.

An extra point and a fumble on the ensuing return and the game is over. The Panther crowd is stunned. The Longhorns led exactly 37 seconds of this game, but they're the right 37 seconds. Cedar Hill is the one seed and will play Copperas Cove in bi-district. Midlothian will face the tougher draw, opening with Midway.

There's a sense of relief and joy on the Longhorn side just for being a part of such a wonderful game. Positive momentum has been established heading into the playoffs, as well as a preferable draw, but there is no feeling of just how *huge* this come-from-behind win would turn out to be. It's only in hindsight that one can truly appreciate how this exciting night at Midlothian would be the start of an incredible run by the Cedar Hill Longhorns.

Getting back to the fieldhouse around 11:00, the players toss dirty laundry into rolling bins before leaving. Several coaches, trainers, and student-trainers put everything away and start the laundry. The other coaches begin breaking down tonight's film. It will be another three hours until the staff leaves before a full Saturday. Tonight will be long, as will the weekend, but every football coach still working is happy for the privilege. The regular season is over; it's playoff time in Texas.

This game also marks a transition for my journey. For eleven weeks, my schedule has been set; I knew where I'd be from day to day and week to week. Now things are up in the air. With ten of my eleven teams in the playoffs, I have many options on where to go from here. My plan has been to stay through the championship games six weeks from now. As homesick as I've become, though, I'm getting apprehensive about another forty-two days in motels. (Yes, it's now a countdown.) I don't know how this will end and only hope some of my teams will give me a compelling reason to stay through the championships.

McGuire is the only Texas head coach I meet who isn't the AD, as well. He prefers it this way. The arrangement lets him focus exclusively on the football program: fund-raising, academic monitoring, and dealing with the huge numbers of college coaches passing through. However, the main reason McGuire is so comfortable not having the power most head coaches enjoy is the woman who holds the title of AD at Cedar Hill High School, Gina Farmer.

Farmer runs the athletic programs at CHHS, the separate ninth-grade center, and two middle schools. In total, she oversees more than seventy coaches on four campuses. McGuire clearly respects Farmer, and talking to Farmer, it's apparent the respect is mutual. She can't say enough about the character of McGuire and the rest of the staff.

"McGuire is an amazing coach. His people skills are amazing. If he has a downfall it's that he cares about the kids too much. He gives everything he can possibly give to these kids, and some of our kids need that."

This feeling is backed up by several players. "I didn't grow up with a dad at home," one tells me. "These coaches are father figures to me."

Not having to worry about AD duties allows McGuire to do a better job as coach and Farmer to make decisions about the entire athletic program without being tied to any one team. Also, she has time to do things most ADs are too busy for.

Farmer creates a very professional annual report in the form of a ten-page brochure outlining Cedar Hill's athletic accomplishments. She presents this document to the superintendent and school board each year. In the opening letter, she writes about the mission of the Longhorn athletic program, "An essential element of educational athletics is the teaching of lifetime values, such as the Six Pillars of Character: trustworthiness, respect, responsibility, fairness, caring, and citizenship." The report also highlights the successes of the program. A few examples: in 2010, student-athletes passed 90 percent of their classes at Cedar Hill; each sports program is required to volunteer for two community service programs; and twenty-two Longhorn football players received collegiate scholarships. Since 2002, the football scholarships received by Longhorn players have a combined value of $8,127,962.

Saturday, November 17—Bi-District at Midway Panther Stadium in Waco Cedar Hill vs. Copperas Cov

Playoff games in large classifications are generally played on Saturday afternoons, while the lower classifications stick with Friday nights. This allows me to cover a lot of ground and follow up with many of my teams. I arrive back at Cedar Hill after a Thursday night in Houston (La Marque-Furr) and a Friday night just a few miles away in Mansfield (Aledo-Cleburne).

It's 10:20 when five buses and two Cedar Hill ISD police cruisers leave the parking lot heading eighty-six miles to Waco. My seatmate on the defensive bus is cornerbacks coach James Sapp. Originally from East Texas, he went to Baylor on a rodeo scholarship before getting into coaching. A man with varied interests, Sapp likes to talk about anything from poker to the hunting dogs he raises, but this morning he sticks to his bus-ride routine on the way to Waco, playing Tetris on his cell phone.

About halfway to Waco, another bus starts billowing smoke. The caravan is delayed while kids and gear are loaded onto the remaining buses. McGuire is on edge. The Longhorn pregame routine is important to him and will be thrown off by the late arrival.

When the buses finally pull up at the stadium, the student-trainers man a table of pregame snacks that the players grab as they enter the locker room: fruit, cracker packets, and Gatorade. The players lollygag too much for McGuire's taste. "In about two seconds," he warns, "someone's fixin' to get it." The kids get the message and pick up their pace.

After a condensed warm-up, the Horns are back in the sweltering locker room at 2:00. With everyone climbing over each other in the too-small room, McGuire sends the newly promoted JV players outside to relieve the overcrowding. Finally, it's time for the highlight film. As the Midlo highlight package ends the picture fades to a shot of the championship trophy from 2006 with the caption, "It Starts Today."

It's a warm afternoon in Central Texas, and the Cedar Hill crowd is a little smaller than the week before. Simply being in the playoffs isn't enough for most of them to make the drive to Waco. Wearing powder blue, the Bulldawgs from Copperas Cove are a tough team but have nowhere near the explosiveness of Cedar Hill.

The Longhorns start the afternoon looking like they're going to show everyone what "Longhorn speed" can do on both sides of the ball. The ground game—with Gonzalez flying to the outside, Hill pounding it up the middle, and Hobbs running zone reads—looks unstoppable. Morales, the running backs coach is feeling good, telling Glaze to keep running the ball. Add to this a much better passing game than I saw last week and it looks like this game will be a rout. The Bulldawgs' offense is just too one-dimensional, and the Horns build a 35-7 lead going into the fourth quarter.

In the final period, however, I learn how volatile 5A football can be and how dangerous the remaining teams are. The Horns take their foot off the gas and make a few mistakes, and the Dawgs seize the opportunity. A Cedar Hill corner lets a Copperas Cove receiver get behind him on third-and-long; the Dawgs complete the pass and score one play later, making it 35-14 with 11:06 remaining.

The Dawgs recover an onside kick and drive again. Another touchdown and the score is 35-21 with 6:38 to go.

Cedar Hill's offense needs to get something going but doesn't, and is forced to punt. Cove pulls out its bag of tricks, throwing a double pass to convert a fourth-and-long, and scores again: 35-28 with 1:36 to go.

Copperas Cove is just an onside kick away from having the chance to tie the score, but the Cedar Hill hands team comes through this time, recovering the ball, and the offense runs out the clock. A scary ending, but Cedar Hill survives. It's clear, however, that if the Horns are going to make a deep run in 2012, they'll have to play better.

Box lunches from Chicken Express are delivered before the buses head back. As we eat, I talk with Oubre, the offensive line coach. Oubre has had an interesting life and plans to write a book about his experiences. Originally from New Orleans, he went to the University of Oklahoma on a football scholarship in 1977, eventually earning a place on OU's "team of the century as an offensive tackle.

Drafted by the New Orleans Saints in 1981, Oubre returned home. Playing time and a starting position came once he learned how to pass block, a skill not much needed in Barry Switzer's wishbone at OU. "My idea of pass blocking was just to fight with the guy across from me," Oubre says.

After five years in the NFL, Oubre retired and worked for the government, spending six years undercover, setting up money laundering fronts for drug dealers, and buying and selling drugs to keep his cover. The stress of the work finally got to him and he retired after thirteen years.

Returning to New Orleans, Oubre got into education, teaching middle school and coaching offensive line at a magnet high school. His life abruptly changed yet again in 2005 when Hurricane Katrina hit the Gulf Coast. Oubre and his fiancée were among the last ones out, leaving the city on August 28 with little more than the clothes on their backs.

"From the causeway over Lake Pontchartrain, we could see the storm coming as we left," Oubre says. "They closed the causeway an hour later. If we were any later we would have been stuck."

He wouldn't return to New Orleans. His home was drowned and his football team was scattered around the country. Refugees now, Oubre and his fiancée headed west, looking for somewhere to sleep. It wouldn't be until they got to Mesquite, on the east side of the Metroplex, that they would find a vacant motel room.

With everything he owned underwater, Oubre turned to his former coach, Switzer. Switzer came through in a big way, sending enough furniture to fill the Oubres' new Texas apartment. Through other connections, Oubre landed at Cedar Hill as offensive line coach in 2006.

Coaching in Texas is different than what he had grown up with and coached in New Orleans.

"Sometimes I have to remember, they are just fifteen- and sixteen-year-old boys," he says. "We put a lot on them. I don't want them to think football is everything, but to some of the people around here it is. It wasn't as much like that in New Orleans. They liked their football, but also other things. Here sometimes, it's just football."

The bus ride back is uneventful. It was a fun game and everyone's happy the Horns' dream is still alive.

I'm in a good mood, too. I have an early flight back to Reno the following morning; it will be my first visit home since I drove to

Texas back in July. I'll celebrate Thanksgiving with my family a day early before returning to Texas for the second round.

Saturday, November 24—Area Round at Southlake Carroll's Dragon Stadium Cedar Hill vs. Denton Ryan

Little is as depressing as spending a holiday alone in a motel room. I fly back into DFW early Friday morning and get a room near the airport. I find a sports bar, watch the Cowboys game, and feel sorry for myself. Five weeks to go, but at least I'm busy. Friday is Aledo-Guyer at Northwest, followed by Abilene-Lamar at the University of Texas at Arlington. On Saturday, I check out of my airport motel and make the short drive up to Southlake.

It's a great afternoon for football. Sunny and cool, the type of day the game was made for. The Longhorns are on the home sideline and dressed in their home black jerseys and pants, with red numbers.

Today's game becomes a track meet. Games like this often come down to possessions, and the Longhorns get an early edge. After the opening kickoff, they drive to the Raider 3. An alley-oop pass from Hobbs to Adeboyejo puts Cedar Hill up 7-0. The Longhorns surprise Ryan with a successful onside kick. A few plays later, Hill plunges into the end zone and the Longhorns are up 14-0 before the Raiders even touch the ball.

From here, both teams are almost unstoppable. The Raiders, finally on offense, score quickly less than two minutes later: 14-7 Cedar Hill.

On the first play of the second quarter, Hobbs again connects with Adeboyejo, this time on a quick slant; he takes it in for a touchdown: 21-7.

Ryan scores on a pass to Jovanta Williams from 4 yards: 21-14.

Hobbs throws a great pass to receiver Jeantavus White inside the 5 and runs it in a play later: 28-14 Cedar Hill.

The second big kickoff play follows. Cedar Hill kicks deep, and Ryan muffs the ball. Cedar Hill recovers. Two plays later, a third touchdown pass to Adeboyejo from 14 yards makes the score 35-14 with 3:49 in the half.

For the first time today the Horn defense makes a stop, and the Raiders punt. The Horns stall on the following drive, missing a 46-yard field goal to end the half. These are the first possessions not resulting in scores. Most often a three-touchdown lead would feel safe, but with neither defense making many stops, no lead seems secure.

On the opening series of the second half, Ryan moves to the 10. On fourth down, they line up for a field goal, but instead of kicking, the Raider holder fires a lateral to the flat. The receiver throws a second pass into the end zone for a touchdown, making it 35-21 Cedar Hill.

Ryan attempts and fails on an onside kick; the Horns score three minutes later on a 4-yard run by Gonzalez and it's 42-21.

Ryan comes right back and scores during the last minute of the third quarter on a dive by Trent Willis. It's 42-28 Cedar Hill heading into the fourth.

Gonzalez scores his second touchdown today two minutes later on a 15-yard run; after a missed PAT, the score is 48-28.

The Longhorn defense gets its second stop of the game, forcing the Raiders to punt. The Horn offense falters for the first time today and punts it back to Ryan. Ryan runs a reverse for a final score, 48-35. The Horns run out the clock and the game is over.

The Longhorn offensive coaches are thrilled. Their unit played a wonderful game, hurting the Raiders up the gut, to the outside, and through the air. They played three outstanding quarters and one very good one.

Defensive coordinator Lemley, however, doesn't look like a man whose team has just advanced to the third round. Too many mistakes, some blown coverages, and a failure to stop Ryan trick plays gnaw at him. The defense *did* make the stops they had to, but they'll have to be more consistent. A win's a win, though, especially during the playoffs. The Longhorns have survived another week.

I congratulate the coaches and quickly take off. I'm heading to West Texas to catch part of the Throckmorton-Water Valley game at 7:00, my fourth game of Thanksgiving weekend.

In 2009, Cedar Hill's regional final was a watershed moment for two very different programs. For Abilene High, it was a historic upset win, propelling them to a championship; for Cedar Hill, it taught a lesson. With twenty-two players receiving scholarships, McGuire believes this was his most talented Longhorn squad, even surpassing his championship team of 2006. Cedar Hill was the number three-ranked team in the nation, undefeated, and a huge favorite. The game was tight until the fourth quarter. A goal-line stand, quickly followed by a 95-yard touchdown run by the Eagles, broke the game open. Abilene went on to win, 41-17.

Having heard about it from both sides, I was struck by the different perspectives from which each school saw this pivotal game. To many Abilenians, their Eagles came out on top because of superior discipline. They saw Longhorn swagger as lack of self-control. They believed that when things got tough, the more talented Cedar Hill team lacked composure and fell apart.

To McGuire, the downfall of his team that afternoon was that they were *too* tight.

It's easy to mistake the exuberance of programs like Cedar Hill for lack of discipline. To West Texans or affluent white programs, the jumping around and whooping and hollering comes across as cockiness and lack of coaching, rather than a calculated style. It's simply a cultural difference. These kids have played this way from a very young age. To require them to play in a more "socially acceptable" way would stifle their natural ability.

This approach can be a double-edged sword. The Longhorns strutting out in their Superman shirts during pregame is partially designed to intimidate suburban opponents before the ball is snapped, and it can be very effective. But unless properly coached, this swagger *can* cross into a lack of control, disastrous in a sport relying so much on precision. The trick is to walk the line between control and chaos.

I wasn't there to judge what happened between Abilene High and Cedar Hill in 2009. But the regional round game against Arlington shows that seeing Longhorn bluster as a lack of discipline is a big mistake in 2012.

Saturday, December 1—Regional Championship at Mansfield ISD Stadium Cedar Hill vs. Arlington High

I don't know Arlington High's offensive or defensive game plan on this chilly afternoon in Mansfield. But one aspect is obvious: the Arlington High Colts would attempt to out-swagger the Longhorns.

It's important to define the difference between swagger and poor sportsmanship. While Cedar Hill plays loose and makes a lot of noise, taunting or trash talking of opponents is rare. The enthusiasm is directed inward, toward teammates, rarely to the other team.

The Longhorns are emotional, celebrating big hits, scores, runs, and passes energetically. It's rare to see a Longhorn flagged for unsportsmanlike conduct. This is very different than the swagger Arlington brings today.

It starts during pregame warm-ups when a group of Colt players break etiquette by not only crossing the 50-yard line but cussing out Longhorns as they casually walk back to their side of the field. The intent is clear: level the playing field by egging emotional Longhorns into taking stupid penalties.

Talking to his offensive linemen, Oubre advises his players how to deal with the trash talk: "Let them talk shit. Beat them with a smile on your face and get back to the huddle."

McGuire addresses it during pregame. "When we circle up, direct everything to the circle, this family, and you direct everything to our fans. When we walk out, we're nothing but stone-faced, stone-cold killers. We ain't going to do anything talking-wise, but with our *friggin' helmets!!* And they're going to know who the Cedar Hill Longhorns are."

As has become my habit, I ask Hendricks, the stadium manager/ "get-back" coach, about the crowd. A big man with a big cowboy hat, he takes a look around and nods approvingly. After two playoff wins the fans are returning.

A "get-back" coach is just as it sounds. During the game, his job is to keep players behind the coaches' box and often to keep the coaches off the field. Football people being as excitable as they are, they slowly and unconsciously creep forward, sometimes getting penalized for it. It's a job few enjoy, but Hendricks does it very well, often grabbing players and coaches, pushing and pulling them to their proper places.

The Longhorns start well, scoring on a 13-yard run by Hobbs on their first possession. The Colts come right back and tie the game, and it looks like this might be a repeat of last week's shootout with Ryan.

A big defensive play sets the tone for the game. With 2:29 to go in the opening quarter, Longhorn safety Jonathan Buffin intercepts a pass on the Horn 44 and takes it back for a touchdown, putting Cedar Hill up 14-7. From here on out, the Longhorn defense is stifling. A three-and-out and a fumbled snap on the attempted punt gives the Horns the ball on the 15. They punch it in two plays later, 20-7.

The Colts fall apart. The early trash talk has devolved into frustration and cheap shots. The Longhorns never take the bait or respond. They play their game as though the whole display is beneath them. Buffin gets his second turnover of the afternoon, this one a fumble, and Cedar Hill capitalizes again, scoring on a quarterback counter to make it 28-7 Longhorns at the half.

It's more of the same in the second half, and my attention turns to following the Abilene High-Midway game on my phone. The winner will play Cedar Hill the following week. With the Eagles leading in the fourth, I'm thrilled that it looks like I'll get the matchup I'd been hoping for, a game between two of my teams and a rematch of the historic 2009 game. The only problem is that it'll be impossible for me to root against either team.

The Colts have quit. Cedar Hill scores two more times, making it 42-7 before putting in their backups and scoring again. Arlington finally gets in the end zone against backup Longhorns during the last minute. Final score: 49-14 Longhorns.

Defensive coordinator Lemley can breathe a little easier. The defense was outstanding, holding the Colts to just 14 points. Of the four Longhorn games I've seen, this was by far the best defensive effort. Winning three straight playoff games in the 5A is always an accomplishment. To win so convincingly after so much early adversity makes me think that maybe this team is peaking at the right time. The playoff shirts say, "One team, one dream, one goal, that Ring" on the back. For the first time it feels possible.

For me, the only sour note happens up the road at Northwest ISD Stadium. Midway makes a miraculous comeback on the final play of the game to beat Abilene High. Of my eleven teams, just four are left. Waco's Midway High will face Cedar Hill next week in the quarterfinals.

Playing all Saturday games at this point, the Longhorns have an abbreviated workout on Monday, mostly just walking and talking though adjustments for Midway. Lemley works with the JV offense today, showing them Midway's plays so they'll be able to give a good scout look tomorrow.

With the college regular season over and the bowls still a few weeks off, a parade of coaches show up every day. On this Monday, coaches from Air Force, Dartmouth, TCU, and various other schools walk into the coaches' office to talk to Longhorn seniors. During spring practices, twenty to eighty college coaches often show up to watch the Horns. A few years ago, Mark Mangino from Kansas brought his whole staff to see receiver Dezmon Briscoe. They got him, and now he's in the NFL.

The competition gets progressively tougher each rung you climb up the ladder, and Midway is a legit contender. For Cedar Hill to make a deep run, they were going to meet the Panthers one way or another. Had the Horns come up short against Midlo, it would have been during the first round. Playing them now, coming off an outstanding performance against Arlington, is much better.

Midway is 13-0 after knocking off the undefeated Abilene Eagles. Cedar Hill's draw may have been helpful during the early rounds of the playoffs, but any weak sisters have turned in their gear. All eight 5A DII teams remaining are here for a reason. When I ask McGuire about the Panthers, he tells me, "It's going to be a war."

Saturday, December 8–Quarterfinal at Midlothian ISD Stadium
Cedar Hill vs. Waco Midway

I've just driven from Beaumont, where I watched Carthage's heartbreaking loss to El Campo the night before. I'm down to three teams. After a few poor hours of sleep in Palestine, I meet the Longhorns back in the Metroplex.

It's a nice, sunny afternoon as the Longhorns return to Midlothian, where this run began. Unlike the regular-season finale, however, the stands on Cedar Hill's side have pretty well filled in. Longhorn supporters finally believe this team may be for real.

Two things have changed about the pregame routine. The coaches' game-day dress has gotten more formal, with more of the staff wearing ties and/or sweaters. Also, the pregame coaches' prayer circle has gotten bigger as friends of the staff have been invited along for the ride. This week, a good friend of McGuire's, a former assistant who took a head job in Oklahoma, is with the team.

Before the game, McGuire reminds his team what's in front of them.

"We're fighting for just one more week together, not another year, just one week. We are a family, and I'll do *anything for my family!!!*"

The Longhorns move the ball efficiently on their opening drive and take the early lead on a 2-yard plunge by Hill. After trading possessions, the Panthers drive to the end zone and tie the game at 7. Midway quarterback Kramer Robertson is a dazzling athlete. He's going to LSU on a baseball scholarship and shows he's a talented football player, as well. He has a strong, accurate arm and fast legs. On their opening drive, Robertson shows each talent, scrambling for a first down on a third-and-long and rifling passes into good coverage.

On their following possession, the Horns take the first of many gambles. On fourth-and-4 from the Cedar Hill 45, the Longhorns pull off a fake punt, letting Gonzalez run for the first down. The very next play, Hobbs pulls the ball on a zone read, scoring from 38 yards out to put the Horns on top, 14-7.

The lead is short-lived. On the following kickoff, Panther returner DeChaar Greer blasts through the coverage and runs 101 yards to tie the game.

Cedar Hill goes right back to work. Hobbs takes advantage of loose coverage by the Panther secondary, hitting Adeboyejo on a quick slant at the 25. Next, Adeboyejo makes a move to the outside and scores, putting Cedar Hill up, 21-14.

The Panthers appear ready to tie the score again. With the ball on the 5, a bad snap is recovered on the 20, setting up an obvious passing situation. On third down, Robertson is hit by Washington and Richard Moore. The ball pops loose, and for the second week in a row, Buffin scores a touchdown on a turnover, scooping it up and returning it 84 yards to give the Horns a 28-14 lead.

The Panthers come right back with an impressive drive, twice converting on third-and-long, again making this a one-touchdown game, 28-21, with 1:38 left in the half.

Just enough time for Cedar Hill. The Horns execute an efficient eight-play drive with Hobbs completing three passes to Adeboyejo, including a beautiful throw to the 1-yard line with 30 seconds left. With no timeouts, Hobbs attempts a sneak on the right side and doesn't make it.

Showing tremendous poise with the clock ticking toward zero, the Longhorns line up. It's Hobbs again, this time to the left and into the end zone with just 4 seconds on the clock. It's 35-21 at the half.

The Panthers immediately cut into the Longhorn lead after the intermission. The drive is highlighted by a beautiful fourth-and-8 pass by Robertson to the 3-yard line. Midway scores on the next play, and it's again a one-possession game, 35-28.

The signature drive of the afternoon follows. As talented as both of these offenses are, there is a definite feeling that the Horns must keep scoring to stay in front. The Longhorns move the ball 74 yards on fourteen plays, including *three consecutive fourth-down conversions*. Any little mistake could end Cedar Hill's season, but they don't make one. The drive is capped by a nice touch pass to Adeboyejo in the right corner from 28 yards out, extending the lead to 42-28.

The Panthers aren't done. They score early in the fourth but miss the PAT, and the Longhorn lead is 8.

Cedar Hill ices the game with less than two minutes to go. On third-and-1 from the 45, Larry Hill breaks a tackle and runs down the left sideline, diving into the end zone for the score. 49-34 is the final.

I'm not sure I've ever seen an offense play as close to perfection as I witnessed this afternoon. In every aspect of the game, the Horns were incredible. They ran fifty-nine offensive plays with no penalties, just three for negative yardage. They were 4-for-4 on fourth-down conversions; Hobbs was 17-of-19 passing with two touchdowns and rushed for 77 yards and two more touchdowns. The Horns rushed for a total of 245 yards with Hill pounding the ball for 105 on eleven carries. Adeboyejo had eleven receptions for 129 yards and two touchdowns. Glaze called an exceptional game, as well, keeping the Panthers off-balance and attacking whatever the defense gave them.

Midway was a great team but made mistakes against a team that was almost flawless. Despite giving up 28 points, Cedar Hill's defense made several key stops, and that was all they needed.

The Cedar Hill family has earned one more week together, and the relief felt after wins in earlier rounds has been replaced by jubilation. The Longhorns are one of four teams left, advancing to the semis for the first time since winning state in 2006. It's truly a great day to be a Longhorn.

Cedar Hill will play Austin Westlake for a spot in the state championship. Lemley goes over tendencies with his group after lunch. Westlake's offense tips its plays by the personnel group they're in. To take advantage of this, the defense must make their calls late. Quick and clear communication will be a must.

Hill hurt his knee on the last play against Midway. As well as he's been playing since taking over for the back who started the season (Rayford, who was lost to an ACL injury during week two), this could be devastating. A converted safety, Bobby Jackson, will get his first carries this season filling in for Hill.

Saturday, December 15–Semifinal at Waco ISD Stadium
Cedar Hill vs. Austin Westlake

Cedar Hill is clearly the better team, but at halftime the Longhorns are up just 14-7. Maybe it's that this game has become so large, but a cloud seems to hang over the game, an uneasy feeling that today, the breaks aren't going the Longhorns' way.

Earlier in the week, McGuire told the offensive players they needed to be loose, that they play best with a bounce in their step, but there's no escaping what's at stake. Since early this morning, when the buses pulled out of Cedar Hill along with supporters' cars, minivans, and SUVs decorated with "Going to State" and other encouragements, reminders of this game's importance have been everywhere. Along with the usual buses and police escort, several charter buses full of students head to Waco.

The players have been hearing it all week. Knowing it was unavoidable, McGuire addressed what's on the line during his pre-game talk.

"I want you to close your eyes. I want you to visualize what I'm saying. I want you to be able to see yourself getting on the bus. We're pulling out of Cedar Hill, and you see us get on 1382, we take a left, we head down 1382, we see the Racetrack minimart on the left. We take a left on 20, we start driving down 20, you see 360 coming up, we take that right on 360. Can you see it!?" They respond, "Yes, sir."

"You gotta see yourself on that bus . . . You see Randol Mill. We take a left, you see the ballpark at Arlington."

His voice is rising now, "As you're coming over, you see that big beautiful stadium! You see Cowboys Stadium! . . . *Let me tell you right now, the only thing between us and Cowboys Stadium are these guys right here! The only people trying to tear this family apart and take that dream from you are these guys right here!* . . . Everything that you've been coached to do is for this moment. And they're trying to destroy it."

The offense is tight during the first half. But even more concerning are the opportunities the Longhorns let pass. A perfectly thrown double pass from receiver Travis Wilson to Gonzalez is dropped in the end zone as Gonzalez is blinded by the bright afternoon sun. The normally reliable sophomore kicker, Brooks Ralph, missed two field goals that would have extended the lead. The defense has played lights out; they've allowed only three first downs and would have a shutout except for a freak special teams play. During a quick punt on fourth down, the ball hits a Longhorn defensive back on the leg. The DB isn't at fault; it's really just a fluke. A Chap player recovers the muff on the 1-yard line. They scored their only points a play later.

McGuire tries to reassure his team, "Things couldn't have gone any better for them and we're still up by seven." But I have a bad premonition that against a team as dangerous as Westlake, failing to capitalize on so many chances is a bad omen. Luck plays a role in any deep playoff run, and so far today, all the breaks have gone to the Chaparrals.

After the half, Westlake's offense starts to pound the ball more effectively, but the Horn defense stiffens and Cedar Hill takes over after a missed field goal. However, on their first play, Gonzalez fumbles, giving Westlake a fresh set of downs and great field position. The Chaps quickly capitalize, tying the game with 4:47 to go in the third.

Cedar Hill comes right back. Playing his first game on offense, Jackson busts out from the 24-yard line on a counter to the left, picks up a great block by Adeboyejo at the 20, and takes it in, putting the Horns back on top, 21-14.

Behind the thick glass of the press box, I can't hear the sounds from the field. I can hear Bill Howard doing play-by-play from the adjoining booth. Ten Cedar Hill coaches, including both coordinators, sit on two tiers. In front, coaches with headphones communicate adjustments and play-calls to coaches on the sideline. On the second level, freshman and junior high coaches quickly fill out stat sheets and chart formations and plays. Periodically coaches in front ask for game data from the back row to study while their units are on the sideline.

Coach Sapp has binoculars trained on the Westlake sideline before each play. "Here comes their heavy package," Sapp tells Lemley when a second tight end leaves the sideline. The tendencies say the Chaps will run, and Lemley tells Jennings on the sideline, "Up Storm." Other sideline coaches make sure correct personnel are in the game, and Jennings signals "Up Storm" onto the field.

After a Chap three-and-out and a long drive by the Horns, Cedar Hill looks like they've put the game away with a 9-yard touchdown run by Gonzalez making the score 28-14 with 9:13 to go.

Westlake is here for a reason, and they get into scoring range with a series of short passes before hitting running back Sean Rollings from 4 yards out. Again it's a one-score game, 28-21, with 6:10 to go.

The Horns go three-and-out, punting back to Westlake. After a sack and an incomplete pass, the Chaps face a third-and-15 when Westlake quarterback Jordan Severt throws a wonderful pass to Brandon Box at the 47 to keep the drive alive. On the next play the Longhorns blow a coverage, leaving Rollings wide open in the left flat. He takes the ball to the 5-yard line before he's brought down. Three plays later, Alex Chavez takes a toss around the right side from the 2, and the game is tied at 28 with 2:33 to go.

After scoring the last 14 points, the momentum is with Westlake. Cedar Hill can't help but be dejected, while the big Westlake crowd has seen this game swing in their favor. The Longhorns have never trailed but let the Chaps hang around too long, and it suddenly feels like Westlake's game to lose.

Starting on their own 27, the Longhorns have one last shot to win in regulation. Three plays later, it looks as though they may be happy to settle for overtime. A sack and an incomplete pass, and suddenly the Horns face third-and-11 from their own 38. A failure to convert, and the Longhorns will have to punt.

Flushed from the pocket, Hobbs rolls to his right and finds Adeboyejo along the sideline. The receiver leaps high and catches the pass over two Chap defenders, somehow managing to stay in bounds at the Westlake 42. Two plays later, Hobbs scrambles to the 25 and the Horns use their last timeout with 8 seconds remaining in regulation.

One of only three white players on the team, Ralph, the kicker known as "skinny pants" to his teammates, is easy to find on the sideline. During the timeout, I look over and try to get a sense of what's going through his head. Forty-two yards, from the right hash mark, and into the wind to send your team to the state finals would be tough for anyone, much less a sophomore kid who's already missed twice today. He either has ice water in his veins or doesn't know what's happening. Standing there joking with the other kickers, he looks about as nervous as someone waiting for a bus. I vote for ice water. Ralph steps in, keeps his head down, and drops the kick over the crossbar. Cedar Hill 31, Westlake 28.

McGuire and his father embrace. Both have tears in their eyes. They aren't the only ones. Cheerleaders, families, coaches, and players are all feeling the same thing. Who could have imagined two months ago that a team with four losses, missing both their starting and backup running backs, would have survived though five rounds to the title game? The Longhorns are going to state. It's a hell of an accomplishment just to still be playing. Of the sixty-four teams who started, two are left. What a wonderful run it's been. For all my hardships and loneliness, I feel I've seen what I came for: how beautiful this sport can be when schools are given the tools to be great. This is what I'd hoped to see when I came to Texas in August.

But for everything the Horns have accomplished, the toughest test comes on the biggest stage of all. The Longhorns will battle the undefeated and top-ranked Katy Tigers.

Out of the Houston suburbs, Katy has been a power in Texas high school football for the last twenty years, winning six state titles, five since 1997.

During 2012 the Tigers have hardly been tested, defeating fifteen opponents by an average of 41 points. Eight times they've scored more than 50 points, a stat made more impressive by the offense they run. They do their scoring the old-fashioned way, pounding the ball into the line from an I-back formation, rarely putting it in the air. The Tigers are ranked third in the nation by *USA Today*. Both Texas high school polling organizations make the Tigers a three-touchdown favorite to win their seventh state championship.

There's no sense of this when I get to Cedar Hill on Wednesday for practice. The workout is pretty much the same as it had been when I first arrived seven weeks ago. Jason Aldean's *Dirt Road Anthem* still blares on the loudspeakers as McGuire starts practice by playing DJ from the press box. As his kids run through their drills, Coach Ingram dances along with the music. Home for their Christmas break, twenty to thirty Longhorn alumni hang out on the track along with the college coaches who are common enough here to go unnoticed.

The staff is confident they can play with Katy. The strength of their defense has been defending the run. Unlike Westlake, not much can be predicted by Katy's personnel groups. Except for third-and-long situations, Katy always has a strong run tendency. There's no secret what's coming, but stopping it's a different matter. The staff acknowledges that the defense must be better against play-action than they were with Westlake, but overall, they like how they match up on defense. On offense, when the Longhorns are executing, they can score on anyone.

The Longhorns borrow the football facilities at TCU in Fort Worth on Friday to conduct their final walk-through, and more importantly, to separate their kids from the craziness revolving around a state championship game. With just four days until Christmas, it finally feels like winter in North Texas. The indoor practice facility at TCU is cold as the Horns run through drills in sweats and helmets. Kenny Perry, coach of Arlington Bowie and a good friend of McGuire, talks about the opportunity in front of them. After lunch, the Longhorns kill the rest of the afternoon with a video: *The U*, an ESPN Films 30 for 30 series documentary about the University of Miami football program in the 1980s and early '90s, a program model that's similar to Cedar Hill's.

In truth, there's little left to say. Through fifteen games and countless practices, athletic periods, and meetings since early August, whatever can be said has already been said a hundred times. The hay's in the barn, and it's time to play the game.

I've made it to the finish line. Cedar Hill has given me an exciting story that takes me to the very last day. Also, whatever happens tomorrow, I have just one more night in a motel room in Arlington, and I can finally go home.

Saturday, December 22–5A Division II State Championship at Cowboys Stadium in Arlington Cedar Hill vs. Katy

December 22 is the last day anyone in the United States plays high school football. This morning, the Longhorns leave the Cedar Hill High School parking lot and make the same drive they'd been asked to visualize the week before. A fire engine joins the usual police cars to clear traffic for the buses. Along Belt Line Road for several miles toward I-20, Cedar Hill supporters line both sides, carrying signs encouraging their team to "Take State" and reminding them to "Turn Those Horns Loose." Whatever questions the locals once had about this team have long been answered.

Playing the middle game of a championship tripleheader, the Longhorns adjust their pregame routine. During the downtime waiting for the 4A game to finish, the staff learns two Katy offensive linemen are out with ACL injuries sustained during the Tigers' semifinal win over Steele. Also injured was Katy's quarterback, Kiley Huddleston, who's expected to play despite a broken tibia. Sixteen games is a long season; nobody stays healthy. Teams who are still playing are often the ones who overcome injuries the best, and with over 200 players on the Katy sideline, depth is something the Tigers have.

Minutes before kickoff, McGuire gives his last pregame talk of the season. He starts, as he often does, by telling his players about his feelings toward them.

"I want you to know, I love you, all of you, unconditionally, like you're my own sons . . ." Talking about the Tigers: "They are a great football team, but the *difference* between us and them is that we are a great *family*! And family will do *anything* for each other!"

Talking about how this game will go: "Handle the highs and lows and we'll be the state champions!" He continues with the reminders I've heard for seven straight weeks. "One: dominate up front and protect the football! Two: cause three turnovers, we win! Three: be special on special teams! And guys . . . if there ever was a day you gotta be at Longhorn speed . . . this is that day. Let's shock everybody in the state of Texas! I believe in this family and I'll protect this family with all that I've got."

Coach Ingram follows with the pregame prayer, "Keep us mindful of our purpose today, Father God. You created us for this moment, God, and we'll play this game the way you designed it to be played. It's been said it can't be done, but we know, Father God, that you're the author and finisher of this story. And it's been a great story, and only YOU can put the ending on this story . . . We give you all the praise and all the glory, in advance for a Longhorn victory . . . Lead us into battle, Father God, allow us to be great, allow us to be supermen."

More than 42,000 fans fill three of four tiers at Cowboys Stadium. Dallas has turned out to support the Longhorns, but even more red-clad Katy fans have made the trip up from Houston. Wearing visiting white jerseys and red pants, the Tigers are impressive just standing there. As you'd expect from a team that's run the table playing smash-mouth football, the Tigers are big and strong. Their offensive line is massive, the biggest I've seen this season. Most impressive of all is tailback Adam Taylor; at 6-foot-1 and 210 pounds, Taylor is a man. Committed to the University of Nebraska, he's rushed for 2,478 yards and thirty-nine touchdowns and runs a 4.5 40-yard dash. He can run around, pull away from, and run over defenses. Slowing down Taylor has to be the key for anybody hoping to bring down the Tigers.

Cowboys Stadium is an awe-inspiring place. Everything is shiny and bright. Even from below, the huge video screen hanging above grabs one's attention. The huge crowd and bands have the place rocking by the opening kickoff.

It isn't surprising that even such polished teams as these would look a little overwhelmed as the game begins. Both teams start slowly; the Horns go three-and-out on their first possession and the Tigers squander great field position on their first drive with a poorly thrown pass in the end zone and a botched field goal attempt. The second possessions go the same way: another three-and-out by Cedar Hill and a fumble by Katy.

Hobbs takes over on the third Longhorn possession, running three straight times to the Tiger 10-yard line. A perfect throw to Adeboyejo on a slant goes right through his fingers in the end zone, and the Horns have to settle for a 36-yard field goal by Ralph. Cedar Hill takes the early lead, 3-0, with 1:45 to go in the first quarter.

The Tigers come right back. The hobbling Huddleston completes two of the three passes he'll connect on this afternoon; the second is a nice throw to Andy Coonrod, who catches it and goes out of bounds at the Cedar Hill 1-yard line. Taylor dives over the top and the Tigers take a 7-3 lead with 11:15 to go in the second quarter.

The two teams trade possessions, and Katy takes over on downs at the Cedar Hill 28.

On their previous two drives, the Tigers have started feeding Taylor. With huge thighs and great pad level, he's a load to tackle. One man can rarely bring him to the ground and he always gains yards after first contact, if he doesn't break free altogether. Capitalizing on great field position, Huddleston gives the ball to Taylor three straight times; on a toss to the left from the 17, he breaks two arm tackles and gets into the end zone, giving the Tigers a 14-3 lead with 3:51 left in the half.

On the next Longhorn possession, a screen pass to Gonzalez from the Cedar Hill 31 shows off some Longhorn speed as Gonzalez crosses the field and nearly scores, taking the ball to the Katy 6. Three plays later, Hobbs finds Brandon Harris on a slant; Harris makes a great catch, going high and bringing the ball in with a Katy defender wrapped around him. It's now 14-10 Katy with less than two minutes to go before the break.

Cedar Hill has a great opportunity to take the lead before the half when Katy fails to recover the kickoff and the Longhorns take possession at the Tiger 24. The Horn offense fails to move the ball, however, and Ralph misses a 38-yard field goal.

Just like last week, there's some frustration that the Horns have left too many points on the field during the first half. A missed field goal and a touchdown that went through the hands of Adeboyejo, and Cedar Hill would be on top. On the plus side, any questions as to whether the Longhorns could play with the Katy Tigers have been answered. This is anybody's game, twenty-four minutes away from the championship.

The first twenty-five minutes of halftime are typical, with players talking to their position coaches and McGuire telling his team, "They're good, but they're human, all we need is a spark. This just makes for a better story." How they get that spark is something nobody who doesn't know this program would see coming. With a few minutes to go before the half ends, McGuire hooks up his iPod and plays the lead song from the practice playlist, *Dirt Road Anthem*.

Lightening the mood, trying to get his tight offense to loosen up, twenty-four minutes away from the ultimate prize, McGuire and his staff encourage their team of South Dallas boys to sing this hillbilly song. Most of them likely see the song as halfway a joke but enjoy singing in spite of themselves. They sing, "I'm chilling on a dirt road, laid back swerving like I'm George Jones. Smoke rolling out the window, an ice cold beer sitting in the console. Memory lane up in the headlights, has got me reminiscing on the good times."

Win or lose, these are the last moments this team, this family, will be together. The sight of them singing just before taking the field for their final half will stay with me forever.

As was true during the first half, neither team can get anything going early after the break. The second Katy possession, the Tigers again begin pounding the middle behind that big offensive line. Taylor up the gut is the main weapon, with an occasional run by the fullback mixed in. The defense sucks up to stop the run, and a play-action pass to Coonrod takes the Tigers to the Cedar Hill 10-yard line. Taylor breaks two tackles on a toss to the left and goes into the end zone for his third touchdown of the game. The score is 21-10.

Cedar Hill puts together its best drive of the night, going 74 yards on eleven plays and scoring on fourth-and-7 from 24 yards on a quarterback sweep. The Horns don't convert on a 2-point attempt and are down, 21-16, with the whole fourth quarter in front of them.

Katy goes three-and-out and Cedar Hill gets the ball back on their own 32. Another screen to Gonzalez—and again, he cuts across the field from right to left and takes the ball into the red zone. Two plays later, Hobbs throws a beautiful touch pass over the middle from the 21 to Harris and suddenly the Longhorns are up, 24-21, after Hobbs converts the 2-point play.

For the first time this season, the Katy Tigers trail in the fourth quarter. The momentum is on the Longhorns' side, and after a Katy penalty, the Tigers face a third-and-9 from their own 36. A stop here and the Tigers will have to punt, giving the Horns the ball with the lead and a great chance to put away the game.

The third-down play won't show up in any highlight reels, but it is huge. Taylor takes a deep handoff on a draw to pick up 8, setting up a makeable fourth-and-1. The Longhorn defense squeezes the inside gaps, expecting an inside run. Instead it's a toss to Taylor. He breaks around the right end and pulls away, scoring from 56 yards for his fourth touchdown today. Katy's back on top, 28-24.

Hobbs throws an interception on Cedar Hill's next possession and Taylor puts the game away, spinning off a Longhorn defender and taking the ball 42 yards for his fifth touchdown and the final score of the game. Katy wins the state championship, 35-24.

Cedar Hill played very well, but not perfectly. They failed to capitalize on too many chances and lost to an incredible football team. Adam Taylor and Katy's running game were just too strong and eventually wore down the Cedar Hill front.

The Longhorns look like they'd rather be anywhere else when they receive their runner-up medals, but maintain their poise and show class befitting an elite team. For the second straight week there are tears, only this time they're tears of disappointment and the breakup of a family.

Back in the locker room, McGuire addresses his team for the final time.

"Hold your heads up," he tells them. "This group right here . . . I'm more proud of than any other time in my life. The stuff that we've had to endure, to be at this point . . . I'm just so proud of you guys . . . Seniors . . . I love you . . . and I'm always going to be there. And if there's ever a time you need me, all you gotta do is call. Because I love YOU . . . and I'm proud of what you did for the team and for this community . . . you be proud of who you are because you are special."

Ingram leads the team in one last prayer, "When [these kids] reflect back on this year, Father God, help them realize they can overcome anything that life can bring them . . . let them know that they have a family that will never die, that will only get larger and stronger as the years go by."

Six Longhorns would sign D-I college scholarships. Quarterback Damion Hobbs signed with the University of Oregon, Quincy Adeboyejo with the University of Mississippi, Laquvionte Gonzalez with Texas A&M, Brandon Harris with Iowa State University, Adonis Smith with Air Force, and Travis Wilson with the University of Nevada, Reno. Four others would sign scholarships to play college football at smaller schools.

It's a lucky accident that I've had the privilege to be on the sidelines for the past seven Longhorn games and many practices and meetings. When I showed up for the Midlothian game in early November, I had no idea of the ride I was about to witness. As this game not only marks the end of the Longhorn season, but also the end of my five-month road trip, saying goodbye is tough. Though I've had absolutely nothing to do with it, by this December evening I'm proud of whatever tenuous association I have with this exceptional program. These are quality coaches working hard to make differences in the lives of the young men they coach. Seeing how these kids respond in both victory and defeat, I know I've been privileged to witness seminal events in building who these boys will become.

Bittersweet is an overused word, but it fits this evening. I'm tired of living in motels, miss my family, and am excited that I'll soon sleep in my own bed. At the same time, I've met so many great people and seen some of the best high school football in the nation. I came to Texas in July knowing the high school athletic system here was something special, but I leave in December with special feelings for Texas and its people, as well. A part of me is envious of those who call this fascinating and exciting place home.

Long after the Cedar Hill buses leave, I linger to watch the Allen-Lamar 5A D-I game, wondering if I'll ever see anything like this again. The crowd has grown to over 48,000. It's one last beautifully played game, with the underdog Lamar squad hanging on until the final moments of the final high school game of 2012. As the Allen Eagles celebrate their hard-fought victory, I head to the parking lot and punch Reno, Nevada, into my GPS. I'm going home.

ADDENDUM

The 2013 Mini Road Trip: Nine Days in Texas

I keep close tabs on my programs during the 2013 season. During games in Reno, it became my habit to check the Texas scores shortly before kickoff. The semifinal weekend is the first chance I get to return to Texas and follow up with my eleven teams. Luckily some are still playing when I arrive.

Nine days aren't enough to visit every school, and I won't decide my exact itinerary until after the semifinals. Nine of my eleven make the playoffs, and eight survive the bi-district round. The following week, three more lose and I'm down to five.

This is where the story gets remarkable. All five teams win both their third and quarterfinal round games, creating some tough travel decisions when I fly into DFW on Thursday, December 12.

That Stamford, Aledo, Carthage, and Cedar Hill are among the survivors isn't surprising. Getting this far is an accomplishment for any team, but these four have been to the deep rounds many times. The fifth is a surprise. Despite finishing the regular season with a record of 9-1, the Calhoun Sandcrabs were expected to bow out early. Instead, Calhoun and their option offense upset defending state champion Cedar Park in the third round, then crushed Alamo Heights in the quarterfinal. For the first time since 1960, the Sandcrabs will play in the state semifinals for a spot in the championship.

The Sandcrab program has continued to rise in other ways, as well. Calhoun County voters passed a $65 million bond to upgrade district facilities. $4.5 million will go into Sandcrab Stadium, upgrading parking and restrooms, improving the field, and adding additional seating and a new press box. On campus, the gyms will be improved and technology will be added.

Day One

After a few hours rest at a Motel 6 in Arlington, I rise early and drive to Aledo to watch practice. It's cold at 7:00, but I'm excited to see old friends and have a taste of Texas high school football after a season in Reno. I'm surprised to find Coach Buchanan very worried about their semifinal game against Ennis the following day. Ice storms in North and West Texas the previous weekend forced most quarterfinal games to be delayed until Monday, so the Bearcats had only four days to prepare for a very tough and rested Ennis team. Despite an incredible 2013 run (14-0, number one ranking in state for 4A, and an average victory margin of nearly 60 points), Buchanan told me he's never been more nervous about a game. He's bothered by the fact that everyone just assumes the Bearcats won't be hurt by the short week and will continue to roll to state. After wishing Buchanan good luck tomorrow, I head over to Cedar Hill for their afternoon walk-through.

Circumstances the previous season meant I'd spent more time with the Longhorns than any other program, so it's great to drive down Belt Line Road and catch up with the coaching staff. Coach McGuire immediately asks if I'm going to travel to Waco for their game against Lake Travis. Honestly, until now, I hadn't decided what I'd do the following day. Four of my teams are playing. As well as Cedar Hill-Lake Travis, Calhoun has Brenham at Reliant Stadium in Houston, Aledo and Ennis will play in Midlothian, and Stamford meets Hico in San Angelo. After having a front-row seat for the entire 2012 run, the Cedar Hill staff sees me as something of a good luck charm. Not wanting to tempt fate, I agree to head to Waco and cross my fingers for my other teams. Unlike Aledo's staff, McGuire and his coaches aren't worried about the short week. Lake Travis is a great team, but the Horns are healthy and feel good about the matchup.

No tough decisions this evening. My fifth survivor, the Carthage Bulldogs, play tonight. I leave Cedar Hill and drive to Mansfield to see them play the La Grange Leopards for a spot in state.

The ice storm is gone, but it's miserably cold in the Metroplex. A cold drizzle is falling as I arrive. I'm early enough to catch up with my third coaching staff of the day during warm-ups. Coach Surratt and his staff seem confident tonight. When I comment on the cold, they tell me this is nothing like what they'd had the previous week in Beaumont.

Carthage is just too strong and executes too well for La Grange. The Bulldogs pull away in the second half and win 51-22. While not very dramatic, it's gratifying to see the Bulldogs happy after the bad taste I'd had from last year's El Campo semifinal. The first part of championship weekend set, I head to Arlington at the end of a very long day.

Day Two

Again, it's a short night. I check out of the Motel 6 early Saturday morning and meet the Longhorns at Cedar Hill. Unsure where I'm going after the game, I follow Cedar Hill's caravan down I-35 to Floyd Casey Stadium at Baylor University. With a new stadium being built on campus, this will be the last football game ever played at the historic venue. It turns out to be a great one.

It's even colder than last night. The drizzle has been replaced by a wet haze and the wind has picked up. I'm having trouble writing notes as my hands go numb as soon as I take off my gloves. It's a defensive struggle most of the day, but the Longhorn run game awakens during the fourth quarter and they finally take the lead late in the final period. Cedar Hill returns to state with a 19-10 victory.

Once again, the Longhorns will play the Katy Tigers for the 5A D-II title. I'm struck by the difference in mood from last year's Cedar Hill semifinal. Last year, there was jubilation about just getting to state. This season the Longhorn family is rejoicing in having "one more week together." A second chance is rare in high school football—that it's Katy again just makes this victory sweeter.

My attention turns to three other games. Unfortunately, the Calhoun Sandcrabs' great season has ended. Several fumbles late in the first half lead to Brenham scores, and the Cubs pull away for a 56-21 win. Stamford leads Hico, 20-12, at the half, and Coach Buchanan was correct to be worried; his Bearcats are in a battle. Aledo-Ennis is 0-0 at the half. My plan is to visit each school still playing. Calhoun's loss means I won't be heading to Port Lavaca. I will go to

Carthage and Cedar Hill, but Aledo and Stamford are still up in the air; I stall at a fast-food restaurant in Waco awaiting results.

This is as good a place as any to recount the 2013 campaigns for those schools that time and geography won't allow me to visit during this trip.

Under new coach Jeff Lofton, the Idalou Wildcats did very well. The Wildcats were 7-3 during their regular season, losing to Denver City for their only district loss but qualifying for the playoffs. The Wildcats won their bi-district playoff game before falling to state runner-up Wall in the second round.

Down in the Rio Grande Valley, the Harlingen Cardinals also had a strong year. The Cards won both signature games, beating San Benito in the Battle of the Arroyo and Harlingen South in the Bird Bowl on their way to another district title. After winning bi-district, the Cards fell, 23-20, on a controversial call to Mission Sharyland in the second round. Sharyland's loss to San Antonio Madison the following week once again assured no Valley school would compete for a big-school title.

In Round Rock, Stony Point showed signs of rebuilding. The Tigers started strong, winning four of their first five games. Unfortunately, they lost four of their final five, and a 5-5 record left them just missing the playoff cut. Realignment numbers released in December 2013 had Stony Point picking up a few hundred students, still far short of the 3,000 they had during their best years, but heading in the right direction.

The story at La Marque is typically complex. The Cougars won their district and finished the regular season 7-3. After beating a Houston ISD school in bi-district, La Marque fell, 37-10, to Coldspring-Oakhurst in the second round. Not surprisingly, the second-guessing of coaches on message boards was vicious, causing Mike Lockwood to shut down Coogsports.net for a time. Coach Jackson was disappointed, but very proud that, unlike last year, his Cougars took the playoff loss like men. As tempers calmed, many message board posters acknowledged this same growth in the Cougar program. The La Marque ISD is in as much turmoil as ever. Both Superintendent Burley and Principal Gurnell are gone, and talk is that the new administration isn't friendly to athletics. It's anybody's guess what this means, but a rabid football community and an anti-athletic administration are a volatile mix.

Both Stamford and Aledo have pulled out their games in the second half. Aledo dominated after the break to beat Ennis by a final score of 29-6. Stamford's game went right to the finish, but a Bo Wimberly interception deep in Stamford territory during the final minutes clinched a 34-26 win for the Bulldogs. I can start moving. I'm heading to West Texas.

Day Three

Yesterday afternoon, I drove a few hours until it got dark and stopped in Gatesville. Today, I arrived in Stamford to catch the end of the staff's scout meeting. It will be a short week, with the Bulldogs playing the Shiner Comanches in the first of four games being played on Thursday. Kickoff is at 10:00. Shiner is well known by Texans as the home of Shiner Bock Beer.

I catch up with the coaches for a while. When the meeting wraps up, I head down to Abilene for an early night.

Day Four

I drop by the Chuck Moser Field House at Abilene High School on Monday morning. It was a frustrating year for the Eagles; for the first time in fifteen years, Steve Warren's team failed to reach the playoffs. Warren tells me he knew this year was going to be tough, as the Eagles had lost many players from 2012. But the extent of the drop was surprising. A star player's unexpected family tragedy took focus away from the field. Injuries and bad luck followed, and before they could blink, the Eagles were 1-6. Sometimes good or bad breaks seem to pile up, and it was just one of those years at Abilene High. Warren is optimistic about the future. The Eagles finished strong, winning two of their final three games. The off-season is going well, and a new star emerged, with freshman running back Abram Smith dazzling the LSWC late in the season. I ask Warren to say hello to his staff and drive sixty miles to Throckmorton.

Coach Reed is surprised to see me when I walk into the gym during his second-grade PE class. Reed asks his daughter (a student in the class) to bring me a Dr Pepper and he tells me about Throckmorton's 2013 season. Like Abilene High, the Greyhounds had some bad luck. Still a very good team, Throckmorton finished 9-1 but were paired with a very tough Ira squad in bi-district and lost, 59-50. Reed isn't complaining. He tells me that after two straight state championships, the Greyhounds were due a few bad breaks. Shockingly, Reed tells me he's interviewing for a 2A Hamilton job, trying to make a rare jump from six- to eleven-man football. He would get the job and leave Throckmorton in January. It's great to see Reed again, but I say goodbye. I have to get back to Stamford.

I drive the sixty miles southwest to Stamford and arrive just in time for afternoon practice. Leaving for Arlington on Wednesday afternoon, the Bulldogs will only have two normal practices this week, but by now this should be enough. I make plans to meet the Bulldogs early Thursday morning, then it's back on the road for my third and longest drive of the day, about 160 miles to Aledo.

Day Five

At before-school practice, several Aledo coaches say they're very impressed with Brenham. "Aren't sure we can beat them," they tell me. I'm in no position to disagree with them but I'm surprised, knowing the Bearcats' record. Buchanan is very busy but great to talk to, as always. After practice, I start driving toward East Texas and Carthage.

I arrive at about 2:00 and spend the afternoon with the coaches. On Friday afternoon the Bulldogs will play Kilgore, the top-ranked 3A team in the state and their East Texas neighbor, only forty-five miles away. The two squads scrimmaged in August and, anticipating this matchup, told each other, "See you December 20," during the handshake. Nobody at Carthage is overly confident. Kilgore is a very tough team, and it could go either way. Practice is held inside the new indoor facility. It's a full 100-yard field with a roof high enough for the kicking game, minus punts. It's easy to forget this is a school with fewer than 800 students. I stick around to watch practice film back in the fieldhouse in both the offensive and defensive offices. It's been great to catch up with everyone these past few days. I feel like I never left.

Day Six

Today is the only day I can sleep late and I take advantage of it. It's only two-and-a-half hours back to Cedar Hill and practice doesn't start until 4:30. I have breakfast (Texas-shaped waffles) in the lobby and check out of the Carthage Best Western. Taking my time returning to the Metroplex, I spend the afternoon in the Cedar Hill coaches' office, watching the parade of college coaches come and ask about various Longhorns. The coaches feel they didn't play well against Katy last season, partially because they went into that game banged up. Now, the Longhorns are healthy and the staff is thrilled to get another chance at the Tigers. After practice, Coach McGuire relaxes on the office floor with his son Garret, a freshman scout team quarterback. His twenty-year-old daughter Raegan comes in, and the remaining coaches, players, and family members enjoy each other's company. I say goodbye and drive up to Arlington and the Hyatt Place Hotel at Six Flags, my home for the next four nights.

Day Seven

I meet Stamford at their hotel at 7:00 AM for the short ride over to AT&T Stadium, formerly known as Cowboys Stadium. Playing in this imposing venue for the third straight year, the early advantage should go to Stamford, but Shiner gets the jump.

At halftime the Bulldogs are behind, 21-7, and Coach Hutchinson reminds his team that they'd trailed by the same margin the previous year. But it's about to get worse; Shiner recovers the ball after Stamford's return team flubs the second-half kickoff and goes up, 28-7. It's hard to believe the Bulldogs will find a way to pull it out. Wimberly is having a bad day at quarterback. He injured his non-throwing shoulder during the first half and has been throwing terribly. During the break, he apologizes for his poor performance and promises to make up for it in the second half, but I don't see how the Bulldogs can overcome such a big deficit. I'm wrong. Wimberly runs for two scores, the defense stiffens, and a 60-yard pass to James Washington ties the game with less than four minutes to go. A Shiner fumble and another Wimberly run put the Bulldogs ahead. A Washington interception returned for a touchdown during the final minute caps the scoring. The Bulldogs win, 41-28. It's an amazing recovery for Wimberly, who finishes with 367 total yards, with three touchdowns rushing and two passing. Like Hagen Hutchinson last year, Wimberly is named both offensive and defensive player of the game.

It's another great day for Stamford, but it would be the end of an era, as well. Defensive coordinator Mitch McLemore was hired as the new head coach at 1A Junction and is moving his family to the

Hill Country. Stamford's phenomenal success attracted the attention of many schools, and in February, Coach Hutchinson took the job at 5A Monterey High School in Lubbock. Stamford stayed in-house and hired longtime assistant Ronnie Casey as their new head coach.

The Holiday Inn looks to have been completely taken over by Carthage Bulldogs and their supporters. I meet them for dinner in a banquet room. During the team meeting, Bulldog players and coaches take turns pantomiming each other, mimicking walking and talking patterns. Players roll on the floor laughing before Coach Surratt informs them about bed check at 10:30 and sends them to their rooms.

Day Eight

It's tense in the coaches' locker room at AT&T. Assistants count the minutes before going out, pacing and stating the obvious like, "We just gotta get after it today." Coach Surratt comes in and says, "Guys, I appreciate all the hard work you've done to get us here and I just want to let you know that if we don't get it done today you're all fired." The joke lightens the atmosphere immediately. The humor last night and today make me wonder if I'd misread Surratt during the week I spent at Carthage last year. I remember him as tightly wound on game day. He isn't today. Loose and relaxed would best describe the Bulldogs and their coach as they take the field.

Over 17,000 East Texans made the trip to Arlington to see the top two teams in 3A. The Carthage Bulldogs are clearly better than the Kilgore Bulldogs, but Kilgore sticks around until the end. The outcome is finally decided when Tevin Pipkin locks up the game for Carthage on a 24-yard touchdown run with 50 seconds remaining. The final score is 34-23. It's another great football game and, this year, I get to see Carthage celebrate.

Day Nine

With Aledo and Cedar Hill playing the first and last games today, I'm going to be inside AT&T for a long time, so I go to the lobby early for a big breakfast. The room is already full of football fans with the same idea. Championship weekend has turned into a huge event in Arlington. Over 200,000 attend the ten games these three days. This afternoon, Allen versus Pearland will set the Texas high school record with over 54,000. I share a table with a red-clad family from Katy who will attend all three games. They moved to Texas by way of Oregon and Arizona, and we discuss Cedar Hill-Katy. The kids play in Katy's middle school program and the family talks favorably about Texas football as compared to what they left out West.

Today, the pessimism of Aledo's staff isn't warranted. Brenham hangs around early, but the second half is all Aledo. It's 3-3 halfway through the second quarter, but four unanswered touchdowns give the Bearcats a commanding 31-3 lead. The backups trade touchdowns and Aledo takes their fourth title in five years and fifth under Coach Buchanan by a score of 38-10. Aledo becomes the first high school team ever to reach 1,000 points during a season, averaging nearly 64 points during sixteen games. Quarterback Luke Bishop is named offensive player of the game and his father, an Aledo assistant, proudly tells me about his elder son winning the same award in 2009.

After watching the first half of the Allen-Pearland game from a second-level end zone seat, I meet Cedar Hill in their locker room. The Longhorns prepare as always, dancing to loud rap music, a coach occasionally joining in, before taking the field. Coach Ingram wears his silver metal from last season's loss to Katy. "I want to remind myself today just how awful a feeling getting this was," he tells me, "Today, I trade this in for a gold medal." Knowing the superstitions here (and even buying into some after attending five straight winning efforts since coming to Texas), I tell them this is the third time I've been in this locker room this week, each time with a winner. (Carthage had been in another room.)

That said, I'm worried for the Longhorns. Last year, as bad the championship loss was, it was a huge accomplishment simply to be there. With the rocky start, the injuries, and the amazing playoff run, the Horns had far exceeded expectations. Although everyone sees them as the underdog now, they *need* to win in a way they didn't last year.

As the Longhorns walk through the tunnel after warm-ups, they pass the Allen Eagles. From their buses, the newly repeated 5A D-I champions encourage their Metroplex neighbors, thrusting championship rings out the windows and telling passing players, "It's your turn now! Get one of these."

The first half is frustrating. To me, the Longhorns seem like the more physical and athletic team. But after controlling most of the early action, Cedar Hill fumbles quickly turn a 10-0 lead into a 21-10 halftime deficit. Coach McGuire reminds his players of the bi-district game against Temple, a game Cedar Hill trailed, 28-7, before winning in the final minutes. "Defense, we don't need three-and-outs, but we do need some stops," he tells his team before leaving the locker room.

The first possession isn't three-and-out. Katy tacks on a field goal to build their lead to 24-10.

A fourth-and-3 gamble turns the momentum. Receiver DaMarkus Lodge takes a direct snap and scrambles 40 yards for a touchdown. The game changes. Great defense and Katy miscues result in a Cedar Hill field goal. Another Katy turnover leads to a Cedar Hill touchdown, and after a 2-point conversion, the Horns go on top, 27-24, with six minutes to go. Katy fumbles the ensuing kickoff for the final nail in the coffin; Cedar Hill recovers, and six plays later, Aca'cedric Ware goes in to put the Horns up by two scores with 3:17 left. Final: Cedar Hill 34, Katy 24.

The celebration continues until AT&T security personnel shoo Longhorn supporters and players off the field. It moves to the locker room as players and coaches sing, dance, and douse each other with Dr Pepper and sparkling cider. It's been three amazing days, watching four of my teams celebrate championships and, this time, the ending isn't bittersweet. The Cedar Hill Longhorns have traded silver for gold.

AFTERWORD

During my five months in Texas I attended thirty-seven varsity football games, (fifty-nine games total including JV, freshman, seventh grade, eighth grade, three college games, and one Cowboys game). I stayed in forty-five motels in thirty cities and put a total of 19,689 miles on my Ford Focus. I also gained seventeen pounds from lack of exercise and eating too much Chicken Express, Sonic Drive Inn, and BBQ.

Some aspects of the journey were tremendously hard, but I'll never regret the season I spent in Texas. I'd coached high school football for twenty-two years before seeing the game Texas style and was never aware of just how limited my perspective was. Hearing stories and seeing something firsthand are entirely different things. Texas high school football has its flaws, but I came away convinced that theirs is the best system of public school athletics in the country. Most people know there are differences, but not the extent of them. This goes both ways. Texans rarely have an inkling of how the sport looks elsewhere. Texas is such a big state and conditions for coaching are so good, it's rare when coaches look beyond the state line for a job. They're amazed to learn things they take for granted aren't done in the rest of the country.

"How do you have off-season without athletic period?" is a typical question I got during my travels. I had to tell them that their concept of "off-season" as well as mandatory athletic periods are largely unique to Texas.

An officer from the American Football Coaches Association, who spent his entire career in Texas, asked me, "Why don't the people where you're from care that things are done so poorly?" People usually take for granted the way things are. Texas coaches can't imagine coaching without athletic period, great facilities, and reasonable pay. Never expecting these *Texas* necessities, coaches elsewhere don't realize what's lacking.

I've always hated when people say, "Everything happens for a reason," after bad events. But I have to admit, in the case of my firing from Wooster High School, the saying turned out to be true. At the time, I was hurt and angry, but it was the best thing that could have happened for me. Without being forced to make a change, I never would have had the adventure of my travels nor the wisdom I gained along the way.

I came to love Texas and was privileged to witness things few coaches ever see. On consecutive days, I stood on the sideline with one team as their championship dream came to an abrupt end and was part of the giddy celebration as another advanced one step closer to theirs. I heard pregame speeches, learned how different schools prepare, and saw how life is different in the various regions of this giant state. It was an amazing experience and taught me much about football and education in general.

I found the Texas experience to be unique. Two factors have kept football here strong: a history of cultural support and the coaches themselves in the form of the Texas High School Coaches Association (THSCA). Coaching was once considered a profession nationwide and athletics played a bigger role in the nation's schools. While other states have slowly but inexorably eroded public school athletics, these two factors have allowed sports to keep its standing in Texas.

Starting in the 1920s, Texans have had a special relationship with football. With a far-flung population and somewhat isolated status, local high schools have had an importance to small towns that universities in other states have enjoyed. During the 1920s and '30s it was common for fans to travel on trains from town to town following their favorite teams. This tradition is still alive today, with fans making road trips to neutral sites during the playoffs. High school football is just part of life in Texas towns in a way that isn't true in most places. As Texas has become more urbanized, the importance of the game has diluted somewhat, but many suburban residents have moved from other parts of the state and brought high school football culture to their new homes.

The coaching profession itself had a big role in sustaining Texas football. The Texas High School Coaches Association was founded to train coaches in 1930, making it the oldest such organization in the country. It's also the most powerful. With more than 20,000 members, the THSCA hires a lobbyist in Austin to protect its interests at the capitol. The THSCA has been instrumental in promoting the professionalism coaching enjoys in this state. While it's not involved in politics, it's often said that *if* the THSCA wanted to endorse a governor, it wouldn't have a problem getting one elected.

The convention itself is impressive. Rotating between the Metroplex, Houston, and San Antonio, this annual "coaching school" begins the season. Staffs from around the state meet for four days, attending seminars, networking, and having some fun before the season starts. The clinic is a gold mine for sports marketers. Most HC/ADs have budgets coaches in other states could only dream of. The clinic is a great gig for those selling uniforms, blocking sleds, technology, and anything else a sports program needs. A general meeting on day four wraps up the convention.

Most important, the THSCA has been a powerful force in keeping the Texas model intact. Whenever the state legislature discusses doing away with mandatory athletic period or allowing volunteer coaches to fill coaching positions, the THSCA has the political clout to block it. The THSCA is instrumental in keeping coaching in Texas a *profession*. The THSCA keeps Texas football from looking like football everywhere else.

I'm often asked which program was my favorite. It's an unfair question. Despite their differences, I'd consider myself lucky to work with or have a son play for any of the programs I documented for this book. When done correctly, high school football builds character traits better taught outside the classroom. By this measure, all of these programs are exemplary and great examples of what high school athletics can offer.

As different as each of these programs is, I found common threads allowing coaches and kids to be successful. Most important is support. Support is a word I found myself using too often as I wrote. It's what separates Texas high school football from most programs outside the state. In picking the eleven teams to focus on, I was aware they had little in common with each other except for being successful. Some have great athletes, others don't. The coaches all have different philosophies and styles. They have different ethnic and socioeconomic breakdowns. Enrollments run from 56 students to more than 3,000. But all have great support.

Support comes from above. The administrators at these schools generally recognize coaches as positive role models and vital members of the staff. Most principals I spoke with stressed the importance of involving kids with activities, often saying coaches were some of their best teachers. Many Texas administrators and superintendents are former coaches themselves, giving them respect for athletics often absent among administrators who have never been on the sideline or even in the classroom—professional administrators who often buy into the testing culture that is infecting schools.

Support is part of the day-to-day interaction between coaches and players in the form of athletic period. Most players told me they have strong relationships with their coaches from working together during all four years of high school, and in the smaller schools, down as far as sixth grade. How many intangible ways can this type of relationship help a student? Janet Thornton, principal at Idalou High School, put it very well, "If our kids can make a real connection with just one adult on campus, they are so much more likely do to well than when this doesn't happen."

Support also comes from below. "Butts in the seats" are part of the equation, but it goes much deeper. Some of my programs spend very little money but find other ways to build success, because it's important to the people. At some schools this means allocating a large salary to attract a quality coach; at another, it may be a principal attracting assistant coaches by giving them good teaching schedules. It usually means a higher than average number of boys coming out for football. There's a belief in these communities, from the superintendent to the families to the clerk working at the Allsup's convenience store, that high school football *matters*. Coaches have some influence in building this support, but it wouldn't make a difference if Vince Lombardi himself rose from the grave and took over certain programs. Without support no coach can be successful.

When I got my head job in Reno, I believed I had good support, and during my first year, by Nevada standards, I did. The man who hired me was a former coach who worked to rebuild the Wooster program and hired me for that purpose. Unfortunately, being a Nevada product, I'd never seen how things could be done and didn't know what I should've been asking for (I know better now). More unfortunately, my benefactor left after that first year. The people who succeeded him often meant well, but their idea of support wasn't to help me build the program, but to console me after the too-frequent losses.

Support in Nevada meant no pressure to win and freedom to build the program, but no help. In Texas, support means higher expectations, but also the tools to make success achievable. I think most coaches would prefer having what's needed and being held to higher expectations.

Something that makes Texas so interesting is that it's an example of both the best and worst of education. I've spent most of the preceding pages documenting the excellence of the state's football programs, but Texas is also the perfect example of what *not* to do when it comes to assessment and accountability. No other state has allowed assessment to overwhelm education like Texas. State-required standardized testing—not only for graduation, but also for individual classes—has stifled teaching. Teachers and administrators are effectively handcuffed into removing creativity or personal initiative from their curriculum. Texas' per capita educational spending is among the lowest in the nation. Texas education has also received national attention for political squabbles over curriculum and textbooks. At first glance, Texas would seem to be a poor model for public education.

I don't think it's exaggerating to say that the excellent condition of the state's extracurricular programs saves Texas from having the worst educational system in the country. I saw this in my eleven schools. They do well despite ridiculous state mandates precisely because those communities and schools believed in something beyond test scores.

Schools work when they offer excellent programs that excite kids. The public support from Texans for non-academic programs allows those programs to thrive. Thriving programs excite students and build life skills; excited students apply those life skills in the classroom. By *not* focusing directly on testing, kids generally perform better than their counterparts in less well-rounded schools. There is a difference between extracurricular and cocurricular. In most places athletics are extracurricular, and seen as a nice way to keep kids off the street after school. In Texas, athletics are as integral to the educational experience as algebra or English. Coaches are viewed as professionals. High school sports are important and coaches are valued.

A three-year study conducted by Dr. Roger Whitley at East Carolina University showed students involved with athletics are significantly more likely to graduate and have higher grade point averages, lower dropout rates, less truancy, and fewer discipline referrals. It wouldn't be a stretch to predict that healthy athletic programs improve standardized test results, as well. Unfortunately, many school districts throughout the country sacrifice the long-term benefit of having robust athletic and extracurricular programs for the short-term fix of replacing coaches with professionals directly connected to test scores. Besides being counterproductive, this strategy forgets why kids *want* to go to school in the first place. Few kids get excited about standardized tests or science class. They *do* get excited for football and band and other "non-essentials"; taking those away removes the motivation for a huge number of kids to attend school at all.

Schools that don't support athletics and arts, both inside Texas and outside, miss the forest for the trees. By focusing so narrowly on objectives required by assessment demands, they've undermined their other programs to the point where their schools aren't attractive to the kids they're supposed to encourage.

It's a common misperception that the extravagance of Texas football is bought by a huge budget. In truth, less than 2 percent of the education budget goes to athletics. The athletic budget of my home of Washoe County, Nevada, reflects a clear difference in priorities. Washoe County spends one-fourth of 1 percent of its education budget on athletics. It's a shame such a significant program is allocated so little. I doubt there's another sliver of the budget that returns so much to so many.

I'm aware that the Texas approach couldn't be replicated nationwide. Too much of Texas high school football culture is deeply ingrained in that state's history for the mind-set to be exportable. Texas is the only state where professional coaches and athletic period are required in every public high school. This would be impossible in most states, where there aren't enough coaches with teaching credentials to fill every job. It works in Texas, due to this state's commitment to providing quality athletics, the huge number of homegrown coaches, and a significant number of coaches who come from other states to work in a supportive environment. That said, parts of the Texas model could and should be copied. Things can be done to improve athletics throughout the country.

Schools *can* make hiring on-campus coaches for teaching vacancies a bigger priority. Nothing has caused more separation between education and athletics than the outsourcing of coaches away from professional educators. Teachers should be hired, in part, based on what they do for the school outside of the classroom. Teachers should be encouraged to coach or help with extracurriculars by being offered beneficial teaching schedules and better stipends.

Rollins Stallworth, former coach and current administrator in Washoe County (Reno-Sparks), Nevada, says that as a high school principal he would "find the best possible candidate for a teaching position who can also coach a sport and add that piece to the interview hiring process. The hiring committee for any teaching position would include the athletic director, athletic administrator, and at least one other teacher/coach on campus."

He further points out the value of coaches as teachers. "Attend a high school football practice and you'll see . . . differentiated instruction, small-group learning centers, scaffolding, athletic engagement, hands-on learning, and independent learning . . . Many administrators do not have the background to understand the dynamics of coaching and athletics."

School districts *can* allocate more funds to athletics and extracurriculars. The benefit athletics provides Washoe County is worth far more than the pittance the district invests. Coaches spend too much time fund-raising for essentials—time better spent working with kids.

Most important, schools everywhere *can* recognize athletics and extracurricular activities as important parts of the curriculum, complementing lessons taught in the classroom by encouraging spiritual and physical growth.

The ancient Greeks recognized true education as being comprised of a triad of the mental, spiritual, and physical. They believed that for a person to be "whole," all three of those characteristics must be present. Education should prepare children for adulthood. For this to happen, all three areas must be addressed. Most of the nation has gone away from the Greek model. Say what you will about Texas' misguided reliance on standardized testing, but its football culture has driven well-rounded, complete education in the Lone Star State.

Shortly after returning from Texas, I interviewed for an assistant job in Reno for the 2013 season. Quickly I realized that the

Texas experience had spoiled me. I'd never again be able to take for granted the crappy conditions coaches in this part of the world don't even think about. When talking about program organization, the head coach told me he couldn't do things a certain way because he wasn't sure it would fly with his off-campus JV head coach.

My mind recoiled. Why was a varsity head coach beholden to part-timers about things that would determine the success of his program?

At the same time, I knew exactly why. This had been me a few years earlier, when Texas was just a faraway place and its football culture was just a magical thing I'd heard about secondhand through books and the few coaches I'd met who'd seen it. My expectation of what a football program should be has changed to the point that it's taking some effort for me to coach here again. The high school stadiums look like middle school fields, and even the facilities at the University of Nevada look somewhat shabby. Watching film of local high school games was painful for all the sloppy play.

Earlier I noted how Texas coaches take what they have for granted, and after only five months, I could see how easily this happens. Having been brought up in a system where athletic periods, fifteen-coach professional staffs, two-story press boxes, and video scoreboards are standard, it's not surprising that Texans would have just as much difficulty envisioning what high school football looks like most places outside of Texas as outsiders have imagining the game in Texas.

As outstanding as the Texas version of the sport is, football is still football wherever it's played. Texas coaches have more resources, support, and time to do their jobs, but the game is the same in Reno as in Round Rock, Harlingen, Stamford, or Cedar Hill. That summer I ran my first padded football drills since 2010. I'd forgotten how much fun it is to be a part of it. I've added a few new coaching points and drills to my arsenal. I have a better vision of what the game can be. But mostly, I have more appreciation for why I've been doing this for so many years. It's great to be coaching again.